Behind the Postcolonial

Modern architecture and urbanism in the colonial and postcolonial world have generally been understood in relation to European domination. In *Behind the Postcolonial*, Abidin Kusno explores this theme from another perspective: as a colonial gift inherited by the postcolonial state. He shows how colonial representations have been revived and rearticulated in postcolonial Indonesia. Using broad but powerful themes, Kusno explores how colonial culture is appropriated to invent a "new" postcolonial identity. He traces the discourses of "Indonesian" identity in architecture at various moments in the nation's history; the shaping of political cultures and their inscription in urban space; racial, class, and national identity and their relationship to the cultural politics of the nation and the city; the significance of space in the making of collective subjectivities, and the formation of a "culture of fear" in the Indonesian capital city.

This book shows how architecture and urban space can be seen, both historically and theoretically, as representations of an emerging as well as a declining social order. It addresses the complex interactions between public memories of the present and past, between images of global urban cultures and the concrete historical meanings of the local. It shows how a political history of postcolonial architecture and urban space can be written that recognizes the political cultures of the present without neglecting the importance of the colonial past. Above all, it poses serious questions about the relevance of contemporary postcolonial theory and criticism for the analysis and understanding of postcolonial states.

THE ARCHI*TEXT* SERIES

Edited by Thomas A. Markus and Anthony D. King

Architectural discourse has traditionally represented buildings as art objects or technical objects. Yet buildings are also social objects in that they are invested with social meaning and shape social relations. Recognizing these assumptions, the **Architext** series aims to bring together recent debates in social and cultural theory and the study and practice of architecture and urban design. Critical, comparative and interdisciplinary, the books in the series will, by theorizing architecture, bring the space of the built environment centrally into the social sciences and humanities, as well as bringing the theoretical insights of the latter into the discourses of architecture and urban design. Particular attention will be paid to issues of gender, race, sexuality and the body, to questions of identity and place, to the cultural politics of representation and language, and to the global and postcolonial contexts in which these are addressed.

Framing Places
Mediating power in built form
Kim Dovey

Gender Space Architecture
An interdisciplinary reader
edited by Jane Rendell, Barbara Penner and Iain Borden

The Architecture of Oppression
The SS, Forced Labor and the Nazi Monumental Building Economy
Paul B. Jaskot

Forthcoming titles:

Moderns Abroad
Italian colonialism and construction
Mia Fuller

Architecture and Language
Thomas A. Markus and Deborah Cameron

Spaces of Global Cultures
Anthony D. King

Abidin Kusno

Behind the Postcolonial

Architecture, urban space and political
cultures in Indonesia

London and New York

First published 2000
by Routledge
11 New Fetter Lane, London EC4P 4EE

Simultaneously published in the USA and Canada
by Routledge
29 West 35th Street, New York, NY 10001

Routledge is an imprint of the Taylor & Francis Group

Typeset in Frutiger Light by Wearset, Boldon, Tyne and Wear
Printed and bound in Great Britain by St Edmundsbury Press, Bury St Edmunds, Suffolk

British Library Cataloguing in Publication Data
A catalogue record for this book is available from the British Library

Library of Congress Cataloguing in Publication Data
Kusno, Abidin, 1966–
  Behind the postcolonial: architecture, urban space, and political cultures in Indonesia/Abidin Kusno.
    p. cm. – (Architext series)
  Includes bibliographical references and index.
    1. Architecture–Indonesia. 2. Architecture, Modern–20th century–Indonesia. 3. City planning–Indonesia–History–20th century. 4. Postcolonialism–Indonesia. I. Title. II. Series.

NA1526 .K87 2000
720',1'0309598–dc21

                                                                    00–028038

ISBN 0-415-23614-2 (Hbk)
ISBN 0-415-23615-0 (Pbk)

Contents

List of figures   vii
Preface   ix
Acknowledgments   xiii

INTRODUCTION   1

PART I: ARCHITECTURE
1   "Origins" Revisited: Colonial Milieu and the Crisis of Architectural
     Representations   25
2   Modern Architecture and Traditional Polity: Jakarta in the Time of
     Sukarno   49
3   Recreating Origins: The Birth of "Tradition" in the Architecture of
     the New Order   71

PART II: URBAN SPACE
4   The Violence of Categories: Urban Space and the Making of the
     National Subject   97
5   Colonial Replica: Urban Design and Political Cultures   120
6   Custodians of (Trans)nationality: Urban Conflict, Middle Class
     Prestige, and the Chinese   144

PART III: (TRANS)NATIONAL IMAGININGS
7   Professional and National Dreams: The Political Imaginings of
     Indonesian Architects   169
8   "Spectre of Comparisons": Notes on Discourses of Architecture
     and Urban Design in Southeast Asia   190

CONCLUSION: Beyond the Postcolonial? 206

Notes 213
References 233
Index 247

Figures

0.1 International reference: the National Mosque in Jakarta, 1962   2
0.2 Back to tradition: the standardized mosque built in every Indonesian province   3
0.3 The aura of the past: Demak Mosque, Demak, Central Java   3
1.1 Marketing tradition: the Dutch Pavilion, Paris 1931   27
1.2 Decentering the pendapa: the Folk Theatre 1920, plan   34
1.3 Modern traditionalism: the Folk Theatre, sectional drawing   34
1.4 Javanese house   35
1.5 Scientific evolution: the development of building structure in Java   41
1.6 Techno-traditionalism: the Bandoeng Technische Hoogeschool, 1920   44
1.7 Ganesha: logo of the Bandoeng Technische Hoogeschool, 1923   45
1.8 Interior design of Henri Maclaine Pont's Bandoeng Technische Hoogeschool, 1920   46
1.9 Sketching tradition: the Institute of Technology at Bandung (ITB), 1950   48
2.1 "Linggam-Yoni": Sukarno admiring a model of the National Monument, 1950s   55
2.2 "Like the Eiffel Tower": the National Monument under construction   56
2.3 Independence Square: the Koningsplein today   57
2.4 Putting the final touch: Sukarno explains the model of the main thoroughfare, 1960s   58
2.5 Sukarno instructs: "Set the wings back 30%" and Wisma Nusantara approved!   58
2.6 Modernist cityscape under construction, 1960s   59
3.1 Miniature Park 1975: the authentic, the beautiful, and the national self   75
3.2 Representing the nation: territory, place and identity in the Miniature Park, 1975   76
3.3 National replica: the Indonesian-ness of "traditional houses"   77
3.4 Colonial replica: the Institute of Technology at Bandung (ITB), 1990   82

3.5	Staging history: the extension of the ITB campus, 1990	82
3.6	Tribute to the master: "zona transisi"	83
3.7	Somewhere beyond the PoMo: "zona modern"	84
3.8	National architecture: the University of Indonesia (UI), c1980	86
3.9	Javanese centralism: the conceptual design of the University of Indonesia	87
3.10	Representing Authority: the rectorate tower of the University of Indonesia	87
4.1	"Rioters Loot": Collective violence, middle class fascination and fear	100
4.2	Mass subject: Sukarno in Semarang, 1950s	101
4.3	Sukarno's national subject	102
4.4	Father of Development: General Suharto, 1985	107
4.5	Guiding from behind: the Javanese philosophy of leadership	108
4.6	Upward mobility: flying over the kampung, Jakarta 1990s	110
4.7	Real estate housing and the "reality" of the kampung	114
4.8	House of Stone Age style	115
5.1	Urban village: skyscrapers rise up from the sea of the kampung, Jakarta 1990s	123
5.2	Kampung improvement under Suharto and the World Bank 1980s: before and after	126
5.3	Kampung improvement under the Dutch, 1930s: before and after	130
5.4	Distance and civilization: posters promoting Dutch "kolonialisasi" project, 1930s	137
6.1	Inverted modernity: the "city" as seen from a kampung	147
6.2	Jakarta 2005: where have all the kampungs gone?	148
6.3	Amnesic Utopia: promotion for the self-contained city of Bumi Serpong Damai (BSD)	159
6.4	Bulwark of resistance: police, workers, and the site of anti-Chinese violence in Sumatra, 1990s	161
6.5	Modern architecture: Indonesian "Chinese" entrance ways, 1990s	161
6.6	Society of spectacle: a view from the flyover	163
6.7	"Us" and "them": securing safety through a sign	164
7.1	Missing: the search for "Indonesian architecture"	186
7.2	Burden of representation: towards an "Indonesian" architecture	187
8.1	Southeast Asian-centric world history	194
8.2	Shared tradition: the geographic spread of Austronesian culture	195
8.3	From house on stilts to the Bank of Bangkok	197
8.4	Centering the region: the theoretical and geographical bases for Asian regionalist architecture	199
8.5	"The ideal is to replicate the tropical forest condition"	201
8.6	Refashioning, resisting or accommodating modernist skyscrapers? The climatic devices of the Menara Mesiniaga	202
8.7	Tropical modernity: the climatic Southeast Asian tower	203

Preface

When I first conceived of undertaking graduate studies in the history and theory of architecture in the United States, "politics" was far from my thought. I was, nonetheless, interested in connecting two problematics that I thought were crucial to many postcolonial urban centers, especially for architects and planners working in such places. The first are the vast environmental and housing traumas presented by continuing urbanization; second, as I became increasingly aware, were the more subtle issues of cultural politics: how can the architecture and spaces of the city be "modernized" yet still retain a distinctive cultural identity? Little did I realize that in this general intellectual quest, sustained by a vision of an unproblematized professional autonomy, I was also, in a way, responding to a specific social and political environment of Indonesia.

The particular critical interest developed in this book arose therefore from both my professional training as an "architect" and my historical subjectivity as an "Indonesian." There was, however, no singular great moment that I could identify as generating my interest to make this experiential connection and write this book. If critical interests are tied to, or emanate from, our autobiographies, it may be useful to think of myself as a second-generation "Indonesian." The second government, the so-called New Order (1966–98) of ex-president Suharto, came to power just a month after I was born. The thrust of "development" and the concomitant discourses of the New Order nationality were, for me, far more familiar than stories of Dutch colonialism, Japanese occupation, and the "revolution" of the early Independence movement. As part of a de-politicized New Order generation, architectural training seemed of immediate relevance. My architectural world was, therefore, strictly circumscribed from the beginning by the values of a professional class largely divorced from broader social and political issues.

Why then do I link architecture and urban space with political cultures? Perhaps it was because of Suharto's regime which, while being closer to my experiences, I still find hard to understand. Perhaps it was because I was educated in a discipline safely separated from "politics" and contained under an aura of "form making." But more importantly, as I understand it today, it was the changing political landscape following the bloody military coup in 1965–6 that made things clear to the generation of the New Order that a serious engagement with the country's political base was something to be avoided.

In this book, with its focus on Indonesia, my aim is to develop a perspective from which to view the emergence and development of the socio-cultural crisis in the postcolonial world, and the ways this crisis both shapes and is shaped by the practices of architecture and urban design. This has involved developing an understanding of architecture and urban design as they are constituted in relation to colonial and postcolonial political cultures. By examining the ways in which architecture and urban design are represented, appropriated and politicized, as well as aestheticized, nationalized and traditionalized, in order to "develop" the nation following the end of formal colonial rule, I aim to open up a debate on the vast shift in the urban norms and social forms of postcolonial space.

In linking the shape of architecture with forms of political imagination, the book aims to accomplish two main purposes. The first is to understand the ways in which collective subjectivities, such as those of "Indonesia(ns)," are constructed, contested, formed and transformed through the mediation of the country's modern architecture and urban space. The second is to address the very particular ways in which these subjectivities were constituted by means of a re-articulation of the colonial politics of representation. By examining a distinct historical moment when colonial and postcolonial spatial paradigms were both assembled and disputed and then put to cultural and ideological use, my aim is to show which frameworks were displaced and which reconstructed, which traditions were appropriated and which neglected. Finally, who represents what is authorized and why?

I have elaborated these issues, questions, and perspectives over a period, moving back and forth between Indonesia, my home country, and the United States, where I undertook my graduate education, carrying a burden of representation and translation associated with work that cut across cultural boundaries. How should a cross-cultural study of modern architecture and urbanism proceed? How might one grasp both the global phenomenon of modern architecture and the specificities of cultural histories in places such as Indonesia, a country that has been the object of colonial knowledge and is also a subject of a postcolonial authoritarian state? How should one address, through urban and architectural knowledge, the idea of the independent nation, the struggle for national identity, and the establishment of postcolonial institutions that are already entangled with the discursive practices of the "West"?

While revising my manuscript, more than three decades of Suharto's rule suddenly came to an end following ten days of savage rioting, leaving more than a thousand people dead, hundreds of (Chinese) women and girls raped and killed and many more (shop)houses, malls, and vehicles looted or destroyed. The sites of this violence were the major cities of Indonesia (particularly Jakarta); the aim of the riots was the renewal of the nation. At that moment, the idealized and official image of an "imagined community" prescribed by General Suharto was openly contested, discursively reproduced and reflectively redefined through both symbolic and physical violence directed to urban spaces and cultural forms that were believed to represent unscrupulous national institutions. Here the practices of "national" discourses took the place of destroying, instead of constructing, the cities from which the national ideal was supposed to emerge. These attacks on pre-existing forms of cities provide some rich and challenging materials to think out more specifically the effects and reception of thirty years' rule of Suharto's official nationalism and understand what the nation and the city have thus far done to each other.

Seen from afar, the "May Reformasi," as it was eventually called, was simultaneously exciting, moving, as well as horrifying and disappointing. I decided not to leave the riots behind, out of the text, or consider them as a logic or mystery of history. Instead, I have put forward my own conception of the current cultural crisis, not about its truth, but about the ways it shapes and is shaped by the political cultures of Indonesia, represented through its discourses of architecture and urban space.

In addressing "internal" affairs relevant for Indonesia, this book, nevertheless, aims to articulate a broader discourse that will not only enable architecture to address the cultural crisis of the larger social field within which it is embedded, but also to engage critically with the questioning of the postcolonial present. As such, it hopes to carry a resonance for issues, questions, and concerns pertinent to larger debates on the political forms of architecture, as well as the architectural forms of politics. "Indonesia" as it is represented in this book is therefore shaped by my own subject position – an Indonesian trained in architecture school – as well as being guided by various social, spatial and cultural "theories." The various concepts used in this book therefore arise from a certain intellectual climate that permeates today's academic environment: a rethinking of "coloniality," "modernity," and "identity" from a transnational and transcultural perspective.

Unless otherwise indicated, all translations from the original Indonesian are by myself.

Four weeks before this book was delivered to the publisher, the capital city of East Timor was brutally destroyed by armed "pro-Indonesia militias." The immediate cause of this violence was the fact that the majority of East Timorese had voted for independence. Violence of this magnitude had also occurred in 1975 when East Timor was "integrated" into the territory of Indonesia. The annexation, supported by the United States, resulted in the death of one third of the island's population, some 200,000 people. Isolated since then for "security" reasons, East Timor became a training ground for the Indonesian military to exercise its various techniques of subjugation. As this book indicates, some of these techniques have also been implemented in the rest of Indonesia, including the urban center of Jakarta. The forms of subjugation exercised in other parts of the country cannot therefore be separated from the violence applied to East Timor. In this context, the independence of East Timor is crucial to the liberation of Indonesia from its subjection to the violence of nationalism which, in the last thirty years of the country's history, has brought a return of colonial conditions. Behind the postcolonial can lurk the spectre of a future more sinister than the colonial past itself.

Acknowledgments

This book developed from a doctoral dissertation completed in the History and Theory of Art and Architecture Graduate Program at the State University of New York, Binghamton. My supervisor, Anthony King, has contributed immensely to my appreciation of the politics of space, as well as the importance of local knowledge, yet also without forgetting the larger world. Tony King has also continued to push me beyond his own work and to ask not just about new scholarship, but also about its underlying relevance and values, especially for Indonesia. I owe him very special thanks for without him, this book would never have been written. Many other scholars in upstate New York helped form this book, though I, of course, am responsible for any errors in it. Benedict Anderson's pioneering work on nationalism and Indonesia opened up a terrain that made this study possible. His critical comments and encouragement have been valuable for me in thinking through issues implicated both in and beyond what have been addressed in this book. John Tagg and Charles Burroughs, through years of interaction, have been immensely important for me in thinking through issues of history, power and representation. My deep gratitude is also owed to John Chaffee, Greig Crysler, Karl Heider, Daniel Lev, Tom Markus, John Pemberton, Daniel Walkowitz, Immanuel Wallerstein and Gwendolyn Wright for reading either part or all of the manuscript in its earlier and later stages, offering valuable suggestions and helping me to formulate various aspects of the book. I also thank Caroline Mallinder, editor of Routledge Architecture books, and two anonymous readers who supported the project and offered valuable comments.

I was fortunate to be a fellow at the International Center for Advanced Studies, New York University and a member of the year-long seminar on Cities and Nations organized by Tom Bender and Harry Harootunian. The series of meetings brought me into frequent contact with a remarkable group of scholars whose engaging and critical discussions provided me with an impressive education on cities and nations: Barbara Abrash, Peter Carroll, Rey Chow, Alev Cinar, Jordana Dym, Camilla Fojas, Benglan Goh, Kanishka Goonewardena, Najib

Hourani, May Joseph, Karl H. Miller, Timothy Mitchell, Leo Rubinfien, Michael Peter Smith, Maha Yahya, Marilyn Young and Xudong Zhang. It was at the Center that this book took a more complete form.

I am also grateful to many others I met elsewhere and at SUNY Binghamton, especially from the Departments of Sociology and Art History, whose friendship and insights sustained this study at various stages. Whatever merits this book may have are due, in no small measure, to the intellectual standards they helped to set. I want to particularly thank Ben Abel, Barbara Abou-El-Haj, Marcia Blackburn, Andrea Frohne, Hong Kal, Young June Lee, Pinghui Liao, Michael Ma, Wentong Ma, Fouad Makki, Larry McGinniss, Walter Melendez, Akiko Ono, Nihal Perera, Kirsten Priest, Ingrid Semaan, Sunaryo, David Wang, and Jiahong Xu.

In addition to the International Center for Advanced Studies at New York University, I would like to acknowledge two other institutions whose financial support made possible the realization of this book: Binghamton University, through the Department of Art History and Graduate School (including the support of Vice Provost Susan Strehle) and Aminef Jakarta Indonesia, through the Fulbright Scholarship Program. To them and their members, I gratefully give my thanks.

I owe a special debt to my friends and teachers in Indonesia: Wastu Pragantha, Josef Prijotomo, Iwan Sudradjat and Gunawan Tjahjono. My adventure into this study was encouraged by them who, within the confines of the technocratic tendency of the architectural school, nonetheless introduced me to issues of ethnicity, globality, coloniality, and nationality. One was to stimulate the study of Indonesian "national" architecture and to make sense of Surabaya, a postcolonial city beginning to experience a "global" transformation; another was to make sense of "modernity" and the increasing authority of the nation's capital city. These teachers, each in his own institution, while remaining loyal to the architectural profession as it evolved in the Indonesian context, were also wholly critical about it. Only much later did I begin to understand, and appreciate, their predicament. I do not know whether this work will contribute in some way to their analytical inquiries; my hope is that it may underline their awareness of the limits of the tradition that both they, and I, have been loyal to. This book is therefore dedicated to them.

Some parts of this book have appeared elsewhere, in an earlier version. Chapter 2 was published in the *Journal of Southeast Asian Architecture*, 2, 1 (1997); some parts of Chapters 1 and 3 in *Public Culture*, 10, 3 (1998). Sections of Chapters 4 and 6 were published in *City, Space + Globalization*, edited by Hemalata Dandekar and published by the College of Architecture and Urban Planning, University of Michigan, 1998. I want to thank the editors and publishers of these journals and book for their permission to reuse these materials.

Introduction

In the mid 1960s, approaching the demise of his political career, Sukarno, the first President of Indonesia and an architect, decided to build a national mosque in a "modern" monumental architectural style at the center of Jakarta. His wish was to mark the capital city as "the beacon of the emerging nations." What was particularly important to the President at that time was not who should design this landmark building but rather that the form it took had to surpass the existing architectural expression of the local traditional mosques. In the words of Sukarno:

> What! Would we build a Friday Mosque like the Masjid Demak, or Masjid Banten. I am sorry! What if I approach Masjid Banten! When it was built it was already great. But if erected today how would it rank, technical colleagues? And in the history of Islam, Masjid Banten, or Masjid Ciparai, Majalaya, or Masjid Bogor, colleagues, near the 'sate' sellers . . . No! It is my wish, together with the Islamic community here, to erect a Friday Mosque which is larger than the Mohammed Ali Mosque [Cairo], larger than the Salim mosque. Larger! And why? We have a great nation which proclaims the Islamic religion. We are always amazed! If we come to Cairo, brothers! If we go to Mokatam, on the left there is a Mosque on the hill. My God it is splendid! Why can't we build a mosque which is larger and more beautiful than that? Let us build a Friday Mosque which doesn't use roof tiles, but one which is built from reinforced concrete ... which is finished with marble, and paved with marble, whose doors are from bronze. And not only must the materials be concrete, bronze and fine stones but of grand dimensions, not just a Friday Mosque, which we already have for Friday prayers or special celebrations, for three or four thousand people. No. Build a Friday Mosque. Let us build a Friday Mosque which is the largest in this world, the largest in the world.
>
> Sukarno (cited in O'Neill 1993: 157–8)

As intended, the Friday Mosque was finally realized with an architectural reference to the great mosques found in the space outside the national territory

(Figure 1).[1] It seemed in many ways what Sukarno was proposing paralleled other post-World War II modernist architectural movements in many places around the globe. However, we need to look inward, to the nation, as well as outward, to the world, to understand not merely the role of nation-building in the formation of modern architecture but also the importance of modern architecture in the making of the nation. In favoring a "modern" architectural image for the Friday Mosque, President Sukarno had also constructed a temporal dialogue with the Indonesian past. By breaking with the traditional form of the local mosque, and projecting the national mosque outward, Sukarno produced a narrative of progress, internally, for Indonesia, and externally, marked the nation on the map of the great countries of the world.

The New Order of Suharto (1966–98), though continuing the construction of the Friday Mosque, began anew the quest for an architecture that reflected its own version of "Indonesia." Here, the repertoire of traditional architectural forms and ideas, "excluded" as a source of inspiration under Sukarno, found its momentum reborn under the aegis of Suharto's New Order. During the early 1980s, a nationally-constituted programme of mosque building was established for remote and less prosperous communities throughout Indonesia (Figure 2). Hundreds of standardized mosques have been distributed in assigned places throughout the archipelago.[2] Unlike Sukarno's Friday Mosque, however, the

Figure 0.1
INTERNATIONAL
REFERENCE: THE
NATIONAL MOSQUE IN
JAKARTA, 1962
Source: Hugh O'Neill,
"Islamic Architecture
Under the New Order,"
in Virginia Hooker (ed.),
*Culture and Society in
New Order Indonesia*,
Oxford University Press,
1993

Figure 0.2
BACK TO TRADITION:
THE STANDARDIZED
MOSQUE BUILT IN EVERY
INDONESIAN PROVINCE
Source: Hugh O'Neill,
"Islamic Architecture
Under the New Order,"
in Virginia Hooker (ed.),
*Culture and Society in
New Order Indonesia*,
Oxford University Press,
1993

Figure 0.3
THE AURA OF THE PAST:
DEMAK MOSQUE,
DEMAK, CENTRAL JAVA
Source: Bagoes
Wiryomartono, *Seni
Bangunan dan Seni
Binakota di Indonesia*,
Jakarta: PT Gramedia
Pustaka Utama, 1995

architectural form of the New Order's mosque-building programme recalls the image of the "classical" great mosque at Demak (Figure 3).[3] The adoption of the image of the traditional Javanese mosque is perhaps an attempt by the New Order to construct its own authority as different from that of its predecessor. The significance of Sukarno's "modern" Friday Mosque, located at the heart of the capital city, is ultimately muffled by Suharto's dissemination of a standardized "traditional" mosque all over the country. As a counter-monument to the "Old Order," the new mosques are believed to have the effect of representing the New Order's image of authority.

One of the premises of this book concerns the meaning of buildings and spaces constructed in and through political memories as a result of what Spiro Kostof (1995: 18) has called the "motivation for sequence." The competition in architectural representation that I have depicted above, within its own scale, projects a construction of the time and space of the nation. The shaping of the built environment is also a writing of the history of a nation. The modern image of Sukarno's national mosque and the standardized model of Suharto's are a way of rewriting national history that is very much concerned with the articulation of sequences, of finding an appropriate time and space. What "Indonesian architecture" is can not be understood without first posing the question of *where* and *when* "Indonesian architecture" should be located, both in time as well as space: where should a "beginning" be placed? How does it come into being? How does it define itself in relation to the architecture of others? How should it be understood in relation to other traditions? How could it be seen as a product of social and political forces in a postcolonial country that it helps to shape?

The sheer competitive drive prompts patrons of architecture to create "monuments" that replenish or even outshine the splendor of legendary master-pieces of the past. What is being recalled after the new monuments are erected is the marking of time and the presence of the past, and this then becomes "tradition." There is no evident similarity between the national Friday Mosque and the Mohammad Ali Mosque of Cairo. And yet Sukarno established a platform of comparison for them. Later on, under the patronage of Suharto's regime, a new genre of mosque building was established in which the meaning could be interpreted as a specific challenge to the previous architectural, cultural and political order. The vocabulary of all these mosques is located, both spatially and temporarily, as here and there, and from which new forms of "heritage" and "tradition" are constructed as well as challenged.

"Buildings" are not only tangible images of the aspirations of the societies that produce them; they are also an attempt to mould social attitudes (Kostof 1995: 19). The idea behind the creation of the mosques, and the building styles they adopt, represents the function of the postcolonial state in its attempt to articulate the basic Indonesian values (the nation as a metaphysical guidance for identity) and how to be a good national subject today. Yet the extent to which these architectural visions are actually absorbed as messages is the difficult question and one that is unsettling. The construction of buildings and spaces contributes to the formation of a collective subject by means of its coherent, yet individualized, vision of the past. But in what ways, and to what extent, are Indonesians of various outlooks influenced by the representations offered to them? There are as many conflicting subjectivities that marked the making and the reading of a built environment, and which an interpretation may tell us about, as there are interpreters. Nonetheless, architectural tactics, as part of the material environment, are crucial in shaping social identities. The material environment, as Lefebvre (1991) has pointed out, is both the product of, and the condition of, the possibility of social relations by which identities are formed and transformed.

This book therefore concerns the formation of collective subjectivities in the postcolonial "national" world by considering the discursive bases of architecture and urban design. It undertakes this issue of subject formation by linking the construction of architecture and urban space to the political imaginings of the colonial and postcolonial world. Using Indonesia as the prime example, I intend to show the importance of the past, including its colonial history, in shaping the present political cultures of the country through discourses of architecture and urban design. I aim to show how and why the past returns, in an active form, in the present, to shape the politics of time and space in the postcolonial regime to form a collective national subject. More specifically, I aim to show the ways in which architecture and urban design has become a *muted* form of colonialism that reigns to guarantee the appearance of the normal life in the peculiar order of the past and present society.

While having its main focus on Indonesia, this book, nonetheless, locates its argument within a much larger historical, political and theoretical context. It provides a socio-cultural and political critique of architecture and urbanism in postcolonial countries by addressing issues subsumed by the impact of urbanization, urban conflict, development, nation-building, and globalization on the identity-forming process of postcolonial cities. Underlying the specific case of Indonesia is therefore the playing out of familiar historical categories: imperialism, economic development, modernity, tradition, colonialism, nationalism, progress and cultural identity. Though making use of these familiar categories, the book also seeks to overturn the common assumptions by which these categories have customarily been used to understand the urban development and identity formation of postcolonial space. It attempts to do this by accounting for the ways in which postcolonial societies alter the space and form of the built environment for themselves, in the process, forming a dialogue with their colonial past (Appadurai and Breckenridge 1995). By reflecting on the ways certain cultural norms and forms, such as "coloniality" and "modernity", are appropriated and transformed in different locales, and at particular moments, the book, without assuming a theory, suggests a wider applicability of its ideas and concerns to other postcolonial conditions.

REPRESENTING COLONIAL AND POSTCOLONIAL SPACE

Dominant forms of scholarly inquiry in architecture and urban design are frequently represented in aesthetic and technological terms with architects, as "master builders," ordering the built environment from a position *outside* the social formation of which they are a part. Here, architecture and urban space have often been treated as autonomous, well-defined fields of practice. In contrast, recent studies of spatial and architectural discourses undertaken from a variety of theoretical perspectives, such as those of King (1976, 1990, 1995), Holston (1989), Rabinow (1989), Mitchell (1991), AlSayyad (1992), Wright (1992), Markus (1993), Crinson (1996), Home (1997), Nalbantoglu and Wong (1997) among others, have argued for a historical construction of architecture and space through processes based on political and social power, contextuality, and resistance. These studies have opened up important new approaches that foreground the active relationship between architecture and its colonial and postcolonial socio-political effects. They have revealed the narrative of colonial exploitation and enlightenment, and suggested a framework within which to address the injustices of colonial space. They have also suggested a way to consider critically the physical consequences of colonialism's architectural tactics as part of the making of colonial subjectivity.

Meanwhile, academics from outside the field of architecture and urban planning began to think about issues of colonial cultures and postcolonial conditions under the rubric of "postcolonial studies." These debates have raised the issues of writing history,[4] and questioned the often over-simplified categories of "tradition" and "modernization," notions inherited from a Eurocentric idea of history as a progression of linear time along "one discourse, one equation, one formula, one image or one myth" (Braudel 1988: 7). They have questioned the ways in which the so-called "non-Western" world has been framed within broad abstractions – modernization, urbanism, nationalism, architecture, strategies of development, the transfer of technology, global cities – whose engagement tends to determine the outcome. What emerges then is an argument that, in the presence of these deterministic frameworks, the endeavors of the inhabitants of that particular world remain insignificant. What are often forgotten are those people and forces *behind* these abstractions, people who rework the categories, cross over them, and use them for different ends.

These debates on how history has been written suggest a series of unresolved questions, not least in relation to the existing works on architecture as colonial enterprise. In generating new theoretical ideas on architecture and urbanism as being the outcome of social, political and cultural forces, to what extent have studies centered on European imperialism themselves "colonized" ways of thinking about colonial and postcolonial space? Is the colony, as well as the postcolonial world, condemned to be a continual consumer of "modernity" and "coloniality"? Viewed from this perspective, critical works on colonial urban development cannot escape from the problematic of writing colonial and postcolonial space. While providing theoretically-innovative and valuable accounts of colonial urban situations, inflected through the practices of a specific colonial power operating in different locales, the standpoint or focus from which these works are written, to appropriate a critique offered by Chakrabarty (1992), still tends to be that of "Europe."[5] In other words, the intellectual focus of these works is still on the "problematic" power of the colonizer.

Logically, as seen from the viewpoint of "postcolonial studies" (though this is, of course, not a singular view or position) one of the ways to expand the limits of existing studies on colonial architecture and urban design is to inscribe the agency of the "Third World," the "subaltern," and the "(post)colonial" subjects, who are either totally, or at least, partially transformed or in other ways, heroically resist the exercise of the "western" power. For instance, in Brenda Yeoh's (1996) study of colonial urban development in Singapore, the limit of colonial power, in its task of "modernizing" Singapore, is exposed by way of re-inscribing the agency of the colonized.[6] Instead of focusing on the power of the colonizer, Yeoh shows the agency of the colonized in appropriating and resisting colonial domination. By showing the contribution of the colonized to the shaping of colonial Singapore, Yeoh argues that the urban form of the city is a product of an interactive history of both the British and the Chinese.

In recent writing more akin to the discipline of architecture, this narrative of "domination and resistance," as demonstrated in Yeoh's study, is utilized to counter the discipline itself as it has been constructed under the cultural hegemony of the "West" (Nalbantoglu and Wong 1997). The purpose is to set "an intervention into those architectural constructions that parade under a universalist guise and exclude or repress differential spatialities of often disadvantaged ethnicities, communities or peoples" (ibid. 1997: 7). This genre of writing, drawing on postcolonial studies, examines the practices of colonialism, and especially, the exclusionary discourses as well as their ambivalent interpretations (Spivak 1987; Said 1993; Bhabha 1994). In large measure, therefore, the critique of colonialist discourse has been constituted around a broad, and often undifferentiated critique of the "West" in order to make visible, on the one hand, the internal economy of colonial power, and on the other, the active resistance of the colonized. What these strategies share is the general problematic that what is really at stake here, as Scott (1995: 192–3) points out, is the "epistemic violence" of colonialism, and the ways in which colonial power works, in the realm of the real as well as the representational, at some times to exclude and at others, to include the colonized.

However, in working on the problematic of "Indonesia," one phenomenon that holds me back from fully merging my object of study into the frame critically provided by "postcolonial studies," is the subject of postcolonial Indonesia itself. As will be shown in the following pages, the political cultures of "postcolonial Indonesia" *do not* seem to acknowledge an awareness of one of the central themes of postcolonialism as it is represented in much of the literature, namely, the "displacement" of indigenous cultures wrought by colonialism (Foulcher 1995). This phenomenon poses a serious methodological question of how to link, in a critical fashion, postcolonial Indonesia to its actual colonial legacies if the issues posed by the latter remain curiously muted within the cultural framework of the former.[7]

This book aims to extend the insights of the existing studies I have mentioned so far to the analysis of postcolonial space, such as Indonesia, in its present form and within a historical perspective. Like the existing studies, its task is to comprehend the different ways specific political cultures have been made thinkable and practicable through architecture and urban space in both colonial and postcolonial time. It attempts, however, to take a new direction in the scholarship by addressing the following problems: How can we recognize colonialism without colonizing our own imagination? How can this historical force be provincialized without reducing the representation of postcolonial architecture and urbanism to a parody of itself? How might one write a political history of architecture and urban spaces of a postcolony that recognizes the centrality of the colonial past without undermining the importance of the political cultures of the present? Finally, how could a critical contemporary Indonesian standpoint be written?

THE SPECTRE OF COMPARISONS

Comparison is perhaps the engine of social change. It is also the only possibility of critical analysis. It is a practice as much as it is a theory of understanding. The "spectre of comparisons," as Benedict Anderson (1998) aptly called it, entails political implications. As such, comparing and linking colonial and postcolonial histories have characterized the past as a contested category and put the political tendencies of the present into question. For the case of Indonesia, the return of the past, in the form of a critical present, is what the late W.F. Wertheim (1987) indicates in his review of current writing on "the Indonesian city," which could actually be understood as "the Indonesian history":

> In several papers of the present volume it is argued that Karsten's (the Dutch town planner of the Indies) main spiritual product, the 'stadvormingsordonnantie,' still plays a significant role in the urban planning of independent Indonesia. However, one may ask whether the term 'arena of conflict,' which was characteristic of colonial urban society in the pre-war Indonesia, would not equally fit urban conditions under Suharto's 'New Order.' Is the social distance between the present Indonesian elite and the still numerous 'urban poor' actually less pronounced than the social distance between the latter and the white 'tuans' in the pre-war colonial society?
>
> (Wertheim 1987: 542)

Here, post-war independent Indonesia seems to share a "modernity," or better, a "coloniality," that is also characteristic of colonial order. The connection that Wertheim made is not only historically sound but also stimulates both a further theoretical thought and intellectual positionality on how to write "colonial" spaces which are, by definition, also "postcolonial."

In perhaps the first critical study of the modern politics of the colonial built environment, Anthony King (1976) began the study of the "mentalities" of the British colonial community and their influence in producing a colonial architecture and urban space for India. King's analysis of the colonial politics of space, from the eighteenth century up to the independence of India, documents a variety of spatial and architectural discourses ranging from those imported from

Europe to others which emerged from an intermingling with the indigenous society. From this study he draws two principal conclusions. The first is that the urban development of colonial India was a product of "colonial third cultures" that are neither exclusively cultures of the metropole, nor of the indigenous society but are a mediation "between the two societies . . . acting as agents by which the two cultures are interpreted and images conveyed . . ." (King 1976: 290). Here we are given an account of "colonial modernity" as an urban phenomenon, a product of overlapping cultures under colonialism. The second conclusion, as a consequence of the first, is that the production of the colonial third culture leads, among other things, to the transformation of cultural institutions in the metropole as well as in the colony. Here, as one among a number of possible examples, the notion of the "bungalow," originally a vernacular form of dwelling in India, was first adopted as a culturally and environmentally appropriate form of house for the European community in the colony and then, as an image or an idea, was subsequently transferred to the metropole to become a "weekend home" for the upper middle class.

King's interpretation of the colonial third culture encourages one to go beyond his immediate analytical concerns. His study of colonial urban development is limited to the colonial period and is primarily concerned with the analysis of the cultural space of the colonial representatives of the metropole and not (at least, not explicitly) with postcolonial indigenous development (King 1976: xiv). The scope of his inquiry was determined by both an intellectual and political position. One is the viewpoint that "cultures are autonomous, to be evaluated only on their own terms" (King 1976: xiv); the other is to counter a neocolonial perspective or position that seeks to continue to represent the postcolony following its independence. His aspiration, in 1976, was to see "newly independent inhabitants adapting the colonial third culture to the needs of a new, democratic and socialist nation" (King 1976: xii). As he concludes:

> With the demise of the third culture brought about by the end of colonialism, such items
> either disappeared, were transferred to the metropolitan society by (colonial) third
> culture members or persisted as part of a westernised indigenous culture sustained by
> the elite in the ex-colonial society . . . [Therefore] the task for the inheritors of the
> colonial society is one of investing it with a new symbolic meaning representative of the
> society of which it is now a part.
>
> (King 1976: 66 and 288)

Here, King's hopes for a decolonized nation, however, only represent one side of postcoloniality. What is not addressed is the failure of decolonization in which the "newly independent inhabitants" still remain victims of their past, half a century after "independence" (Said 1989).

It is the task of this study to explore episodes in the aftermath of colonization, a time when the "newly independent inhabitants" seek to construct their own version of modernity, and one which is ultimately held back by the shadow of its own political pasts. The politically contradictory space of a "colonial third culture" is examined from the perspective of the "newly independent inhabit-ants." Seen from that position, and in the time of the present, this "colonial third culture" has become a cultural replica, an "empty" but still powerful framework of the past, which is subjected to site-specific rearticulation.

In showing the articulation of this colonial replica by Indonesians through the discourses of architecture and space, my position in this work is less con-cerned to promote an "indigenous" contribution to the study and understanding of "colonial urban development." My aim is rather, following Wertheim's (1987) suggestion, to trace, in the manner of a diachronic spectre of comparisons, the genealogy of a still persistent coloniality in present day, postcolonial Indonesia. It is in this way that I understand Indonesia as undergoing a "postcoloniality," a condition with the mixed characteristics of those "who had freed themselves on one level but who remained victims of their past on another" (Said 1989: 207). This book suggests that the appearance which postcolonial Indonesia produces for itself in order to appear as "normal," brings to the surface memories of its political past, including those of colonialism, revealed, yet simultaneously dis-guised, under the present forms of subjection.

I put forward this argument not for the reason of claiming a truth. Instead, the objective of this study is rather more experimental, and also more ambitious. It includes not only an identification of the colonial conditions that have made possible the political cultures of the present, but also the demonstration of a way of representing this "cultural crisis" through one particular field of knowledge and practice, namely, that concerning its built environment. But how could a few examples of buildings, cities and architectural writings be made to stand for the larger movement and crises of Indonesian societies and cultures? How should this inquiry begin?

ARCHITECTURE AND POLITICAL HISTORY: A CRITICAL DIALOGUE

In 1985, in a special edition of a professional journal, *Arsitek Indonesia,* Indone-sian architects declared for the first time their position in regard to the socio-political context of the country. The announcement, which appeared on the editorial page, confirms an often forgotten fact that architects and urban plan-ners are not only specialists of a particular knowledge, but also members of a particular social and cultural order. The article indicates, at a curious time when there was no serious oppositional politics in existence, that the professional association had decided to maintain its integrity by standing outside the bound-aries of any political ideology battleground. It follows then that the decision to assume an objective professional subjectivity is built upon a memory of recent political developments in Indonesia. It comes to this conclusion by referring to the earlier period of decolonization (the late 1950s) when the professional association of architects was born:

> At that time all organizations, be they trade, professional or student, were forced to
> choose a political affiliation. The criteria for the right to live were based on the power of

the masses rather than on moral issues. Thus, the Association of Indonesian Architects, as a new organization with different aspirations, had no chance at all to develop because it is grounded on the principles of non-affiliation to any kind of political ideology.

(*Arsitek Indonesia* 1985: 9)

Writing in the midst of the increasing authority of the economic development and political control of the 1980s, the concern over "moral issues," which in fact is highly contested and could be turned to many different purposes, could not be other than metaphysical. These fellow architects (including myself at the time) were framing architecture as having within itself a coherent account and representing a major creative and technological breakthrough as being beyond any political and ideological contexts or concerns.

The separation of the socio-political from the imaginative space of architecture seems to emanate largely from the shape of professionalism and the *logic* of the discipline itself. However, in the context of Indonesia, the deliberate exclusion of socio-political inquiry from the discipline projects a style of governing architecture and urban design which was quite particular to the country. Since the bloody military coup of 1965–6, the notion of "politics" has entered into the public imagination as something suspicious, distrustful, dirty and ideological. It thus makes sense that the discipline of architecture today represents itself as apolitical and the inquiry into architecture and urban design is better off without a deep investigation of what is known as the political.

The avoidance of architecture as a political force that is deeply embedded within the social and political shape of today's Indonesia nevertheless says something about the latter. One of the principal reasons behind this compartmentalized vision of the discipline is closely related to the political regime of the New Order in Indonesia, the aim of which is to produce "technicians" to function in a society increasingly dominated by de-politicized technocratic and consumerist cultures. Within an inaccessible political climate, apolitical professional subjects are constructed and the terrain of architecture is kept separate from political symbolism. While the modern politics of Indonesia has used architecture to symbolize its power (Anderson 1990; Hooker 1993), architecture, as a discipline in Indonesia, still finds it difficult to acknowledge, let alone engage critically with, its relation to power.

This book begins with this "problematic": How to situate the book in a way that emphasizes the political dimensions of architecture and urban design, and how to locate it in a disciplinary space that considers politics as something beyond the field of inquiry? How could one then articulate a critical discourse: to call into question the cultural and social political frameworks that established the material and intellectual grounds of architectural culture? How can we open up a debate which sees architecture and urban design as a representation of political forces that shape an emerging as well as a declining social order?

COLONIAL MISSION AND PROFESSIONAL SUBJECTIVITY

In articulating the relations of postcolonial identity formation, the muted legacies of colonialism, and the "higher commitment" of architects working in and for the nation, I appropriate some of the interpretative frameworks of Paul Rabinow (1989) and Edward Said (1993). Rabinow studied the formation of the "modern" social environment of France through an examination of the field in which power operates, namely, urban planning. Through a series of interlinked studies, he examines the various ways in which social spaces are represented in a series of historically heterogenous social missions, including overseas colonialism, that ultimately constitute what, at home, he terms "French modern." Here, the organization of space serves to represent and improve society, within the national territory and abroad, by giving it a representable spatial and architectural form. As the work of scientists and social reformers overlap with the French imperial project, a political culture of French "society" – which justified colonialism as the practice of the "ethical" – took shape.

What is remarkable about Rabinow's analysis is that the ordering of architectural space by architects and urban planners is not read as a plot of one dominant group over the subordinated others, nor is it analysed in terms of any law of history or an essential determinism (Rabinow 1982). Following Foucault's analysis of the panopticon as a form of modern power, Rabinow shows the ways in which all subjects involved in, and the target of, the spatial formation are necessarily constituted under, as well as contribute to, a commitment towards a universally understood "social modernity." The architects, planners, and social reformers that filled the panorama of Rabinow's account all worked heterogenously, but managed to articulate themselves to a single purpose: to achieve social modernity. Yet while the claims of these "specific intellectuals" are universal, the nation of France continued to serve as the natural if unspoken frame of the whole professional dream. Rabinow is perfectly aware that the huge œuvre of his "actors," from Hubert Lyautey to Tony Garnier and Maurice Halbwachs, should be understood *within* the scopic regime of France of their times even though these actors spoke in the "universal" language of their social mission.

In a similar way, but from a distinct political position and different disciplinary and theoretical terrain (a Foucauldian "humanist" approach), the later work of Edward Said begins to suggest the importance of looking at the formation of the "ethics" of colonialism that generates the politics of domination and resistance itself. Indeed the most interesting part of Said's later work lies not in the connection he makes between empire and culture (or culture as a form of domination and discipline), but in the fact that the European civilizing mission of the late nineteenth and early twentieth century was conducted, not really as a form of colonialism, but more as a "social mission." There are very many reasons, of course, to criticize this political culture and indeed Said, in much of his work, has usefully done so. However, what makes Said's *Culture and Imperialism* distinctive is that it addresses the question of how colonialism, or nationalism for that matter, was naturalized as culture and represented as the practice of reason and the ethical. This practice of the ethical, most clearly demonstrated in Said's reading of Conrad, is derived from a conscientious belief on the part of the colonizer that the colonies *need* to be colonized in order to develop.

Here, the way Joseph Conrad was read by Edward Said and Hubert Lyautey was represented by Paul Rabinow is particularly instructive. In Rabinow and Said's accounts, these two practitioners of colonial power do not conceive of their practices as a form of politics; instead, they both see colonialism as an ethical solution to the problems of the colonial world. Lyautey and Conrad had the means of colonialism, yet in Rabinow and Said's accounts, they are not fully in control over them; instead, each in his own way negotiates with colonial power by working for, as well as against it. Colonial urban planners, in Rabinow's "anti-humanist" approach, are not "colonizers," they are simply "specific intellectuals" who devote themselves to the idea of "social modernity." In Said's "humanist" account of Joseph Conrad, we find Conrad, in his *Heart of Darkness*, facing colonialism with two contradictory visions. One is the need of colonialism to fulfill its inevitable historical role. The other is the awareness that colonialism carries with it the moment of menace and horror that overruled its enlightening vision. By representing the darkness of colonial enlightenment, Conrad struggled for, as well as against, the rationality of colonialism. This kind of interpretation presents a more complex history of colonialism beyond the binary opposition of the colonizer and the colonized. More importantly, it also opens up a way to think about the subject formation of those involved in the shaping of colonialism within his or her own particular field of cultural power.

Following Rabinow and Said, what I will show in this book are the ways in which individuals or groups of architects and political social reformers try to come to terms with imperial and, for the postcolonial era, the national, reality; how they ignore the empire and how they represent it. Though aware, and even critical, of the interests of colonialism (and postcolonial "official" nationalism) they, who live in its social field, did not stand "in the way of the accelerating imperial process" (Said 1993: 81–2).

I appropriate this insight first in the chapters on colonial discourses, and later in the discussion on postcolonial architectural discourses. The problem I encountered in writing colonial architecture and space is actually the problem I have of writing about the present. I represent some of the New Order's architects, who are working within postcolonial "official nationalism" of the late twentieth century, as an inappropriate reincarnation of the Dutch architects, Thomas Karsten and Henri Maclaine Pont, who worked within the scopic regime of colonialism at the beginning of the century.[8] They are the "specific intellectuals" or the "technicians" working within a particular constraint of power that makes them appear to be *both* the colonizer and the colonized.

Karsten and Maclaine Pont were both critical towards colonialism yet they did not stand in the way of the accelerating imperial process because they considered themselves as working for a higher rationality, namely, social modernity

for the colony. Their ambiguities towards imperialism can be compared to my own ambiguities towards my fellow postcolonial architects who are also ambiguous towards the (often unspoken) *national* framework they have to cope with. For in a similar way, the postcolonial architects and urban planners try to come to terms with a "national" reality, contributing to the ideology of "development" while imagining themselves as occupying a higher ethical position as "objective" specialists. I understand these figures as specific intellectuals who find themselves working within, as well as contributing to, a political culture that is advantageously problematic.

HISTORY OF THE PRESENT AND THE FORMATION OF A POLITICAL CULTURE

This book is an attempt at showing the reciprocity that exists between the society and politics of Indonesia on the one hand, and Indonesian architectural culture on the other. In doing this, I aim to respond to what has customarily been neglected in the culture of architecture in Indonesia, namely, its social and political significance. In inquiring into the political form of Indonesia, I am not suggesting here that architecture is a mere reflection of the state, or that architecture in Indonesia could be understood sufficiently through an analysis based on an idea of "embedded statism" (Taylor 1996). It is rather that both the style and the paradigm of architecture in Indonesia could only be sufficiently grasped through a serious interpretation of their relations to the "political cultures" of the regime in power.

By "political culture," I mean a powerful, socially shared interpretative framework that operates and develops consciously as well as unconsciously in the political and cultural life of a country. It evolves through practices of representation, such as those of architecture and urban design, that mediate the relationship between social structures, such as between the state and civil society, in such a way that the *effects* of daily life can be seen and felt in the state, and vice versa. In this sense, my understanding of the "state" goes beyond the customary state and civil society division. Through the discourses of architecture and urban space, I intend to see how these social structures, instead of occupying a separate realm, mutually constitute each other in forming and transforming the political culture of a postcolonial country (Mitchell 1997).

In his comparative analysis of the design of parliamentary complexes in four postcolonial states in the Middle East and Asia, Lawrence Vale (1992) discusses the struggles of these states to build the symbols of national unity after decolonization and during periods of rapid political and economic change. Starting with the idea that government buildings, through their architectural representation, expressed the character of a political regime, Vale shows the struggle of the architects to deliver "national identity" as part of their design commission. Vale's interest is limited to a particular building type, namely the capitol, seen as embodying the identity of the state, and the problem of nation-building.

The limit of this illuminating comparative approach proposed by Vale is not merely that there is not enough space to treat each of the country's colonial histories, but it has also not allowed sufficient exploration of the complex making of the contemporary cultural formations of the postcolonial countries. By positing the capitol as the embodiment of the dilemma of the postcolonial state, it overlooks the blurred division of the state/civil society dichotomy, and the discursive constructions of postcolonial societies beyond the symbolic representation of the capitol complex. As a result, issues of subject formations, such as the ways in which "identity" prescribed by the state and the designers is absorbed and challenged are neither analysed nor historically explored. In this present study, I attempt to go beyond a study of the state's "monuments" to capture not merely the "political cultures" of a postcolonial country but also to conceive the making of the "national" subjects. My aim is to examine the discursive construction of diverse infrastructures of "everyday" urban life: buildings, settlements, highways, and professional cultures, and understand them as embodying, as well as shaping, the state's activities. In this way, I attempt to show the broader material effects of the mutual relations between the state and the civil society beyond those represented officially and exclusively in, for example, the form of a capitol complex. My aim, therefore, is not merely to conduct a study of how politics necessarily takes a particular architectural form but, more importantly, why this has become the case at particular moments in the history of the nation.

This book is written, deliberately and/or unconsciously, after the excavation, reinterpretation and refashioning of a limited, but endless array of tangible structures of knowledge about the past and present. The African historian, Achille Mbembe (1992), has explored issues of power in relation to postcoloniality understood as "the specific identity of a given historical trajectory, that of societies recently emerging from the experience of colonization" (Mbembe 1992: 2). Mbembe's discussion links a series of seemingly unconnected locations or incidents like commemorations, disciplinary practices and rituals; figures and commodities are put together without any total history attached to them. Each example, together with a series of general propositions, demands its own logic of inclusion and exclusion and selective incompleteness.

A similar logic organizes my own studies. But unlike Mbembe's "postmodern" treatment of events that are represented as self-contained and self-evident units,[9] I propose a historically grounded argument. The fragments (a disparate series of actors and circumstances in more than one time period) are all compiled, comparatively, under various themes that allow architectural events and urban planning discourses to be understood as involved in the making of Indonesian political cultures.

Entangled in the time and space of the colonial and postcolonial, this book engages in the ongoing "invention of tradition" and the shaping of modern Indonesia. It is about what has been forgotten from the understanding of architecture in Indonesia, namely, its relations to social and political forces, its services to power and its potential of rupturing power itself. Pierre Nora (1989) indicates the dialectic between "souvenir" and "amnesie" of historical memories. Such an interaction between remembrance and amnesia defines the discipline of architecture as much as it marks the historical memories of the generation under the New Order Indonesia.

The "essence" of the nation, according to Anderson (1991), lies in its capacity to foster its citizens, by means of representations, to collectively imagine a range of things. In this sense, what should be officially recalled to foster a sense of national identity implies a cultural consensus as to what should be overlooked. It is within this spider's web of what to remember and what to forget that this book is undertaken. It tries to remove existing Indonesian architectural memories in order to make room for new ones. As such, it does not seek to excavate the "truth" and to represent the past in order to render it intelligible, but to make the past usefully speak of the present. It wants to be a "history of the present."[10]

THE SHAPE OF THE BOOK

The choice of the early twentieth century as a starting point for the study of subsequent developments in Indonesia has a certain significance.[11] It marks a remarkable turn in Dutch policy concerning the Netherland Indies, from a "liberal" toward an "ethical" policy (Ricklefs 1993). In 1899, Van Deventer's article, "A Debt of Honour," was published in Holland. It pushed the Queen of the Netherlands to speak clearly to her nation in 1901 of an "ethical obligation and moral responsibility to the peoples of the East Indies" (cited in Van Doorn 1982: 1). A year later, a decision was made to open an inquiry into what was called "the diminishing welfare of the native population" (cited in Van Doorn 1982: 1).

"Development," serving as the prime mandate of the Ethical Policy, marked the emergence and expansion of technical services in the Dutch East Indies, displacing the prestige of the Colonial Civil Service (Van Doorn 1982). Yet of perhaps greater significance was the change in the colony. At about the same time, the mass debut of the railways and the circulation of newspapers in vernacular languages, among others, opened up new means of communication between the colonizer and the colonized.[12] The opening up of space and time by these technologies provoked fantasies of liberation in the colonial world (Shiraishi 1990; Ingleson 1981). Meanwhile, the plurality of the society in the Dutch East Indies became manifest; groups became aware of their identities (Van Doorn 1983). While sealing themselves off from each other, they shared an intensive interaction generated by communication technology that compressed the sense of time and space. Many new key words such as "equality," "politics," "revolution," "organization," "progress," and "modern" entered the imagination of various groups. All contributed to the sense that everyone was living in a new age, a time which Takashi Shiraishi (1990) has aptly called "the age in motion." It is at this time that the colonizers reorganized their attitudes by courting what was identified as "local" cultures and traditions. Here architecture became profoundly political in its role in responding to the demand of the "new age" and remolding an ideal colonial society based on "ethical" principles.

I have chosen to open my analysis with this moment, for this time marks a period of "nationalist" awakening, the reorganization of colonial attitudes, experiments in the science of the city, and the remolding of society through an ideal of architecture. Along with these are subjects concerning culture, heritage, tradition and identity, on the one hand, and the idea of the modern, modernization and progress on the other, subjects that shaped the memories of the following generations. What concerns me here is not so much the changing mode of conceiving the social and cultural, but the ways in which the new imaginings were also restructuring the politics of time and space of the later postcolonial regime. I aim to show how the generation which spans the twentieth century has been struggling over the politics of space and time and, as such, how it is obsessed with the meanings and uses of urban knowledge and their inscription in the built environment.

This book is organized in three major, inter-related parts, bearing the themes of architecture, urban space and (trans)national imaginings. Part I addresses three episodes in the discourses of "Indonesian" identity through spatial and architectural representation: late Dutch colonialism (1920), early post-independence Jakarta (1950–65), and contemporary postcolonial Indonesia (1975–98). The main thrust of this part is to trace the ways in which colonial and early postcolonial architectural representation restructures the present politics of time and space.

Chapter 1 traces architectural discourse in the Dutch East Indies and its relations to the colonial politics of pacification (1920–40). Here, the colonial technocratic tendency emerging in the early twentieth century was coupled with the collecting of art and culture. The aim of this cultural enterprise is to revitalize architectural culture in the metropolis on one hand, and to re-articulate the politics of Dutch colonialism in the colony on the other. The Dutch architects involved in representing the architectural cultures of the Indies are understood as hybrid subjects whose relation to colonialism, I argue, remains ambiguous. The major theme in this chapter concerns the larger political implications surrounding the architectural construction of "Indonesian" culture by Dutch architects. Its main purpose is to address the cultural "origin" of contemporary discourses on Indonesian identity and their spatial and architectural representation. The colonial tracing of the indigenous civilization and of its urban spaces was one of the first steps to construct a "modern" indigenous space and architecture crucial for subsequent postcolonial discourses of "cultural identity." This chapter focuses on "Indies architecture" as this short-lived architectural experiment represented in a most sophisticated way the dynamics of the time. Most importantly, it also provided an earlier grammar by which the postcolonial subjects could imagine an "Indonesian architecture."

Chapter 2 analyses the representation of Jakarta as the "portal of the country" and "beacon of the emerging nations" of Asia and Africa under

Sukarno's Guided Democracy (1957–65). The concern of Sukarno, the master-architect of Indonesia's capital city, was not so much about whether the architecture, planning, and spatial concept of modern Jakarta was "East," or "West," Stalinist, Maoist, or Corbusian, as about how they could possibly place Jakarta on the same platform with the contemporary "modern" world. The force of this (inter)national imagining of Jakarta's leader, I argue, was derived, curiously enough, from the "old" mentality of the dominant male Javanese cultural and political milieu. The general and theoretical theme of this chapter concerns the question of the local reception of the global cultural flows of modernist architecture and the distinctive historical and political meanings that are invested in this.

Chapter 3 discusses the representations of architecture under the Suharto regime (1965–98), as they undergo unprecedented pressure from the forces of global capitalism and a relentless search for a cultural identity characteristic of the New Order. I argue that the New Order gave birth to the idea of "tradition" in architectural culture. This national discourse interacts with international architectural movements on regionalism. The major themes of this chapter concern the crisis in the production of a national ("Indonesian") culture and the appearance of contradictions in its origin. Read in comparison to the first chapter, this chapter addresses the collusion of colonial and postcolonial time and space and the interaction between local and global cultural flows.

Part II comprises three inter-related chapters discussing different discourses of urban renewal in both colonial and contemporary cities in Indonesia. They are discussed in regard to the ways in which subjectivities are formed and transformed through urban spaces. The theme of Part II is written as a reflection of the May 1998 riots that toppled Suharto from power. The three chapters are assembled to provide, first, the inscription of the nation's political cultures in the urban spaces of the postcolonial regime; second, the different sense of continuity between the colonial dominant paradigms and those of the postcolonial; third, the formation of a "culture of fear" in the urban spaces of contemporary Indonesia.

Chapter 4 begins with an examination of the politics of city building under the first president, Sukarno, and ends with a "journey" through the urban structures built under the New Order of the second president, Suharto. In between the journey are attempts, first, to examine the ways in which the techniques of representing architecture and urban space constitute collective subjectivities that generate two profoundly contrasting social categories, namely, the "underclass" and the "upper-middle class" Indonesian. Second, to consider how this identity formation contributes to the legitimacy, as well as to the fall, of the ruling power. The main argument here is the construction of alterity *within* the national "self." The envisioned "threat" of the previous populist politics of Sukarno has been transferred to the present, in the form of an imagined "threat" of the poor urban neighborhood of the kampung. The postcolonial city, while modelling itself upon modern cities of the "West" is, I argue, constructed out of an internal, contradictory relationship with the country's political culture, and concurrently with the kampung, with which it lives side-by-side. Through the discourses of fly-overs and the "real estate" housing, the New Order erases its political past, and controls the present. In this way it represents the city as the showcase of the future in the form of "discipline" and "development." The theoretical question here is what makes the city a legitimate focal point for inquiry into the "nation"? What is the role of the physical characteristics of the city in shaping/forming national and class identities? This chapter also deals with the complexity of the interactions between images of global urban cultures and the need to address the very concrete historical specificities and meanings of the local.

Chapter 5 studies the discourse of Dutch urban planning in the early twentieth century at the time of the nationalist awakening in the Indies. The zoning system of modern urban planning, introduced by the prominent Dutch architect, Thomas Karsten, produced a class-based society, replacing the one based on racial "census" categories. I argue that this has the effect of concealing social inequality based on race, while at the same time pacifying the increasing threat of anti-colonialism. This chapter also discusses the project of colonial transmigration founded upon the notion of redeeming the urban poor through the reconstruction of ideal Javanese (agri)cultural traditions in the Outer Islands. This method is later re-fashioned by the postcolonial New Order regime to manage the overcrowding of the urban center and to consolidate the integrity and security of the nation–state. I raised the issue of how one could conceive the ways in which different rationalities, of colonial and postcolonial time, interact with each other to form a common conceptual framework, one in which society is to be thought as best governed and ruled. The general theme here is to show the ways in which "old" colonial imaginings – found to be useful in the memories of the "modern" postcolonial governing elite – continue to surface and to structure the politics of time and space in the later postcolonial regime.

Chapter 6 represents the postcolonial city as what Wertheim (1987) called an "arena of conflict." It brings together arguments posed in Chapters 4 and 5. Instead of focusing on the discourses of the "powerful," the postcolonial city is seen as containing many modernities that contradict the basic premise of a disciplined city. It shows how the transformation of the urbanscape constitutes a "culture of fear" that carries with it the perennial conflict of class and ethnicity that is inseparable from the political economy of postcolonial Indonesia. The issue of Indonesians of Chinese descent is discussed, particularly how this group is implicated in the politics of the built environment, and the making of Indonesian subjectivity. Here I argue that a "culture of fear" has been constructed in the mentality of the Indonesian middle class in their relations to the majority of the poor "kampung" inhabitants (as demonstrated in Chapter 4) and the economically dominant and politically pariah Indonesians of Chinese descent. This emphasis on the urban conflict and the subject formation of the Indonesian "middle class" will modify prevailing interpretations of transnational flows of culture which, to date, have predominantly been conceived in terms of East/West encounters.

Part III considers the thinking of Indonesian architects as they live within the social field of the postcolonial nation. The professional and national subjectivities of Indonesian architects are "compared" with other Southeast Asian architects working with similar "problems" but are provided with a different alternative.

Chapter 7 traces the memories of the architectural discipline through a reading of some Indonesian architectural debates. It explores the construction of nationality and the creation of value-free specialists in the discipline from the 1950s to the present New Order. This chapter provides an account of the grafting of "Indonesian" on their identity as an "architect." What can these professionals tell us about the socio-political milieu in which they are embedded? It demonstrates the ways in which the theory and practice of "modern architecture" elsewhere, instead of dominating, has allowed Indonesian architects to define their professional identity in relation to the official construction of a national culture. The general issue here is that of professional identity – how it is formed in relation to the national "reality" which demands a suppression of the architects' subnational specific cultural practices and social orders. And where does "modern architecture" stand in relation to specific local political conditions?

Chapter 8 extends the inquiry of the previous chapter. It seeks to examine the shared culture of architecture as it now circulates in the postcolonial countries of Southeast Asia. In writing the previous chapter, I indicated certain paradigms that could be used to explain some of the postcolonial architectural discourses in Southeast Asia. If Singaporeans, Malaysians and Thais are also "architects," what are they doing and writing about? What are their political imaginations? What paradigms are they using to define themselves and their disciplinary identity in relation to national and transnational forces? In this chapter I show that the architectural discourse of "regionalism" remains a central trope to "re-write" architectural history and re-define architecture and urbanism in Southeast Asia. I suggest a reflection on the ways certain cultural norms and forms, such as those provided by "modern architecture" (elsewhere), are appropriated and transformed in different locales and at particular moments. The general theme concerns the relations between architecture and its Utopic visions on society, the structure of Eurocentrism in the production of knowledge, and the interactive self-construction of architectural histories and identities in Southeast Asia.

The Conclusion provides, first, a discussion on the postcoloniality of Indonesia and the major impasse in current postcolonial studies. Second, I suggest that an understanding of the connection between the built environment and subject formation is what is missing in the current debate in postcolonial studies. Scholars of colonial discourse continually discuss "space," but often their works hardly touch on the real, physical representation of colonial encounters.[13] While spatial metaphors are used (such as "third space"), the making of colonial subjects as hybrid, contradictory, and ambivalent are seemingly unmediated by the material properties of architecture and space. I suggest that this study on the political history of architecture and space shows that space is not only metaphorical; instead its materiality helps to construct social identities. These, I suggest, are important issues for a reflective social and political treatment of architecture and space in postcolonial societies.

Part I

Architecture

Chapter 1: "Origins" Revisited

Colonial Milieu and the Crisis of Architectural Representations

This first chapter has two purposes. The first is to reframe the formation of "modern architecture" by considering the history of Dutch colonialism in Indonesia. Recent works on architecture and urban design of colonialism have prepared a way for this consideration.[1] However, despite their valuable insights on architecture and the colonial enterprise, they are nonetheless limited in terms of the theoretical power they bring to other situations. In these works, the metropolitan "West" is largely – if not entirely – represented as controlling knowledge production in the (post)colonial or dependent world, and this is then countered or contested by the indigenous agency, through resistance, appropriation, and accommodation. The problem in these narratives of domination and resistance is the assumption of an oppositional identity between the metropole and the colony, a narrative of a dichotomous negotiation between West and East; one dominates and the other resists. I want to go beyond this narrative of "domination and resistance" by showing the complex relations of power, unresolved contradictions and the ambivalence of colonialism which often exists in both colonial and postcolonial situations. I approach this subject by looking at Dutch architects involved in representing the architectural cultures of colonial Indonesia in the early twentieth century. I argue that some of these Dutch architects working in the colony, such as Henri Maclaine Pont and Thomas Karsten, should be understood as "hybrid subjects" whose professional identity was formed as neither colonizer nor the colonized.

The second, and more important, purpose is to show the ways in which architectural techniques of representation are replicated and transformed over time as a framework that allowed the imagining of both the colonial and, particularly, the postcolonial "national" world. Dutch architects, in coping with the colonial situation, preserved what was considered to be an authentic indigenous domain which, as a result, carved out an authoritative realm for the later postcolonial architects to insert the national self. The "Indonesian architecture" (more fully explored in Chapter 3) which in the view of nationalist architects ought to represent the uniqueness of the postcolonial nation, when understood historically, is the basis for Dutch colonial domination. Its appearance in the postcolonial imagination has to be read under the sign of inauthenticity, in what Partha Chatterjee (1993) has called a "derivative discourse," no matter how much contemporary architects have insisted on its integrity.

As a "derivative discourse" it might seem as though the argument is meant to emphasize, once more, the power of colonial domination. In fact, however, the objective of this chapter is rather more complex. I first want to identify the discursive conditions that make such an invention of "Indonesian architecture" during the colonial period possible; but I also want to suggest a rethinking of the dilemma of postcolonial identity formation, to reflect on the question of agency, and finally, address the problem of re-writing architectural history. The agenda is therefore to provide a new arena of debate beyond that already established by orientalist and anthropological scholars that have championed authenticity, originality and spirituality in Indonesian architecture. This chapter seeks to ask: What if Indonesian architecture did not originate from the "inside"? What if it was constituted within a colonial politics of representation? Would this genealogy challenge the originality and creativity of future architectural and urban design?

THE INTERNATIONAL COLONIAL EXHIBITION AND THE DUTCH ETHICAL POLICY

At the International Colonial Exhibition in Paris in 1931, the Dutch delegation sought to represent its distinctive style of colonial governance to the European public. By exhibiting the architecture, cultures and arts of the Indies, the Dutch delegation was determined to make a statement about the unique management of its overseas colonies. What made the Dutch colonial practice different from that of other European nations, according to the Dutch delegation, was the emphasis the colonizers put on "their careful study and profound understanding of the complexity of native cultures" (Gouda 1995: 220).

The Dutch Pavilion (Figure 1.1), praised in the French press as the most impressive building of the entire exhibition, conveyed, in the words of historian Frances Gouda (1995: 194), "the metaphor for the Dutch pride in being able to forge political unity among the diversity of sophisticated ethnic cultures and religions that flourished in the Indonesian archipelago." Unlike other colonizing powers participating in the Exhibition which largely presented replicas of temples and picturesque grass huts, the Dutch displayed a truly creative synthesis between East and West, a genuine creative innovation. A colonial journal reported that the monumental structure was "composed of different architectural styles linked to each other by Dutch building motifs; hence we see the work of ordering and association which the Netherlands accomplishes among the people of the Indonesian archipelago" (as cited in Gouda 1995: 210). The Dutch pavilion brought together the Hindu temple of Bali, the roof type of the Sumatran Minangkabau house and the Javanese mosque, and shingles from

Figure 1.1
MARKETING TRADITION: THE DUTCH PAVILION, PARIS 1931
Source: Nederland te Parijs 1931 Geden le boek Van de Nederlandsche deelneming dan de Internationale Koloniale tentoonsfelling Uit gave Van de Vereeniging „Oosten West," ten Bate Van Hef Steuncomite-Párijs

Borneo resembling what Clifford (1988: 13) has called "modernist collage." The collage seemed to suggest the rational form of a colonial authority that, it claimed, had amalgamated the disparate cultures of the Netherlands Indies into a coherent political whole (Gouda 1995: 210–11).

The architectural collage of the Dutch pavilion was a by-product of the maturing age of mechanical reproduction. Technical and evocative images from maps, drawings, photographs, books, and postcards provided the possibility of envisaging architectural fusion.[2] The impressive parts, as well as a sketchy whole of the buildings and monuments of the colony, immediately suggest their reproduction in the actual form and space of (modern) buildings that were "objective," evocative and picturesque.[3] This reproduction and transfer of various images in order to convey a sense of European mastery over its colony was also enabled by detaching building elements from the "real" sacredness of local sites and repositioning them in quite a different setting. In this respect, the Europeans who showed interest in the architecture of the Indies probably also saw it as an example of the reintegration of place and sacredness lost in Europe.

In addition to mastery, nostalgia, and reflection, the display of the Dutch pavilion was also considered as representing a humanitarian purpose. In showing "a culture that is more ancient than that of Western Europeans," though "illiterate and uncivilized" (as cited in Gouda 1995: 218), the Dutch colonial authority exhibited the benevolence of its regime. Through "the assiduous labors of two generations of European scholars" (as cited in Gouda 1995: 218), this had exposed "native" intellectuals to the value of their own cultures as well as their own well-being.

The "sensitivity" towards Indonesian cultures accompanied the implementation by the Dutch of their "Ethical Policy" in the colony at the turn of the twentieth century (Ricklefs 1993: 151–62). This policy had roots both in humanitarian concern and economic advantage. Following the "liberal" period (c.1870–1900) private capitalism came to occupy a powerful position in shaping colonial policy. Yet it also came face to face with the "awakening" of social conscience, a feeling of guilt and moral responsibility on the part of the Dutch against the free play of economic progress. Caught between the need for economic progress and the "moral" duty to safeguard "humanity," the new Minister of the Colonies, A.W.F. Idenburg, declared in 1901 the new mission of Dutch colonialism:

> Not an increase in our possession, an increase in our power, an increase in our honor, an increase in our capital is the aim of colonial possession, but the advancement of the native population. Egoism is not the basic principle of our colonial policy, but higher motives. Power is not its legal basis, but the moral mission of a more advanced people toward less advanced nations, who are not of a lesser species than the western peoples, but who join with them in a single organism of humanity.
>
> (Idenburg, as quoted in Schmutzer 1977: 16–17)

Seen from a Machiavellian perspective, this colonial benevolence is an innovative strategy for maintaining colonial order. First, the attention given to creating a profound knowledge of the wide range of cultural practices within the archipelago produced a perception that the people of the Indies were ignorant about the complexity of their own world and were thus in need of colonial tutelage.[4] Represented as a mission to protect the indigenous population from the onslaught of Western enterprise, the Ethical Policy was meant to educate and uplift the Indies population by introducing modern European educational values and standards and promoted the "traditional" civilization of the Indies. Second, it sought to secure a "peaceful" space for the increasing number of Europeans who either came to or were born in the Indies and were being tempted to make it their home (Doorn 1983: 11). The Dutch business community began to see more than before its colony as at once a great place for living as well as for the world market, and thus required the raising of living standards there, including the provision for communication, stability and safety. Business interests therefore supported more intensive colonial involvement in matters concerning justice, welfare, and development. Humanitarian concerns coincided with the interests of business. Third, it was a response to the growing economic importance of the Outer Islands where international as well as Dutch capital began to diversify investment and sought to extract further raw materials. The immediate consequence of this was the need to train Indonesian skilled labor in modern enterprise and the reconceptualization of the colonial state as encompassing the whole of the present Indonesian archipelago.[5] While pressures of population growth, most notably of the Dutch community, demanded special attention, the penetration of the colonial apparatus in both the economic and social fields of the colonized was intensified. Under this new regime of power, it was not merely the state, but also the civil society of the colony that had to be rebuilt. Finally, the Ethical Policy was also the outcome of a fear of the increasingly politicized social groups organized, at that time, around issues of ethnic and religious "nationalism" and which often took the form of anti-colonialism (Doorn 1983: 11). Indeed, the coercive role of the Ethical Policy is indicated by the modifications implemented in response to disparate nationalistic tendencies, both ethnic and religious in character. Thus, the Minister of Colonial Affairs wrote to the young queen Wilhelmina in 1904 that a lasting possession of the colonies could be best secured through a "peaceful, righteous, and enlightened administration" (as cited in Gouda 1995: 24).

On this final account, the Ethical Policy could be seen as a conquest through pacification, instituting a multi-cultural partnership in which all participants were ordered by, and ultimately in the interests of, "humankind" under a benevolent, if not patronizing colonialism. Since then, the Indies state "embraced its role as a faithful sponsor of ethnographers, and information about local cultures improved in terms of quantity as well as quality" (Gouda 1995: 225). The practical task facing its "specific intellectuals" remained one of how to represent colonial "problems."[6] More specifically, it was a question of how to restore colonial order characterized by images of co-prosperity, peace, progress and achievement. This also meant a call for the creation of a representation which all the segmented colonial societies were supposedly willing to share. Here, a particular representation of architecture was to be thought out that would associate the colony with an ideal system of colonialism that was more efficient, productive and, not least, more humane. It is in this capacity that architecture was profoundly political.

GREATER NETHERLANDS: IMPORTED MODERNISM

In 1914, a report by the colonial Department of Agriculture, Industry and Commerce on the state of the built environment in the colony pointed out the general, if not total, lack of architectural principles in the design and construction of buildings in the Indies (Snuijff 1914). S. Snuijff, an architectural engineer in the Public Works Department, established only in the late nineteenth century, deplored:

> No national colonial architecture exists at present even after the three centuries during which the Dutch have been established in the East. Political and economic conditions have never promoted this, whereas the mild climate and the fertility of the soil have never created anxiety on the part of the uncivilised population to acquire better and more permanent dwellings . . . neither as regards size nor with a view to construction do the native buildings occupy a place of the slightest prominence in the architecture of the present time, the less so as an appreciable influence has never been exercised on the constructional works of the foreign races . . . Boroboedoer and similar temples, which although highly interesting, cannot serve as a sample of local architecture . . . not to mention the fact that already then their structures were mere ruins.[7]
>
> (Snuijff 1914: 1–2)

The arrival of many Dutch architects in the Dutch East Indies set up debates in architecture,[8] not least on how it could situate itself in a colony undergoing a new imperialism. The debates and contending practices showed, however, that the Ethical Policy did not manifest itself in a single architectural phase. The translation of the Ethical Policy into architecture produced many tendencies, each one in competition with the others.

The view of Snuijff, as quoted above, belongs to one side of the debate on how best to represent the new Ethical Policy. To Snuijff, the non-permanent dwellings of the indigenous were trivial when viewed within the grand structure of the Borobudur, conceived to be inherited from the Great Tradition of India.[9] Following the thesis of the "Indianization of Southeast Asia," fashionable at the time, Snuijff held the idea that the high civilization reached by the kingdoms of Java and Sumatra in the early centuries was largely due to the infiltration of Indian culture. Along this line, Wolff Schoemaker, Professor of Architecture at the Technical College in Bandung, West Java, argued in the 1920s:

> The Indies does not have an architectural tradition . . . Old forms are often no longer
> suitable to satisfy the practical and spiritual needs, anyway, so far as one can say about
> indigenous building methods. Architecture in the sense that it has for us does not exist
> in Java.[10]

(As cited in Jessup 1989: 132)

In denying the existence of an indigenous "architecture" this faction was conceived of "the irresistible advance of western civilization" leading to the complete assimilation of colonial society into the transformed modern metropole in the interest of the Netherlands (Doorn 1983: 12). In this view, the colony is subjected to a construction along the lines of the "metropole." Yet to make this practice work, the policy required the colony always to remain "backward" and thus "different" so that the process of "modernization" made sense to both the colonized and the colonizer. Accordingly, if the colony was to achieve a mutual partnership with the metropole, the indigenous culture that shared none of the "western" norms had to be marginalized and the norms of the West centralized. The ultimate outcome of the Ethical Policy would therefore be a "Tropical Netherlands" so that, in the long run, "there will be only eastern and western Netherlands, a unity in the political and national sense" (as cited in Doorn 1983: 12). While there is no evidence that a policy on architecture was imposed by the colonial state, the architectural implications of the adherents of the "Tropical Netherlands" tendency was most closely represented in the great variety of buildings that made explicit references to the architectural trends developed in the metropole. The first two decades of the twentieth century witnessed an expansion of architectural services in the colony to fulfill the demand for public buildings, commercial facilities, and housing. The architects, mostly Dutch and working privately and/or in the Public Works Department under the colonial state, favored Neoclassical styles, often with slight modifications according to the requirements of the climate.[11]

Other architectural movements included "international modernism" and "art deco." Reacting against the eclecticism of European classical architecture, these movements shared a conception of architecture as an artistic expression capable of transcending the social and the political. Influenced by the Dutch avant-garde in the metropole, "international modernism" believed in the universality of form; whereas the art deco movement aspired to the artistic conception of originality based on individual expression.[12]

These specific architectural tendencies discussed so far, each with its own ideologies, represent the experiments of the ideal of architecture in the late Dutch East Indies. Despite their different ideologies, they shared one tendency: the marginalization of the indigenous from the mainstream architectural cultures of "Europe." However, these architectural movements were only a specific tendency within a historical phase of architecture in the late colonial Dutch East Indies.

INDIES ARCHITECTURE: SYNCRETIC MODERNISM

Against the largely Eurocentric architectural vision of the Tropical Netherlands arose the vision of an "Indies architecture." This short-lived architectural movement, emerging only in the 1920–30s, was consciously developed by a distinct group of architects who shared the objectives of a Dutch intellectual movement of the time that proposed the idea of an "Indies society." According to this perspective, the Indies was made up of "a synthesis of interests and ideas to be borne by an increasing number of the archipelago's residents, a synthesis, therefore, neither 'Indonesian' nor 'Dutch,' but a combination of what all the participants had to offer" (Doorn 1983: 12). This cultural enterprise was not so much to represent the indigenous as having his/her own autonomy, nor to support the metropole, but was rather to provide the vision of a new colonial "Indies" society. Advocate of the self-reliance of the colony, the underlying cultural strategy of this group was, on the one hand, to resist mounting indigenous nationalism and, on the other, to avoid the provocation of Holland in the Indies (Doorn 1983: 11).

The central issue of the "Indies society" concerned the "development" of the Indies by means of exposing and cultivating the civilization of the colonized people. This subtler version of the Ethical Policy believed that the indigenous civilization had, on the one hand, to be protected against the destabilizing effects of European culture and, on the other hand, to be cultivated according to what Rabinow (1989) has termed "techno-cosmopolitanism." Techno-cosmopolitanism understands that society must be designed, planned and organized through art and science. It seeks this end through the use of the already existing cultural spaces seen to embody "modern" elements but which need reorganization. It is technological in that the operations are scientifically arrived at. It is cosmopolitan in that these technological operations themselves are applied in and through the context of specific cultures. This double vision of colonial power produced a discourse of modernizing the "indigenous" by carefully representing its "cultural heritage."

The architectural vision of "Indies architecture," according to its most prominent Netherlands architect, Henri Maclaine Pont, was to bring "west and east together without suppressing either ... Some typical differences between the architecture of the modern western and that of the eastern people were to have been expressed" (as cited in Jessup 1989: 211–12). This perspective was also shared with H.P. Berlage (1856–1934) who visited the colony to advance the course of "modern architecture." Berlage formulated "Indies architecture" as a synthesis of two elements: the modern constructive spirit, born of a rationalistic and intellectual knowledge that is universal and therefore eternal, and the spiritual aesthetic elements that are particularistic and therefore everywhere different. The task was to integrate the two elements, one representing the modernist "West" and the other, the localized "East."[13]

The two best known members of the "Indies architecture" movement, Henri Maclaine Pont and Thomas Karsten, arrived at this position not only through this academic conceptualization, but also through their historical background.[14] Henri Maclaine Pont (1884–1971), a liberal Dutch architect critical of colonialism, was born and grew up in the Indies before graduating from the Technische Hoogeschool at Delft, Holland, in 1902. Thomas Karsten (1884–1945) was also educated in the same school almost at the same time as Pont. He was known there as a member of the Housing Committee of the "Sociaal-Technische Vereeniging van Democratische Ingenieurs en Architecten" (STV-Social-Technical Society of Democratic Engineers and Architects) before he joined the architectural firm of Pont in Semarang, Central Java in 1914.[15] Critical of the general practices of colonialism, both Pont and Karsten, however, were also products of the Dutch intellectual environment of the time whose sympathy and interest towards Indonesian cultures remained within the scopic regime of Dutch colonialism.

For Karsten, the colonizer's assertion of Western style led not only to his growing isolation, but to the exposure of colonial contradictions. In 1914, he reflected on what he saw in the colony, and wrote:

> The absolute, inevitable, insoluble duality, lies in the essence of the colony: the contrast in tradition, degree of development and aims between dominating European and dominated indigenous life ... A successful architecture must express a unity of the spiritual and material needs ...
>
> (As cited in Jessup 1985: 138)

By imposing "the imperialistic Western ideas of the East," the colonizer not merely ran up against the "genius loci" of the Indies, but also confirmed the violence of colonialism which would eventually provoke the rebellion of the colonized, with "every 'tukang' " (workman) potentially a member of "a rebellious proletariat" (as cited in Jessup 1985: 138). In formulating the idea of "Indies architecture," Thomas Karsten began to see the advantages of bringing to the surface not only the different architectural narratives of the indigenous population but also the nobility and achievements of their civilization.

Karsten's concern with the state of architecture in the colony, in contrast to his contemporary, Snuijff, marks the growing awareness of the expanding Dutch community. A sense was developed that the values of indigenous culture, as understood by the colonizer, were to be taken as "real," at least, as construed through the optic of colonial knowledge of the indigenous civilization.[16] With Karsten, architecture not only played its role as a sign of foreign domination but also as a symbol of colonial pacification. Architects working on "Indies architecture" were convinced that the best way to achieve an "Indies society" was not by alienating the colony through an overwhelming architectural sign of "west(ernization)." Couldn't an "Indo-European Architecture," instead of a "European" one, play a more effective role in the process of cultural integration in the Indies?

In her study of the politics of design in French colonial urbanism, Gwendolyn Wright (1991: Chapter 3) has used the term "modernization and preservation" to describe an architectural effort aimed at achieving colonial pacification. It seeks to involve or indeed transform the colony in and through the "participation" of the indigenous counterpart. Rather than imposing a supposedly universal aesthetic, the technique comprised a blending of modernistic forms with traditional motifs, understood as a way of responding to the local "indigenous" context. In a similar line, Henri Maclaine Pont suggested in 1923:

> The invading people ultimately have an eye for the culture of the conquered and may prove receptive to it . . . Then no clash, no demonstration of supremacy is necessary, and the peoples draw together . . . [If there is] a living architectural tradition, a new mighty architecture can arise, heterogenous and not pure in style . . .
>
> (As cited in Jessup 1985: 144)

Here, the theme of a combined culture, and the possibility of the heterogenous display of culture in architecture suggests a more appropriate place for architecture in the colony. To achieve this, it became necessary for architecture to create a style that affirmed a genuine faith in the ability of indigenous architecture to provide a basis for future development. This suggests not merely a technique of architecture, but also a search, within the scopic regime of the discipline, for what are considered to be a "living architectural tradition" of the colony.

THOMAS KARSTEN AND THE DISPLACEMENT OF AUTHORITY

The architectural implications of the colonial Ethical Policy can be illustrated in the light of one of the most celebrated works of Thomas Karsten himself: the design of the People's Theater at Semarang, Central Java in the 1920s (Figures 1.2 and 1.3). Colonial interest in collecting and performing the culture and art of the Indies opened up this possibility. Karsten himself also enthusiastically embraced this idea with his designs for the Yogyakarta Sonobudoyo Museum.[17] Here we will look at the Semarang People's Theater as representing his desire, through a general colonial policy, to develop indigenous buildings without losing their "essential" identity.

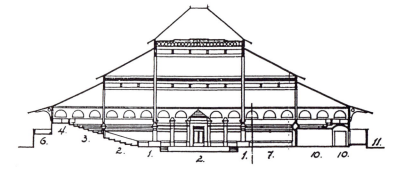

Figure 1.2
DECENTERING THE
PENDAPA: THE FOLK
THEATRE 1920, PLAN
Source: Thomas Karsten,
"van pendopo naar
volkschouwburg," *Djawa*,
1e jrg, no. 1, 1921: 21–9

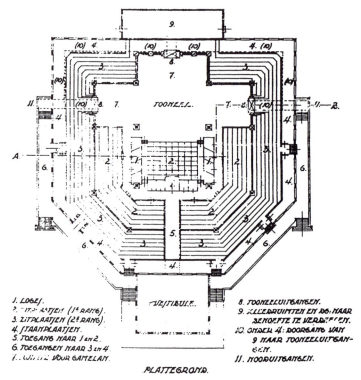

1. LOGES.
2. ZITPLAATJEN (1e RANG).
3. ZITPLAATJEN (2e RANG).
4. STAANPLAATJEN.
5. TOEGANG NAAR 1 en 2.
6. TOEGANGEN NAAR 3 en 4.
7. ... VOOR GAMELAN.

VESTIBULE.

8. TOONEELUITGANGEN.
9. KLEEDRUIMTEN EN R6. NAAR
   BENOEFTE TE VERDEELEN.
10. ONDER 4: DOORGANG VAN
    9 NAAR TOONEELUITGAN-
    GEN.
11. NOODUITGANGEN.

PLATTEGROND.

Figure 1.3
MODERN
TRADITIONALISM: THE
FOLK THEATRE,
SECTIONAL DRAWING
Source: Thomas Karsten,
"van pendopo naar
volkschouwburg," *Djawa*,
1e jrg, no. 1, 1921: 21–9

The project was intended to restore the popularity of the shadow "wayang" puppet performance which, according to Karsten, was more "profound, finer and more fantastic," (as cited in Jessup 1982a) than other performances of the Indies. The "wayang" show was normally maintained, performed, and promoted by the "kraton" (palace) or, more generally, by the middle and upper class Javanese, but, in Karsten's time, it was seen as more profitable to be adapted to a commercial proscenium theater independent of aristocratic patronage. The design programme was how to restore Javanese "civilization" and adapt it to "modern" times on one hand, and how to redefine the "people's" taste for cultural performances on the other.

By tradition, the "Wayang" puppet performance was staged in a Javanese elite house which is composed of three pavilions – the "pendapa," the "pringgitan," and the "dalem" – representing the public, intermediate, and private sections of the house (Figure 1.4) (Prijotomo 1984; Tjahyono 1989). In the

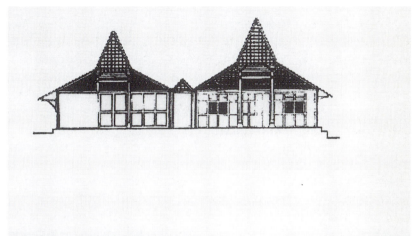

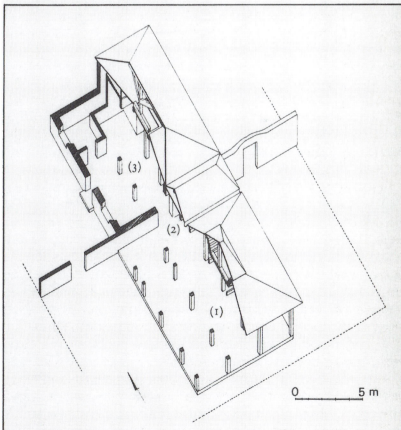

Figure 1.4
JAVANESE HOUSE
(1) PENDAPA
(2) PRINGGITAN
(3) DALEM
Source: J. Dumarcay, *The House in Southeast Asia.* Oxford University Press, 1987

"original" setting of "wayang" performance, the "pendapa" (an open pavilion supported by four central columns) is the place where the puppeteer and the gamelan orchestra are located. Here is also the place of the lamp that casts light onto the flat puppets which, in turn, cast shadows onto the screen. The screen itself is located in the "pringgitan" (the space in-between the "pendapa" and the "dalem" of the Javanese house). This setting provides two sides for viewing the screen: first, the side of the shadows cast by the wayang puppets visible from inside the "dalem" and second, the side of the puppeteers and its gamelan troupe visible from the "pendapa." In this sense, there is no fixed perspective from which the members of the audience can anchor their gaze in a frontal direction *vis-à-vis* the stage, as in the western theater. We are thus literally provided with two perspectives of the performance: in front of and behind the screen where the spectators see one another.

Karsten proposed his version of the Peoples' Theater by first detaching the (public) "pendapa" from the (private) spaces of the "pringgitan" and the "dalem." The separation of the "pendapa" from the body of the Javanese house seems to symbolically represent the detachment of Javanese performances from the princely patronage. The "pendapa" had to stand alone self-sufficiently as the ultimate space of performances so that it could function as a public as well as commercial "theater." The second architectural surgery is the incorporation of what Karsten considered to be the positive elements of the "pendapa," but at the same time eliminating its chief drawbacks, namely, its poor sight lines. According to Karsten, the sight lines of the traditional wayang performance, its two sides viewing, was "nothing less than a great disadvantage, and the 'pendapa' can have no future whatsoever as a theater if this is not taken care of" (cited in Jessup 1982a: 28).

To resolve this, the open spaces of the "pendapa" had to be spatially re-planned and formally re-defined. The "pendapa," organized around its four "soko-guru" master-pillars at the center, was thus divided by Karsten into a stage *vis-à-vis* the area of the audience. A background wall, defining the area of the stage, was thus built into the "pendapa" in order to provide for "modern" requirements (provision of dressing area, space for changing the background scenery, etc.) and make a varying performance easier. Along with this, the seats in successive tiers were raised above the floor level of the central area as in the European theater. In this way, the authority of the center from where the "soko guru" (master pillars of the "pendapa") stood was effectively dwarfed. The hierarchical system of the central arena and its surrounding areas were not only disrupted but also displaced by a new order. The center is no longer a space from which the performance takes control of the audience but instead it is "commanded" by the downward gaze of the audience.

The provision of the back stage made possible the accommodation of various types of entertainment, from different versions of "wayang" to modern drama and concerts, at once smoothing the way for a practical mode of flexible management associated with the notion of show business. All these transformations were conducted in the language of 'traditional" architecture. The result was, as Karsten indicated, "the ideal theater . . . for the traditional Javanese drama, but also . . . an extremely useful public building with a typical character of its own, the realisation of which would have idealistic, national and practical value" (cited in Jessup 1982a: 32). Thus the various kinds of "wayang" performance or other kinds of show were ready to be performed in the People's Theater, to be used "democratically' by the people for entertainment outside the structure of princely authority.

What is of interest in Karsten's architectural discourse is the metamorphosis of preservation, starting with the fully-fledged inventiveness towards the indigenous culture, and seeking to rescue its "deterioration" through architecture, inflecting it with rational modernist categories of efficiency, envelopment and containment. The People's Theater, while representing the traditional Javanese "pendapa," is nonetheless a kind of modern traditionalism. The traditional norms and forms were represented through the spatial and formal organization of modern architecture. The People's Theater was internally transformed into a "rational" space yet externally it retained the image of indigenous representation.

In his study of Victorian architecture, Mark Crinson (1996: 97–123) has discussed the attempt of British architect, James Wild, to design the church of St Mark in Alexandria, Egypt, to stand for a sympathetic colonialism. Wild's church, built in the form of an early Christian "basilica," was fashioned with remarkable Islamic details. Aimed at mediating two cultures, the Anglican community and Egypt's Islam, Wild's church represented the image of Islam. The Islamic components, gained through Orientalist scholarship, were shown, in Crinson's words, as "outwardly showy, non-figurative, intricately decorative, and even ceremonious" (Crinson 1996: 122) in their attempt to mask what is essentially an early Christian form of church. By incorporating certain passages in Egypt's history, this "localized" church depoliticized the British presence. Wild's use of architecture to represent a sympathetic colonialism might be appropriately compared to Karsten's efforts to come to terms with Javanese culture.

Karsten's working concept, however, while sharing the Orientalist paradigm of the East and the West binarism, was, nonetheless, a deconstruction of Orientalism. Whereas under Orientalism, the former was static and the latter dynamic, the progressive thought of "Indies architecture" refashioned the passivity of the East into an active one and thus enabled the two separate realms to constitute each other. Indigenous traditions, to quote Karsten's associate, Henri Maclaine Pont, were far from static; under the discourse of "Indies architecture," they "remain the basic element of the new formal language" (cited in Jessup 1985: 144).

For the Karsten we have so far evoked, if his work is characterized only in terms of the desire called "rationality," there was a risk of his being assimilated back into the "western" realm from which he had, quite consciously, distanced himself. To anticipate the argument, he came to terms with the "traditional" fabric and cultural image of the indigenous. It is my understanding that this solu-tion emerged from a premise that a total adoption of "modernist" architecture was pathological to colonial relations. It was the task of "Indies architecture" to overcome and propose the linguistic version of colonial pacification. Architects in the Indies ought to speak the "language" of the indigenous architecture and not import European modernism. It is in this manner that architecture at the time was implicated in the colonial Ethical Policy in its task of seeking a peaceful, righteous, and enlightened colonial administration.

REPRESENTING ARCHITECTURE: SEPARATING THE "PENDAPA" FROM THE JAVANESE HOUSE

The creation of a transformed "tradition" of the indigenous, as demonstrated by Karsten's People's Theater, no doubt owed much to the colonial classification of knowledge into "East" and "West," but it also emerged from a concern specific to the discipline of architecture. Here, the "indigenous" component, namely, the "pendapa," selected to represent the "civilization" of the Indies, was defined according to the architectural principles of the "West."

Before turning to the incorporation of the "pendapa" into "architecture," let us again take a brief look at the prototype of a Javanese house (Figure 1.4). As described above, the basic scheme of a Javanese house is composed of three structures, each with its own roof marking three different spaces, which formed a united whole (Prijotomo 1984). The first structure, situated at the front part of the house, is called the "pendapa," an open pavilion that is used for the recep-tion of guests and for performances. The second structure, called the "pringgi-tan," is a passage way to the back part of the house, thus forming a connecting space between the "pendapa" and the third structure of the house, the "dalem." Situated at the farthest access from the main gate, the "dalem" is the only walled-in structure in which the Javanese family lived.

The transformation of a Javanese house from its status as a "building" into that of "architecture" has recently been elucidated by Stephen Cairns (1997). Cairns traces the complex process by which the "pendapa," the verandah-like pavilion of the Javanese house, qualified as "architecture" in the 1920s after going through a set of specific disciplinary specifications established by promi-nent Dutch architects working in the Indies. The "pendapa" form became the highest manifestation of the Javanese "art of building in wood" because it satis-fied the structural, functional and formal requirements of representation in the discipline of architecture (Cairns 1997: 79).

Cairns also points out that the appeal of the "pendapa" to contemporary architectural sensibilities has resulted in the exclusion of other parts of the Javanese house, namely, the "pringgitan" and the "dalem" (see Figure 1.4). These two "inner" structures were considered as hidden. The "dalem" was somewhat enclosed, private and dark, like a cave, whereas the "pringgitan" is "invisible" because it is neither structurally spectacular nor spatially impressive;

instead, it is only a passageway, a "line" separating the public "pendapa" and the private "dalem." According to Cairns, for the Indies architects, these two structures did not fit satisfactorily within the conventions of representation in architecture (such as in drawing) which seek structural clarity.

But Cairns' imaginative investigation encourages one to go beyond his immediate analytical concerns. The representation of the public "pendapa" as the most developed example of "living architecture" suggests an "ethical" consciousness on the part of Dutch architects to leave intact the other half of the Javanese house (i.e. the "pringgitan" and the "dalem"). They are, after all, "private" spaces, an appropriation of which would certainly be an intervention into the supposedly "spiritual" domain of the indigenous. Only the "public" space and form of the "pendapa" then, according to the standard European architectural paradigm, was subjected to the imperative of rationalization. The political implication of this architectural surgery is a suggestion that there is an inner spiritual self of the indigenous (represented by the other half of the Javanese house), that in the minds of the Ethical architects, should be left intact. This other half is considered an unrepresentable "spiritual" domain of the indigenous. This working concept is more profoundly articulated in the works of Henri Maclaine Pont.

HENRI MACLAINE PONT AND THE RATIONALIZATION OF INDIGENOUS BUILDING TYPES

Along with Karsten's "modernization" of the Javanese building, architectural experiments were also conducted to discover if there was an indigenous tradition that would meet contemporary economic and construction standards and public health guidelines. Here, Henri Maclaine Pont, once an associate of Thomas Karsten, drew on his knowledge of the (grand) vernacular Javanese architectural scale and examined its style, its structure, and its common roots from the viewpoint and principles of Western "rational" architecture.

During his time in Holland, after returning from the Indies, Maclaine Pont undertook a study of the mathematics and physics of Javanese buildings in order to locate his architectural experiments in the colony on the "solid" terrain of the science of architecture. Imagining the structural principles of indigenous architecture was thus conducted through an analysis akin to that of a modern theory of structure. As a result of this scientific analysis, Maclaine Pont discovered a light and economical construction akin to modern architecture. In a word, it was found that the indigenous architectural tradition fitted perfectly with the principles of "modern" architecture. Only some architectural operations were needed in order that it could enter the modern world.

Maclaine Pont's intense study of Javanese building construction was published in 1923 in his best-known article: "Javaansche Architectuur."[18] In this article we find a diagram outlining the structural principles of the most representative buildings of Java (Figure 1.5). Maclaine Pont collected examples of prototypical Javanese architecture ranging from domestic to public buildings and subjected them to scientific scrutiny. The analytical framework was no doubt derived from European principles of structural architectonics. Selected types of Javanese architecture, arranged in a generic diagram for comparative study, were abstracted into a sectional drawing that shows only the structural principles of their buildings. Hierarchy was formed according to the hypothetical "development" of the structural principles, starting from the outline of a "tent." This mode of representation constructs a position for an evolutionary account of buildings in the Indies, from a "simple" type into a more complex one. Each type was given a caption showing the name and site of the buildings. However, as the diagram is based exclusively on a structural and formal appropriateness, all socio-cultural differences were effectively suppressed.

Based on this "technological" account, Javanese architecture was deemed as qualified to enter the modern age. In an account of Sudradjat (1991: 171–2), an Indonesian architectural historian, Maclaine Pont's study convinced him that "Javanese architecture is adaptable to present day purposes and is well suited with the Javanese way of life. Although this architecture does not yet fulfill modern hygienic, economic and constructional requirements, through significant modification some limited adjustments can be made."

In "modernizing" Javanese architecture, Maclaine Pont seems to have felt that his intervention in no way violated the "culture" of Java. Instead he believed that he had contributed to the culture of the indigenous society by elevating the form of their architecture into the realm of scientific progress, thus turning "handicraft" into developed architectural science and technology, based on representable "rationality." The rational enclosure of indigenous building types brought about a sense of control over the otherwise chaotic, unrepresentable "spiritual" world of the indigenous.

THE CONTRADICTORY VISIONS OF MACLAINE PONT

The architectural experiments of Maclaine Pont were two sided. They were motivated first by a concern to salvage the further development of architecture, and second, by the search for an appropriate architecture in the colony that was ultimately an attempt to help the indigenous people regain self-confidence.[19] Writing in *Djawa*, a periodical published in the colony for Dutch and Javanese elites interested in the study of Javanese culture, Maclaine Pont situated his discipline within the framework of this social mission. "Architecture is the environment man creates for himself from subjected nature, to create conditions . . . to make possible his own attitude to life, to bring about the required atmosphere and permit the demands of status" (cited in Jessup 1985: 141). The possibilities of architecture to improve human behavior permitted Maclaine Pont to imagine that a new architectural style would be an expression of the will to progress on the part of the indigenous people.

This professional benevolence, under the colonial situation, as Gouda

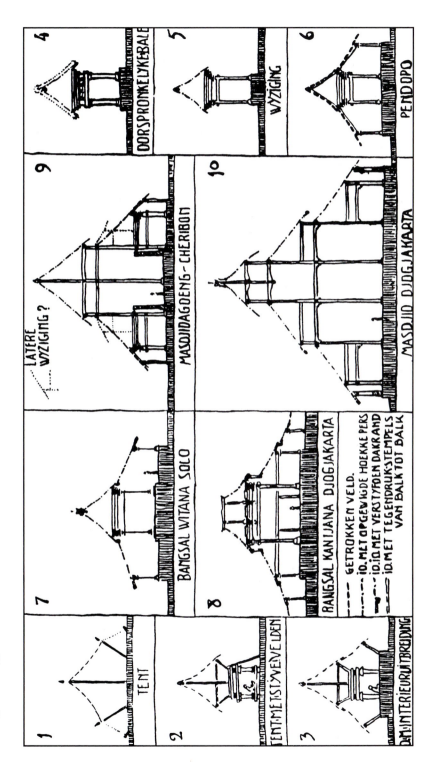

Figure 1.5
SCIENTIFIC EVOLUTION:
THE DEVELOPMENT OF
BUILDING STRUCTURE IN
JAVA
Source: Henri Maclaine
Pont, "Javaansche
Architectuur," *Djawa*, 4e
jrg, 1924

(1995: 221) points out, resided in a curious paradox. While the Indonesian people and cultures were theoretically allowed to speak for themselves, it was the Dutch archeologists who identified, excavated, and analysed a previously unmapped landscape and the long-forgotten "monuments" and other examples of vernacular architecture.

Maclaine Pont's architectural work was derived as much from his understanding of the local traditions as from his own professional subject position. His architectural enterprise to "modernize" Javanese architecture was built upon an analysis of its "structural essence," methodologically based on the "rational" principle of modern architecture. The contingency and the specificity of his architectural discourse suggested that his contribution, if not intervention, to the material culture of the indigenous remained incomplete. Colonial social structure allowed him to participate in institutionalized cultures of the colonized, but prevented him from becoming an "everyday" member of the indigenous society.[20] What he could do, on the basis of architectural form, was to demonstrate the capability of the material and rational progress of the indigenous people.

Yet, Maclaine Pont was also perfectly aware that for all his ingenuity in bringing together the technology of the "East" and the "West," he was disappointed that the cultural realm of the indigenous, the potential basis of architectural progress, remained inactive. His Javanese contemporaries showed no concern for the achievements of their ancestors whom Pont celebrated as the source of his architectural inspiration. Unable to adopt a Javanese identity within the colonial structure of power which he uneasily inhabited, Maclaine Pont was determined to give the Javanese the confidence that "they" were capable of achieving works of high quality, that they were equal to the "West." His conflictual subjectivity is well illustrated in the following exhortation to his fellow engineers:

> We, Dutchmen, in our support for the strivings of Javanese craftsmen and technicians
> for development and professional knowledge, have enough critical sense to discern and
> point out all that has become routine and continues to exist as untruthful ballast. But let
> us do it wisely.

> (As cited in Sudradjat 1991: 174)

There are many sides to this statement. First of all, traditional feudal values were outdated in Java, then the subject and object position; the implication of an outsider and insider; the professional vision of value-free specialists that contradicts the desire to be part of the routine culture of the Javanese, and to transform it from within. Here, neither "science" nor his professional "identity" could penetrate what Maclaine Pont thought of as the indigenous realm except by standing in the position of the observer and critically "discern and point out all that has become routine and continues to exist as untruthful ballast." Following these concluding remarks, as if inhaling a last breath of air, with a sense of loss that what *we*, the scientist, the professional, the heirs of rationality, the Dutchmen, could do towards the improvement of *our* fellow Javanese is merely to "do it wisely."

Pointing out the milieu of Maclaine Pont suggests that his work does not provide a full view of what is *outside* the all-encompassing attitude of his architecture. The "rationalization" of indigenous architecture implies the existence of an "other" dimension of indigenous architecture that he, consequently, assumed, but could not enter. Because of this impossibility to penetrate the indigenous cultural realm, Maclaine Pont implied the possibility of an alternative architecture that was not at all based on the rational "sign" of architecture. The Western architectural principle of "logos," which Maclaine Pont shared with the metropole, presumably closed down the possibility of thinking in terms of its "other."[21] In his view, this different and unspecified "other" does exist but is unthinkable. Maclaine Pont could only imagine the architecture of the indigenous from the "Western" position of dominance. He identified himself with the force of "logos" in Western architecture that he was supposed to serve in order to make possible the process of architectural development. His highest achievement inevitably was to function, albeit in a critical manner, according to the "Western" architectural system of thought within which he was intimately produced.

Pont's working concept, not unlike that of H.P. Berlage in Europe, suggested a division between the "rationality" of the West and the "spirituality" of the indigenous architecture. He came to terms with the "traditional" fabric and cultural images of the indigenous by elevating the form of their architecture into the realm of scientific progress, while leaving behind what was considered the "spiritual" world of the indigenous. In this sense, what the "modern" framework of indigenous building types brought was merely a sense of control over the otherwise unrepresentable "spiritual" world of the indigenous.

As a result, besides the structural principles of indigenous buildings, what finally becomes important to Pont's "Indies architecture" was the visible marks (the formal elements of the building itself) that represent a familiar or authoritative colloquial image of the indigenous traditional buildings (Figure 1.6). This is perhaps best represented in one of his most famous buildings in the Indies: the Bandoeng Technische Hoogeschool (Technical College of Bandung), today's Institute of Technology of Bandung (see Chapter 3).

THE BANDOENG TECHNISCHE HOOGESCHOOL

One of the most crucial aspects of the Ethical Policy was the education of Indonesians. The *Nieuwe Rotterdamsche Courant* had suggested that the idea of bringing young Indonesians to study at Dutch institutions in the Netherlands had created a "political problem." Such eager young men went socially and ideologically astray, and they began "to espouse extreme forms of nationalism because Moscow was searching for Revolution against the West through its mobilization of Asians" (as cited in Gouda 1995: 218). Hence, it became politically relevant to establish a technical college in the Indies.

Accordingly, the Bandoeng Technische Hoogeschool (Figure 1.7) was built

Figure 1.6
TECHNO-
TRADITIONALISM: THE
BANDOENG TECHNISCHE
HOOGESCHOOL, 1920
Source: P.H. van
Moerkerken Jr., and R.
Noordhoff, *Atlas
Gambar-gambar Akan
dipakai untuk
Pengadjaran Ilmoe
Boemi*, Amsterdam: S.K.
van Looy, 1922

and, concomitantly, became the best known "Indies architecture" of Maclaine Pont.[22] If the Paris Exhibition was an international statement of the Dutch to convey its colonial vision of the Ethical Policy, then in the colony, the message was communicated more directly to the indigenous people by the first technical college in the Indies, established in Bandung in 1920. Here, MacLaine Pont was given the opportunity to formulate an architectural rationalization of indigenous building. The university was established to provide the indigenous elites with the requisite technical knowledge. Commissioned by Dutch industrialists under the Ethical Policy, the building was a modern institution consciously designed to display an idiom of indigenous architecture. The concern to honor, conserve, modernize and integrate the myriad native cultures of the Indonesian islands was a central part of the programme in designing the campus. Just as the indigenous people were incorporated into the technocratic tendency of late Dutch colonialism, the building incorporated the roof shape of the indigenous Minangkabau house, responding simultaneously to the regional climate and local building materials. Maclaine Pont selected some of these indigenous architectural elements considered as "broadly based, relevant to the entire people" (as cited in Jessup 1985: 144).

Formally, the dominance of the indigenous idiom in the exterior and interior of the school ultimately dispels any illusion of the possibility of a "European" architecture. The buildings and interior spaces are furnished with local arts and crafts, as if the rationality of the engineering school, along with its institutional management, is contained by a series of grandiose traditional chiefs' houses of a particular region in the archipelago. On the one hand, the curving, multilayered roofs supported by a series of arched structures were a technologically advanced construction (Figure 1.8). On the other hand, the interior details of joints, the ornamented windows and doors, the exposed stone walls and columns, and the lucid composition of building materials, all exposed in their "natural-ness," was the epitome of Arts and Crafts design. The details of the buildings and the clear exposition of the structural logic intensify the rationality of the local arts and crafts. Presupposed here is the ultimate reconnection of the indigenous

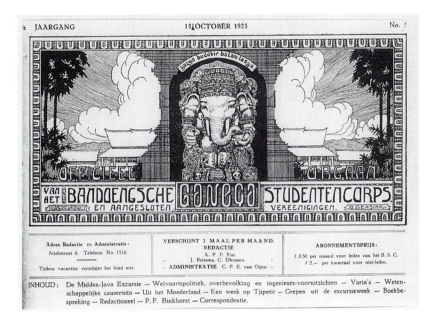

Figure 1.7
GANESHA: LOGO OF THE
BANDOENG TECHNISCHE
HOOGESCHOOL, 1923
Source: *Ganeca*, 1923

architectural style with the mechanistic activities but within a functional, structural and formal appropriateness of an architectural order of things.

Not unlike his architectural analysis of the indigenous buildings, Pont's design for the Bandoeng Technische Hoogeschool was limited to the visual aspect of indigenous cultures. The material culture of the Indies was exposed as highly technological. The Minangkabau roof of the Technische Hoogeschool was left as a trace of the indigenous rationality that has nothing to do with the socio-symbolic values of the "real" roof in the land of Sumatra. The visual cultures of the indigenous were adopted to represent an entirely new socio-cultural signification.

The Bandoeng Technische Hoogeschool could therefore be seen as the outcome of Maclaine Pont's experiment on how to integrate the scientificity of the institution, the Arts and Crafts movement he had sympathy with, and the indigenous culture he was emotionally attached to. It also represents the efforts of Pont to resolve his own ambiguous identity by integrating the best of both the indigenous and the metropole as suggested by the "new society" of the Ethical Policy. It also shows his ambiguous position towards colonialism, as how to think of a building as a statement for the changing colonial policy, from force to hegemony, from violence to pacification, demonstrating the subtlety of Dutch colonialism in coming up with new, more "sympathetic" symbols of power.

However, as a space where a post-enlightenment rationality was disseminated, higher education inevitably contained a gap which resulted from its internal contradiction. On the one hand, it sought to sustain colonial policy, but on the other hand, it sought its own disinterested coherence regardless of its ideological supports as an instrument of the colonial state. Made to be

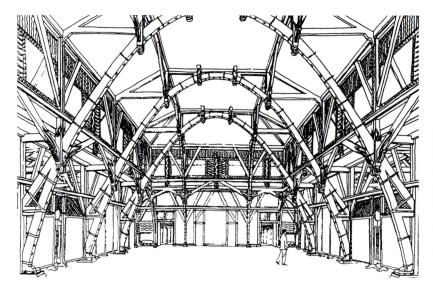

Figure 1.8
INTERIOR DESIGN OF
HENRI MACLAINE PONT'S
BANDOENG TECHNISCHE
HOOGESCHOOL, 1920
Source: Ben Leerdam,
*Architect Henri Maclaine
Pont*, Den Haag: CIP-
Gegevens Koninklijke
Bibliotheek, 1995

egalitarian within a colonial structure of inequality, higher education entered the history of colonialism in an ambivalent way. It produced "indigenous" professionals trained to sustain colonial hegemony, but it also unintentionally provided an intellectual basis for the emergence of elites who worked against colonialism. It is appropriate to recall that Sukarno, the first president of Indonesia, was himself the first graduate of the Bandoeng Technische Hooogeschool, choosing to design his nation instead of designing buildings for the Dutch elite.[23]

Sukarno's memories of the curriculum in the 1920s Bandoeng Technische Hoogeschool are worth recalling:

> Our curriculum was geared to a society of Dutch rule. The science I learned was science of a capitalist technique. For instance, the knowledge about irrigation systems. It was not how to irrigate rice fields in the best manner. It was only about the water supply systems for sugar cane and tobacco. This was irrigation in the interest of imperialism and capitalism, irrigation not to feed the starving masses, but to fatten the plantation owners. Our instruction in road building could never benefit the population. Roads were not engineered to be cross-jungle or intra-island so people could ride or walk better. We were taught only to plan byways along the seacoast from harbour to harbour so factories might have maximum transportation of goods and proper communication between sailing vessels. In sketching class, when we drafted a model town we also had to indicate the residence of the 'kabupaten,' the District Chief who watches over the slaving peasants. The week of graduation I discussed this with the Rector Magnificus of the Technical Faculty, Prof. Ir. G. Klopper, M.E., [who explained] 'this Technical Institute was established primarily to promote The Hague's policy in the Indies. To keep pace with the rate of expansion and exploitation, my government feels more engineers and skilled workers overseas are needed.'

> (Sukarno 1966: 67)

CONCLUSION

In this chapter I have shown that one of the most remarkable products of "Indies architecture," as exemplified by Karsten and Maclaine Pont, was the "essential modernity" of "indigenous" architecture. The Dutch architects showed the "nobility" as well as the "activity" of indigenous architecture by elevating it to the level of its Western counterpart. Yet in "modernizing" the architectural image of the indigenous, they also suggested it had an inaccessible spiritual realm.

Homi Bhabha (1983: 202) has written about the ambivalence of colonial discourse as a construction of the "indigenous" by the colonizer in a form of contradictory belief that moved between the recognition of difference and the disavowal of it. As a discourse "at the crossroads of what is known and permissible and that which though known must be kept concealed," (Bhabha 1994: 89) colonial discourse produced its "other." This presumably "other" narrative, which may not have an object, was seen as an "inside" of the cultural realm of the indigenous which the Dutch architects did not enter as a result of both their social and disciplinary constraints. It is this supposedly inner space of authenticity, left open by colonial discourse, which later on becomes the repertoire from which official Indonesian nationalism is able to claim its "authenticity" and suggest "Indonesian architecture."

The myth of an "authenticity," existing outside colonial power, suggests that Indonesia, while "materially" colonized for "three hundred years" under Dutch colonialism, "spiritually" remained intact. Indeed, this is also an aspect of the Ethical Policy that did not aim at a wholesale transformation of Indonesian society. Despite its more or less revolutionary appeal, the experience of the 1900–30 period of Ethical Policy did not affect the totality of the social and cultural structure of Indonesian society (Wertheim and Giap 1962).

"Indonesia" was thus never remembered as a colonial construction. In one of the most well-known rhetorics of Sukarno, Indonesia was represented in terms of its "own" development "from a glorious past" to the "time of darkness (Dutch colonialism)" and later on, in a matter of fact way, to "the promising, pure, and luminous future" (Sukarno in 1930, as cited in Oetomo 1961: 75). Colonialism's cultivation of "indigenous" identities and civilization placed "Indonesia" within its own genealogy and (apparently) outside colonial legacies.

This, as I will argue in the following chapters, also suggests the cultural strategy of the postcolonial discourse on "Indonesian architecture" which seeks to imagine its own "new" identity drawn from the material progress of the "West" and safeguarded by the spirituality of the "nation." Yet, since "Indonesian architecture" is anticipated by the Dutch late colonial representations of "Indies architecture," its identity is fundamentally split. For while it is a mark of the "indigenous," it is also haunted by its colonial construction (Figure 1.9).

Partha Chatterjee (1993; 1996) has argued that the fundamental feature of anti-colonial nationalism in Asia and Africa lies in the separation in the world of

Figure 1.9
SKETCHING TRADITION:
THE INSTITUTE OF
TECHNOLOGY AT
BANDUNG (ITB), 1950
Source: Bandung
Institute of Technology
Prospectus, 1950

social institutions and practices of two domains – the material and the spiritual. The former has been the domain of the economic and technological development dominated by the West; the latter is the "essential" marks of cultural identity generated by the nationalists *outside* colonial power and which then provides them with a means to negotiate with the "West." What I have tried to show in this chapter is that this "authentic" spiritual space eloquently preserved by Chatterjee so that the nationalists might gain their agency, owed much to such colonial "middle" subjects as Thomas Karsten and Henri Maclaine Pont who both remained ambivalent towards colonialism.

Chapter 2: Modern Architecture and Traditional Polity

Jakarta in the Time of Sukarno

> Despite all the political rhetoric that has been invested in arguing that one can
> differentiate decisively between variants of modern culture – that certain architectural
> styles are inherently "fascist," that constructivist principles are intrinsically "progressive,"
> or that heroic iconography is uniquely "socialist" – these cultural forms have shown
> themselves remarkably resilient, adaptable to the most diverse social and political
> purposes.
>
> (Buck-Morss 1995: 4)

Recent studies on culture and imperialism have put forward the importance of European colonialism (often under the curious notion of "modernity") in the formation of what is generally known as "modern" architecture and urban design.[1] These studies show that architecture and urban design, instead of being just aesthetic and technological issues, become an integral part of European political and cultural domination providing a way to establish order, regulate activities, and separate populations especially during the nineteenth and twentieth centuries.[2]

This genre of scholarship has made possible analyses of modern architecture and urbanism within the distinct socio-political contexts of postcolonial countries in a similar manner – that is, to see them as part of given political strategies at particular historical moments. Indonesia, for instance, can first be seen as a postcolonial country which inherited colonial space and is now investing it with a new symbolic meaning representative of the society of which it is now a part. Second, the contemporary Indonesian state can equally be seen as a colonizing power where architecture and urban design are political representations and instruments of control.

Yet, in adopting the categories of European "colonialism," "modernity" or its expression, "modern(ist) architecture," as something of an "ideal type" which I can use to explain the dynamics of a postcolonial condition, I also put myself in a position of treating the latter as part of a "universal," if not "European" history of the modern world. I have, of course, no essential objection to this approach, one that is both powerful and important. However, I also realise that if the discourses of architecture and urbanism in the rest of the world have to choose "colonialism," "modernity," or "modernism" as forms of categorical analysis, already made available to them by "Europe" and the Americas, what conceptual or categorical apparatus do they have left to think about the transformation of their own social and spatial environments?

In this and the following chapter, I consider the question of the local reception of the global cultural flows of modernist architecture and the distinctive historical and political meanings that are invested in this. To begin with, I consider architecture and space as a representation of local objectives and not as a variety of historical concerns that amount to an "essence" of the historical object being studied, such as European "colonialism," or "modernism." With this understanding, different techniques of representation and strategies of identity formation will emerge.

This chapter analyses the representation of Jakarta, the capital city of Indonesia, in the early days of Independence when it was conceived by the first president, Sukarno, as the "portal of the country" and the "beacon of the emerging nations" of Asia and Africa. I argue that, in adopting modernist architecture for Jakarta, architect Sukarno's concern was not so much whether the concept was from the "East" or "West" but rather how he could best put Jakarta on the map of world cities. Nonetheless, the driving force of this modern international imagining was still to stem from the "old" cultural milieu of Java.

The purpose of this chapter, however, is not to emphasize once more an "oriental exceptionalism" (Chatterjee 1996: 224). Instead, it seeks to demonstrate that the presumed exceptions, not unlike their European "modernist" counterpart, are only a particular form of a different and more contradictory conceptualization of a global culture. In other words, seen from Jakarta, through what Anderson (1998) calls "an inverted telescope," European modernist universalism in the eyes of the Jakarta leaders is no more than a particular form of a much richer and more diverse set of cosmologies of the world.

This chapter, therefore, has as its main purpose the reframing of the problem of understanding "modernism" in other parts of the world. Its second purpose is to draw an analytical line between "universal" modernism and "particular" nationalism by showing the ways in which the former's expression of architecture and urban design are used to construct a particular "national culture" in a postcolonial country. The third is to demonstrate the profound ambivalence of the postcolonial nation–state in its effort to construct a "national culture" that generates a mutually constitutive, yet contradictory identification: an attitude to "modernity" that is simultaneously an acceptance and a rejection of it.

HISTORICAL ANOMALY OR ALTERNATIVE MODERNITY?

The history of independent Indonesia after 1950 is a story of the failure of successive leadership groups to meet the expectations of democracy generated by the successful struggle for independence (Feith 1962). Already by 1957 the democratic experiment had collapsed. A historian of the country reported that "corruption was widespread, the territorial unity of the nation was threatened, social justice had not been achieved, economic problems had not been solved, and the expectations generated by the Revolution were frustrated" (Ricklefs 1993: 237).

Between 1957–65, Sukarno, installed in 1950 as the first president of independent Indonesia, instituted the so-called nation-building Guided Democracy project. Central to Sukarno's policies of these years was the reconstruction of Jakarta to demonstrate the regime's commitment to a form of national discipline and the need to attract international recognition.

Sukarno's "urbanistic" projects have been characterized by some scholars interested in the field of urban symbolism as representative of the competitive (inter)national order of the time. In this account, the urban design of central Jakarta is seen as part of Sukarno's larger political plans to enforce his authoritarian regime (Boddy 1983).[3] Several studies have considered the built form of the transformed capital city – the modernist "international style" architecture, current in the 1950s – as an attempt by Sukarno to foster a national unity and identity for the Indonesian people (Sudradjat 1991; Leclerc 1993; Macdonald 1995; Wiryomartono 1995). In this interpretation, the "modern" part of Jakarta was intended to raise the self-esteem of the Indonesian people after a long period of colonization.

While providing valuable accounts of the spatial "modernity" of Jakarta, these studies are hardly adequate in themselves. Other studies have been made of this period, by scholars from different disciplines, which accept Sukarno's own view that Guided Democracy was a return to something more in keeping with Indonesia's, and specifically Java's, past (Anderson 1990: 73). In this account, as this chapter will show, the building of a stadium, monuments, grand avenue and vast public spaces as a central part of the capital city were meant to convey an expression of, or a struggle over, legitimacy similar in function to the court ceremonial of the pre-colonial age.

Following this perspective, it is nonetheless worthwhile to ask why Sukarno, the latest Javanese ruler of the time whose Guided Democracy policy represented itself as a continuation of Java's past, did not revive features of traditional architectural culture such as the classical "Joglo" roof, the "sokoguru" column, the "pendapa" form, or the traditional layout of the royal court. In other words, in harnessing architecture in support of the traditional Javanese conception of political power, why was so-called modernist architecture and urban design chosen, when centuries old Indic-Javanese architectural traditions, canonized by both the ancient courts and the late colonial Dutch orientalist society, already existed? How could modernist architecture be reconciled with, and ultimately represent, a national polity which claimed descent from an ancient "indigenous" political system?

This chapter suggests that, in harnessing modernist architecture to the cause of his nation-building project, Sukarno's aim was to put into place a much older cultural and political matrix from pre-colonial Java. The modernity and monumentality of the capital city owed as much to a spatial conception derived from the traditional polity of the ancient Javanese kingdom as it did to the tradition of "modernism" that dominated political imaginations in both Eastern and Western Europe for most of the century. Modernist architecture and urban design are never transhistorical, transcultural or transpatial: they always carry different meanings wherever they are located. My aim in this chapter therefore is to interpret architectural modernism historically *within* the political culture of Indonesia's Guided Democracy in order to show its role as both a progressive national unifier and a reinforcer of traditional values. Rather than attempting to discover a universal explanation of modernism that accounts for various kinds of "monuments" in Sukarno's Jakarta, I explore local spatial concepts within a Javanese political tradition to grasp the otherwise invisible conservatism of Jakarta's elites. My aim is to contextualize the flows of architectural culture in specific situations.

There is, in fact, a remarkable paradox in Sukarno's "nation-building" of Jakarta that is central to the production of postcolonial Indonesian identity. This, I argue, was constructed out of a complementary contradiction of identity and difference, of juxtaposing local tradition and global modernity. On one side, Sukarno claimed that he (and his government) embodied traditional Javanese conceptions of power; on the other, when manifesting these ideals in the built environment, he eschewed traditional architectural expressions of that conception. In conceptualizing this paradox within Sukarno's "nation-building" Guided Democracy project, this chapter shows how the complementary identification of both local and global is mobilized.

The period of Guided Democracy is chosen because it most effectively frames the discourse of "nation-building." For Sukarno, this literally means the covering of a central part of Jakarta with representative buildings of a "modern" kind, marking it as a new national space that was different from both the colonial towns and the surrounding sea of poor urban neighborhoods collectively described as "kampung" – "a residential area for lower classes in town or city" (Echols and Shadily 1992).[4] It was also a period in which Sukarno, who prided himself on being a "megalomaniac architect,"[5] was given, legislatively, full powers to take control of the country in general and the capital city in particular.

THE UNITED NATION'S MASTER PLAN: CONFLICTING ASPIRATIONS AND REALITIES

Soon after the transfer of sovereignty from the Dutch in 1950, the capital of the newly independent nation witnessed the most rapid population expansion in the city's history, bringing tremendous urban pressure on the municipality.[6] The aftermath of Revolution, the unrest that plagued the outskirts of Jakarta and its surrounding regions, and the unfavorable economic conditions in the villages of Java and outer islands where production was down and fewer goods were available were the principal reasons (Abeyasekere 1987: 172–3). These contributed to the attraction of Jakarta as perhaps the ultimate symbol of security, opportunity and, not least, "modernity."

Writing in 1953, sociologist J.M. van der Kroef (1954) described the aura of Jakarta in terms of this "modern" experience:

> Life in a 'kota Parijs' like Djakarta has cast a magic spell even on those who live far from the city's crowded, bustling roar. A modern city, with modern ways and urban conveniences is a concretization of revolutionary aspirations, affording education, material comforts and an escape from ennui, or so it is hoped.
>
> (As cited in Kroef 1954: 157)

The concentration of "aspirations, affording education, material comforts and an escape from ennui" after decolonization inevitably replicated the hierarchical Dutch colonial geography that had established Batavia, the future Jakarta, as the center. However, the postcolonial image of Jakarta as the "center" hardly matched the reality of the city, marked by massive population increases and their attendant squalor, popularly simplified as the problems of the kampung. As Kroef (1954) pointed out:

> Existing 'kampungs' are long since filled to the brim and new arrivals in the city are thrown largely upon their own resources, roaming around by day, and finding a place to sleep in whatever unoccupied nook or cranny they can find.
>
> (As cited in Kroef 1954: 158)

Arriving in Jakarta as a boy in 1951, and sharing a bed with two other men in a small room inhabited by five people, novelist Ayip Rosidi recalled:

> It was entirely beyond anything I had imagined before actually coming to Djakarta, and I felt nauseated. I had never, never thought I could live in such squalor. Yet little by little . . . I grew familiar with Djakarta housing, knowing that it was sometimes possible to live in a row of shacks, as we did, only after some stroke of good luck.
>
> (As cited in Abeyasekere 1987: 174)

Although the city boundaries were altered to take in the sparsely populated surrounding regions, making the Jakarta of 1950 three times the area of the old municipality, the bulk of the (poor) population was still concentrated in the old center (Abeyasekere 1987: 171).[7] An early response, in an attempt to discipline the city center, was the planned removal of the homeless. In an official history of the municipality, the mayor reveals that, in the early 1950s, in an effort to beautify Jakarta, he took steps to clear the city of homeless people. "Unlike now, they were sleeping in shop verandas, under bridges, in little huts alongside railway lines, so that foreign people stared at them and they lowered the status of the nation" (as cited in Abeyasekere 1987: 198).

Figure 2.2
"LIKE THE EIFFEL
TOWER": THE NATIONAL
MONUMENT UNDER
CONSTRUCTION
Source: Karya Jaya, *Karya
Jaya: Kenang-kenangan
Lima Kepala Daerah
Jakarta, 1945–1966,*
Jakarta: Pemerintah
Daerah Khusus Ibu Kota

years of war with the Indonesians who proclaimed their Independence in 1945, left the plan incomplete. The architectural execution of this square of governance, its surroundings and the new southward thoroughfare had to wait until the postcolonial regime to be completed.

It was not by chance that the city's first priority was to host the fourth Asian Games in 1962 and, a year later, the First Games of the New Emerging Forces (GANEFO).[11] It was clear that, for Sukarno, the Games had a ceremonial function. They could project a future in which Jakarta, in the eyes of neighboring nations, could be seen as "the beacon of the New Emerging Forces" of Asia.[12] The spectacular events in which thousands of people took part were represented with the six-lane thoroughfare from Independence Square, passing south through a series of newly built highrise office buildings, the Hotel Indonesia, the Sarinah Department Store, the clover-leaf bridge, to the Asian Games Complex and the Convention Hall of the New Emerging Forces, all in the form of a modernist urban environment (Figures 2.4, 2.5, 2.6). They were organized as part of exciting occasions at which the "modern" environment within Jakarta was made to envelop the crowds of the transnational alliance.[13]

Internally, the new cityscape demonstrated the power and the splendor of the ruling regime. Orchestrated by the state, the Games and the built environment of Guided Democracy attained a status very close to what Clifford Geertz (1980: 123) has called the "exemplary center." Here, "the state drew its force . . . from its imaginative energies, its semiotic capacity to make inequality enchant." However, this political function of ceremony was not an end in itself but represented to the participants the conjuring up of the power of the ruling

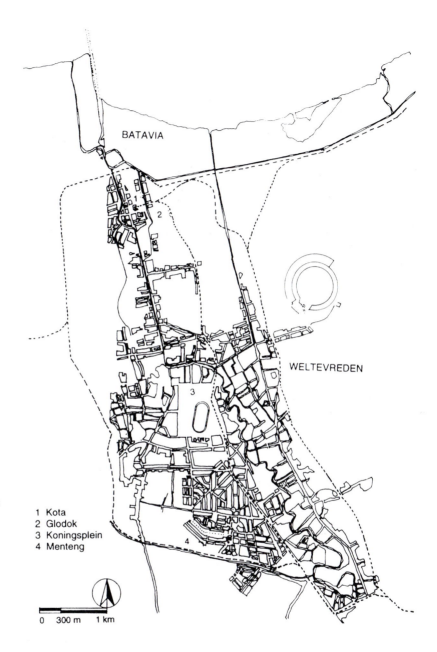

Figure 2.3
INDEPENDENCE SQUARE:
THE KONINGSPLEIN
TODAY
Source: Bagoes
Wiryomartono, *Seni
Bangunan dan Seni
Binakota di Indonesia*,
Jakarta: PT Gramedia
Pustaka Utama, 1995

1 Kota
2 Glodok
3 Koningsplein
4 Menteng

0 300 m 1 km

realm which is both active and aggressive. The large-scale entertainment provided a spatial focus for the people to witness that the nation–state existed and
was moving forward, generating its power by organizing extra-national events.
The President proclaimed:

> Projects such as the Asian Games, the National Monument, Independence Mosque, the
> Jakarta By-pass, and so on, are examples of 'Nation-Building' and 'Character Building'
> . . . of the whole Indonesian people striving to recover our national identity. Who is not

Figure 2.4
PUTTING THE FINAL
TOUCH: SUKARNO
EXPLAINS THE MODEL OF
THE MAIN
THOROUGHFARE, 1960s
Source: S. Damais, *Bung
Karno dan Seni*, Jakarta:
Yayasan Bung Karno,
1979

Figure 2.5
SUKARNO INSTRUCTS:
"SET THE WINGS BACK
30%" AND WISMA
NUSANTARA APPROVED!
Source: S. Damais, *Bung
Karno dan Seni*, Jakarta:
Yayasan Bung Karno,
1979

aware that every people in the world is always striving to enhance its greatness and lofty ideals? Do you remember that a great leader of a foreign country told me that monuments are an absolute necessity to develop the people's spirit, as necessary as pants for somebody naked, pants and not a tie? Look at New York and Moscow, look at any state capital, East and West it makes no matter, and you always find the centers of nations' greatness in the form of buildings, material buildings to be proud of.

(As cited in Leclerc 1993: 52)

Loaded with male metaphors, drawing on lessons from the world, claiming universality for monumental cities, a stable polity had to show signs of an ability to maintain and extend its influence further and further afield. For Sukarno, it was

Figure 2.6
MODERNIST CITYSCAPE
UNDER CONSTRUCTION,
1960s
Source: Dean Conger,
National Geographic,
January 1971: 6

the representative structures of a state capital that Jakarta badly needed. Such monuments were a necessity not a luxury, "pants and not a tie." For Sukarno, "problems of identity are problems of daily life" (as cited in Leclerc 1993: 52).

In her study of Italian city planning for the "Esposizione Universale di Roma" (Rome Universal Expo), Mia Fuller (1996) indicates the importance of international exhibitions for the legitimation of power in the Fascist regime of Italy. The exhibition for the (European) world of the spatial possessions of the Italian empire and the historical continuity of Italian civilization served to transform Italian society. In this way, they were made to believe in the progress of the country and the necessity of colonization abroad. Fuller's account of the importance of spatial and architectural representations in the making of Italian political culture provides an earlier, though parallel example, to the efforts of Sukarno in quite a different social formation to convince Indonesians that the transformation of Jakarta was a necessity, if not a natural progression, of the whole Indonesian people. With this glorious vision of Indonesia, Sukarno wrote:

> Man does not live by bread alone. Although Djakarta's alleys are muddy and we lack roads, I have erected a brick-and-glass apartment building, a clover-leaf bridge, and our superhighway, the Djakarta Bypass, and I renamed the streets after our heroes: Djalan Diponegoro, Djalan Thamrin, Djalan Tjokroaminoto. I consider money for material symbols well spent. I must make Indonesians proud of themselves. They have cringed too long.

(As cited in Abeyasekere 1987: 210)

In the mid-1950s, the municipality began to build up Jakarta as the idealized center of power. They immediately encountered what Abeyasekere (1987: 197) sees as "the three main sources of conflict: illegal occupation of land, homeless people, and street traders and buskers." Under the martial law of early Guided Democracy, 47,000 people were moved to make way for the 1962 Asian Games project. The six-lane thoroughfare required the moving of hundreds of houses from the site, their inhabitants transported to resettlement areas elsewhere. Uncontrolled street vendors and entertainers were relocated to a "proper" place under the patronage of private and public institutions (Abeyesekere 1987: 197–9). A limit was thus set to the excessive over-flow of the kampung by means of monumental structures that ordered and symbolized the capital city as a center of Indonesian postcolonial power.

Sukarno, himself an architectural engineer and early product of the Bandoeng Technische Hoogeschool – today's Bandung Institute of Technology, established by the colonial government in 1920 (see Chapter 1) – was seemingly devoted to the modernist idea of architecture and city planning of the 1950s, one that could serve his vision of a new society. A "universal" modernist vision of a capital city was appropriated to establish a new center of power, externally for the gaze of neighboring rulers, and internally for the admiration of national territorial subjects.[14]

It is possible to view Sukarno's architectural and urban discourses as part of a more general trend toward the hegemony of the modernist paradigm worldwide. But it is also not difficult to see that there is something else behind Sukarno's obsession with a "modern" city. When Sukarno envisioned Jakarta as the portal of the country and the beacon of the new emerging nations, he was also speaking about the importance of having an authoritative center akin to the Javanese spatial concept of power. The concern therefore is to restore the authority of the ruling regime *vis-à-vis* its allies and also its enemies in other realms.

RESTORING TRADITIONAL AUTHORITY: JAVANESE CENTRALISM AND THE TRANSLATION OF MODERNISM

In his studies of the Southeast Asian traditional polity, Benedict Anderson (1990: 17–77) indicates the driving forces of the pre-colonial Javanese concept of power which, he argues, still significantly marked the cultural values of postcolonial ruler(s).[15] Drawing from various sources, Anderson indicates that the spatial representation of power in the classical regime of Southeast Asia (up to the fifteenth century, before European colonialism) is based upon the concept of the "mandala" that is composed of a center surrounded by a complex of hierarchically, but mobile, lower satellites.[16] The spatial dimension of power is not determined by well-defined territory but by the amount of power a regime can concentrate in the center. The center therefore, as Anderson (1990: 36) illustrates, works like the casting of a light, the radiance of which decreases as it travels outwards. The real challenge of the ruling regime is therefore to concentrate power in the center so that the neighbors would be made to voluntarily submit themselves, by means of tribute and acknowledgment, to the superiority of the supreme power of the ruler. The ideal form of power is achieved when all conceivable political entities are absorbed in a coherent unity centered on the Supreme Ruler ("Chakravartin") that made him the "world" empire.[17] This centripetal character of the Javanese polity explains the reason why the names of empires and kingdoms in Javanese tales and historical traditions are those of the capital cities.[18] Working like a "beacon," the center demands a concentration of power on one particular space that, for our case, is Jakarta, the capital city. To avoid the dispersion of power, which indicates a looseness at the center, a representation of a central symbol of power is necessary.

Within this logic, the concentration of large populations, important monuments, and arts and cultures from the (imagined) territories of the state signify that the power is still in the possession of the designated ruler. Similarly, the attraction and accommodation of many disparate groups, and particularly certain elite circles to the center, with its displays of power taking many different forms, would be deemed necessary (Geertz 1983: Chapter 6). Here, political buildings of monumental scale and commercial and cultural facilities fashionable at the time, are but one of the organizing principles to attract loyalties and possibly dispossess rivals of their hegemonic claims. They are signs that people were able to imagine – as verification – that government was in the correctly designated hands.

Since the concentration of power in the form of unity is a central symbol of power itself, fragmentation, multiplicity and competition are signs of weakness, the occurrence of which will lead to the disintegration of power (Anderson 1990: 36). This anxiety about the dispersion of power underlies Sukarno's centralism. His aspiration to put Jakarta on the map of the world's capital cities was, therefore, built not merely on the glories and binding power of decolonization; more importantly, it stemmed from a recognition of internal conflict, divisions, and danger *within* the territory of his imagined space. For some considerable time, the newly independent country faced disintegration, signified by inflation, factionalism and regionalism. Sukarno pointed to the rebellions of internal insurgents, regularly emerging in the islands beyond Java, against the authority of the new central government. These rebellions indicate the looseness of the center that, in turn, needed what Sukarno in 1952 considered as "authorities [that] should be bold enough to reestablish the instinctive and natural respect for Authority" (as cited in Feith and Castles 1970: 75).

In 1958, as unrest in the regions outside Java continued and conflicts between parties under Parliamentary Democracy remained unsettling, Sukarno in 1957 determined to recall the Authority of Javanese centralism by implementing his policy of "Guided Democracy"[19]:

> I merely wish that Indonesia may become whole again, that the state becomes whole again . . . I want to propose something that is in harmony with the Indonesian spirit, the real spirit of the Indonesian Nation, that is: the spirit of family life.
>
> (As cited in Feith and Castles 1970: 88–9)

The realm of government was going through a chaotic phase. One-man rule was deemed necessary to restore the well-being of the "national family." The move from "liberal" to "Guided Democracy" meant a change to one-man administration in Jakarta, a form of unity which in itself is a central symbol of Javanese power. It appears that the change to "the centralized and personality-centered type of administration was generally felt to be more consistent with the institutionalized authoritarian structure of Indonesian society at large" (Selosumardjan in 1961, as stated in Feith and Castles 1970: 129).

What I am suggesting here is that there is a sense in which there is an appropriation of modernist architecture and space to sustain the presentation of "power" that is peculiar to the political culture of traditional Java. The constructive principle of Sukarno's Jakarta, the modern architectural language it adopts, was seemingly shared with the Utopian iconography of Maoist socialism and also resonated with pre- and post-war architectural movements in the West – the German Bauhaus, Italian Futurism, and Le Corbusier's modernism – but these cultural forms were adopted by Sukarno's regime to represent what is remarkably indigenous to Indonesia – the "power" of Javanese culture.

MONUMENTS, EMPIRE AND SPACE

Twenty years earlier – on 3 January 1946, a year after the proclamation of independence – Sukarno left Jakarta, which was unsafe at the time, and stayed in Yogyakarta, Central Java, a city where one "ancient" Javanese court is located. Yogyakarta served as a provisional capital of the Republic of Indonesia up to the middle of 1950. A day after his arrival, Sukarno broadcast on the radio his thoughts on the "national state" and the function of the "capital city" as the center of power and leadership. "No 'nationale staat' can endure without co-ordination. No 'nationale staat' can exist without centralism. Russia has Moscow, America has Washington, England has London. Mojopahit had Wilwo Tikto" (as cited in Leclerc 1993: 56). Here, the identification of the national state with the influential fourteenth century Mojopahit kingdom of Java, whose power is said to have gone beyond today's national territory, suggested a return of a spatial and political imagination centered on the exemplar of a capital city. Sukarno was sometimes critical of the ancient regime of Majapahit as a symbol for the new Indonesia because "the imperialism of Majapahit which dominated almost the whole Archipelago plus Malaya were not different from any other forms of imperialism" (as quoted in Supomo 1979: 183). Nonetheless, the "political culture" on which Jakarta is based appears to derive from the idea of the "center" of this ancient political and spatial representation. Sukarno's Jakarta was imagined through the image of the ancient Wilwo Tikto, the center of the Majapahit kingdom. To this extent, Sukarno's Jakarta was a manifestation of Indonesia in which the city, the state, and the nation came together, their imagined spaces collapsed into simultaneity.

In a similar way, the early nationalist, Muhammad Yamin (1948), represented an ideal national polity in his account of the Majapahit kingdom:

> Between the beginning of the fourteenth and the middle of the fifteenth century many books were composed, while the number of *monuments* in Eastern Java increased very much . . . In Gadjah Mada's time many inscriptions *on stone or copper* were published in order to commemorate important events or to be used as pieces of evidence. All recent as well as obsolete documents were kept and great care was taken that they would not just disappear.[20]

(As cited in Oetomo 1961: 77; emphasis added)

It is my understanding that the quest for permanency, the aim of making and establishing monumental "stones," was to impress the surrounding social environment, and thus contribute to a raising of the status of the ruling regime. The seeking for permanency and monumentality as represented in the time of Gadjah Mada and in the "capital city" of Majapahit is complemented by the beginning of a new age in which the urban center was symbolized by all traces of civilization. Under a colonial regime of power, the young Sukarno had, in the 1930s, been dreaming of an Indonesian future which "will live in peace and friendship with other nations and the Indonesian colors will constitute an ornament at the firmament of the East. A powerful, outwardly and inwardly sound nation will be ours" (as cited in Oetomo 1961: 83).

It was only at the time of Guided Democracy thirty years later that "the powerful outwardly and inwardly sound nation" was finally represented in Jakarta. The building up of Jakarta can thus be seen as a building up of a national network of vassals, forming a circle of alignment and alienation. The capital city becomes the symbol of power, the beacon of the center for both surrounding rulers and subjects who could, potentially, seek power of their own.

In the center of the Koningsplein, once the main square of colonial Jakarta surrounded by Dutch government buildings and other city facilities, the National Monument, as Sukarno conceived it, "like the Eiffel Tower in France," was erected (cited in Abeyasekere 1987: 169).[21] The center, "the heart of the town surrounded by public buildings,"[22] was renamed Lapangan Merdeka (Independence Square) and all temporary structures were demolished in order to provide a perfect perspective for the Monument (Figure 2.2). The form of the National Monument, curiously enough, was inspired by the ancient Indic form of the "linggam-yoni," reported to be Sukarno's idea. It was officially explained in *Tugu Nasional* that:

> linggam and yoni are ancient symbols which denote eternal life; there is a positive principle (linggam) and a negative one (yoni), as day and night, male and female, good and evil . . . linggam is the pestle-like 'tugu' which soars high up into the sky, and 'yoni' the mortar-like bowl-shaped hall. Mortars and pestles are everyday utensils owned by every Indonesian family, particularly in the country-side.

(As quoted in Leclerc 1993: 44)

In his study of the monument, Anderson (1990: 175) points out that the tall stele, crowned with a golden flame, and implanted in a large flat-topped base, did not commemorate any specific event or achievement, but was a mere commentary that sought to connect the present Indonesia to the past. The National Monument was "less a part of tradition than a way of claiming it" (Anderson 1990: 175). It stands as a monument claiming to emerge from a long tradition of the (for)ever existing "Indonesia." As a sign of "continuity" that links the present to the past, temporality was at once collapsed into simultaneity. The image of the National Monument could therefore be seen as an abstraction of the "power" of Javanese culture. Externally, the phallocentricity of the "linggam" seeks to capture the attention of competing allies and enemies beyond its perimeter. Internally, the maternalistic "yoni" houses the obedient allies that made up the nation.

On a larger scale, the radiance of power emanating from the National Monument was replicated in the way the city of Jakarta is made to represent itself. Sukarno thus declared:

> Comrades from Jakarta, let us build Jakarta into the greatest city possible. Great not just from a material point of view; great, not just because of its skyscrapers; great not just because it has boulevards and beautiful streets; great not just because it has beautiful monuments; great in every respect, even in the little houses of the workers of Jakarta there must be a sense of greatness . . . Give Jakarta an extraordinary place in the minds of the Indonesian people, because Jakarta belongs to the people of Jakarta. Jakarta belongs to the whole Indonesian people. More than that, Jakarta is becoming the beacon of the whole of mankind. Yes, the beacon of the New Emerging Forces.
>
> (As cited in Abeyasekere 1987: 168)

Perhaps there can be no more joyous expression of the "architect's dream" approach to city planning, oblivious of the socio-economic consequences, than this statement.[23] The perspective is vast. The "architect's dream" is joined with the will to secure an internal Power *vis-à-vis* the competing supra-national regions. During the confrontation with Malaysia in 1963,[24] Sukarno was particularly anxious that Jakarta should outstrip Singapore in rehousing people in high-rise buildings. Young Indonesian architects were thus challenged, not really to rehouse people but, as one Indonesian diplomat recalled, to "build more skyscrapers, more parks, more hospitals, more schools and clear more slums . . ." (as cited in Abeyasekere 1987: 202).

In 1963, under pressure from the Army and the sponsorship of the United Nations, Dutch New Guinea (Irian Jaya) was integrated into the territory of Indonesia, thus completing the colonial map of the Dutch East Indies and the imagined space of postcolonial Indonesia. A 35-meter-high commemorative monument, "Tugu Irian Barat," was erected in Banteng Square in Jakarta, formerly a parade ground of the Dutch. This depicted a man who had broken his chains, with arms stretched into the air and legs spread. After securing Irian Jaya, by spending three quarters of the entire national resources and designating 1962 as "the right year to give the rebel gangs the 'coup de grace' . . . in connection with the international situation of 1962 (Asian Games)" (as quoted in Feith and Castles 1970: 117–18), Indonesia was again envisioned by Sukarno as a beacon for other states:

> Who is not proud that he is a member of a nation that is not stagnant, of a nation that is moving, moving, moving on swiftly towards a building of a great state, whole and strong, that stretches from Sabang to Merauke, a great state that moves forward fast toward a life that is noble and respected, just and prosperous, that is a beacon to others, that has no exploitation de l'homme par l'homme, and that is rapidly becoming one of the champions of the new emerging forces, a nation that is moving to realize socialism based on its own identity?
>
> (As quoted in Feith and Castles 1970: 118–19)

Here the Indonesian state and national identity are inter-changeable with the aspirations of the capital city. In 1963, a new map of the world was issued which relocated the zero meridian from Greenwich to Jakarta; along with this, the Indian Ocean was renamed the Indonesian Ocean (Vittachi 1967: 28).

Yet it is important to note that Sukarno's understanding of "nation-building" as covering Jakarta with monuments to represent spectacular achievement and greatness took place within the weaker form of the Indonesian polity that was the product of specific social and political forces. "Nation-building" centered on Jakarta occurred largely in the period of Guided Democracy when a series of political events threatened the central government in Java. The PRRI (Revolutionary Government of the Indonesian Republic) rebellion in the Outer Islands (supported by the United States and other regional countries) and which involved groups from Sumatra and Sulawesi was proclaimed in 1958; the Darul Islam rebels in Aceh, West Java and South Sulawesi continued to put up resistance. Along with these events were the internal conflicts within powerful groups of the army, the Communist Party and other political organizations.[25] Though the series of rebellions was eventually suppressed by military force, these events also called for a "ritual" performance of "power" that attempted to pull together (once again) the differentiated whole of the country under the "monumental" image of the capital city. The modern Jakarta of Sukarno, its spectacular spatial and architectural representation, was a significant part of the construction of a powerful state by a leader facing a crisis of authority. The ordering force of display of national achievement in Jakarta thus constructed a master image of the nation seeking the restoration of its declining power. The "nation-building" discourses appeared to be the last spark of the exhausting force of the ruling realm.

The dignity of Jakarta as the symbol of the nation was related to Sukarno's role as the apex of the political system of the state. Considerations such as the threat from within and outside the imagined national space appear to generate the creation of exemplary monuments in the center in order to signify the authority and to exorcise the weakening of the polity. Despite the energy put into erecting monuments to establish the "exemplary center," Guided Democracy eventually led to Sukarno's fall.

INTERNAL CRITIQUE AND THE END OF SUKARNO'S POWER

The growing authoritarian rule of Sukarno's regime under Guided Democracy and the internal impasse to which his policies led ended the social visions which had been represented in the grandiose and ill-founded display of the city as the "beacon." The "modern" part of the city, named after heroes, decked with brick-and-glass buildings, opened up by a clover-leaf bridge, the Jakarta Bypass, and financed as a material symbol, while illuminating the power of "nation-building," also illuminated the presence of the rotten (and rotting) kampung. About the same time Sukarno left the presidential office, the young poet Taufiq Ismail wrote:

> What we ask is just a dike
> No monuments or football stadiums
> Or coloured fountains
> Send us lime and cement

> (As cited in Teeuw 1967: 254)

As a mode of governance, a representation of a declining social order, the display of modern space and architecture of this period did not exist in isolation. As only a fragment of the whole city, they were at once juxtaposed to the sea of the kampung and the older "colonial town."[26] These latter components, however, were seemingly outside the realm of "nation-building," yet they were needed in order to cultivate, or better, to define the "modern" achievement of Sukarno's regime. As the elite city dwellers were looking for housing closer to the center, the kampung dwellers were further displaced, either to multistorey accommodation or the outskirts of Jakarta. The beacon of Jakarta, while built by the kampung dwellers, was less to enlighten their kampung than to restore the darkening realm of power in the "center." Here, the establishment and maintenance of the hierarchical priority, monuments over a dike, appears to have been one of the main means of authority for the center. The ignorance of the "center" towards its peripheric kampung of this period was best told by Pramoedya Ananta Toer (1990) in his satirical story about Jakarta:

> You too, friend, can come to my kampung sometime. My kampung also can become a
> tourist kampung that will enrich the soul. Finding it is not hard at all because everyone in
> Jakarta knows where the national palace is. Five hundred meters in a straight line
> toward the Southwest, there my kampung stands in all its glory, challenging the ranks of
> doctors and technocrats. But all this does not surprise residents of my kampung itself. If
> surprising, it is only so for tourists – among whom you are also included – because it is
> located so near the palace where everyone's health and every little detail is guaranteed.
> But my kampung remains tranquil and has not been penetrated by agitators. Only later

when there is another person who is escorted away by diligent old Djibril (the imagined nemesis), and after the drum sounds, people will just say coolly: 'who died?' Someone else will answer: 'Mr. So-And-So.' And then the talking will end with mutual understanding.

(Toer 1990: 29–30)

Sukarno's "beacon" was eventually dimmed. It was in Jakarta too that the eventful night of 30 September 1965 ended his power.[27]

Towards the end of the 1960s, the older polity and newer signs, rigorously organized by Sukarno to save the national realm, could no longer coexist effectively. A new style of managing the Indonesian polity was called for. Following the change of political climate in 1966, the consolidation of the vision to signify "modern" Indonesia through a series of monumental modernist architectural forms was pushed further by the new regime officially and popularly known as the New Order. It is also under this order that architecture and its practitioners started to gain their "liberation" from the state. It was a liberation enabled by the New Order's pursuit of its own architectural sign and, most importantly, one characterizing the rapid penetration of capitalism. This demanded its own signature.

CONCLUSION: SYNCRETIC MODERNITY AND THE AMBIVALENCE OF SUKARNO'S JAKARTA

What I have tried to argue so far is that material "progress" during the "nation-building" period can not be adequately seen simply (and only) as a sign of "westernization" as manifested in the hegemony of a modernist architectural and urban paradigm. It is rather an attempt, on the part of Jakarta's leaders, to create a national political "tradition," based on a traditional spatial and political representation, to restore the crisis of the national realm experiencing an unrest that threatened its authority. Yet if this argument has any validity, we still need to ask why the representation of the exemplary center of the capital city was conceived in the form of a modernist built environment rather than in any other architectural and urban languages.

In his comprehensive study of the formation and transformation of Brasilia, James Holston (1989) has pointed out that no single meaning can be attributed to any sign of architecture, not even to the supposedly most universal aesthetic of modernism. Holston has demonstrated the various ways in which the sign of the "modern" was appropriated by the subjects it was supposed to transform. In the study he shows how the architects and planners saw the sign of socialist revolution in the modernist city they built; the right-wing military commissioner appreciated it as the most powerful symbol of the nation's modernization, demonstrating progress, industrialization, independence, and national identity and that shared nothing of the political beliefs of the designers; the inhabitants of the city understood it as a "white" canvas awaiting the inscription of social cultural values that the government sought to eliminate. The architectural image of modernist architecture, namely, the so-called international style, may be constant, but its denoted meanings are subject to changes according to the context, use and intention.[28]

The adoption, or indeed, the appropriation, of modernist architecture to represent the new nation–state of Sukarno's Indonesia was the result of many historical conjunctures involving local political cultures. For the argument I have laid out so far, modernist architecture in the time of Sukarno was not merely a representation of an intellectual break with tradition, the spiritual formation of the new generation, and a radically different episteme from that which had gone before. Instead, it also came as a manifestation of the "power" of "traditional" political culture. Here, "tradition" appeared to be something more attached to the holder who struggles to overcome and/or surrender to it.[29]

The intriguing question remains why modernist architecture was understood by Sukarno in a way that expressed the aspiration of Indonesia under Guided Democracy. No doubt this idea reflected a general formalist argument. But there are also many non-aesthetic reasons. In the first place, the modernist architecture of the 1950s suggests not only an advanced architectural discourse, a Utopian vision of socialism, as conceived initially in Europe, but also a rupture with the colonial legacies of underdevelopment. Secondly, and this appears to be more important, both Neo*classical* European architecture and the living Indonesian *traditional* architecture could no longer facilitate the *national* aspiration of the elite. They were perhaps incompatible with what Sukarno (in 1960) understood as "the ideals of the Revolution of August 1945, that is, a fully independent Indonesia clean of imperialism, a democratic Indonesia, clean of the remnants of feudalism, an Indonesia with Indonesian socialism . . ." (as quoted in Feith and Castles 1970: 112). Here, the "international" image of modernist architecture seems to provide an internal commentary on the national crisis that seeks to transcend the "suku" (ethnicities) and join world socialism understood, according to the Minister of Basic Education and Culture, as "the good international morality" (as quoted in Feith and Castles 1970: 329).

Although Sukarno's Guided Democracy was guided by a rigorously sought for, everlasting, if not essential sign of the past to represent the narrative of "continuity," to a (for)ever existing "Indonesian spirit," his regime of power was not that of the fourteenth century Majapahit, but of a *present* kind, signified not by the "roof tiles," but by the "reinforced concrete." Yet, in identifying, or better, countering the ancient regime he appeared to seek "continuity" with its glorious past, a source for the authority of the "modern" present. In this sense, the modernist architecture of Sukarno could be seen as a replica without origin in which it appears as both a sign of rupture as well as continuity with the (pre)colonial past. The conflictual positions of Sukarno problematizes any analysis intended to fix him as either a "traditionalist" or "modernist." His "traditionalist" discourse of nation-building cannot be considered as the other side of "modernist" discourse. It co-presents with it and intervenes in it, but does not do so in opposition to it. Homi Bhabha (1994: 241) has written about the postcolonial translation of modernity that, he claims, rests in its representation that "does not simply revalue the contents of a cultural tradition, or transpose values 'cross culturally.' " Instead, as I have shown in this chapter, concepts pertinent to a cultural tradition are dynamic; they are exposed to as much experimentation and negotiation with modernism as to their own milieu.

It is important to note that modernist architecture did not first appear in Sukarno's Jakarta; Dutch architects, since the 1920s, had already spread modernist design in many major cities of Indonesia, including Batavia (Jakarta). But the choosing of modernist architecture as a symbol of Sukarno's Jakarta occurred not in relation of the postcolonial subject to his ex-colonial master but in his relation to the external world. Unlike the dominant First World postcolonial discourses of identity which occurred around the negotiation between (post)colonial subjects and their (ex)masters, what we have in Sukarno's Jakarta is a disinterested relation to the colonial past.

When Sukarno claimed the centrality of Jakarta in the national struggle for decolonization, he also recommended the nation to "look at New York and Moscow, look at any state capital . . ." and so on, so that Jakarta could look like them. What this suggests is a transposition of identity, from inside to outside, from self-identification, to identification by reference to others, from a self-referential history to an externalized globality. In this account, Sukarno's Jakarta, instead of being self-sufficiently "powerful," demands recognition from the world that is not fully met. The appearance of modernist architecture in Jakarta tells the public that the city has something from a world to which Jakarta wants to belong. Modernist architecture is endowed with the capacity to evoke recognition of the modern look-alike; the effect of recognition is to complete the (trans)formation of what was thought to be the "spirit" of Indonesian identity.

The phantasmagoric illusions fostered by the appearance of modernist buildings and the changing arrangement of streets within Jakarta appeared to provide the imagery of a world in which Sukarno's Indonesia wants to be a part. It was considered to be a new space, an architecture of authority to which the imagined communities of the nation were asked to aspire and within which all the opposing forces embedded within the nation could be overcome. It is as if, through the representation of modernist architecture, the postcolonial nation could be thought out and a "common" traditional spirit at once imagined and transformed.

In this context, modernist architectural and urban paradigms may well be understood less as an "imported" technology to which the recipient subject responds according to local circumstances. Instead, it is a product of what Appadurai and Breckenridge (1995: 5) have termed "public culture." Here, the modernist architectural and urban design paradigm becomes a replica without origin that has been "emancipated from any specific Euro-American master narrative and indicates an arena of cultural contestation in which modernity can become a diversely appropriated experience." Their paradigms are subjected to appropriations by those who, among others, hold power to construct, contest and rule societies. However, as this world-wide paradigm enters into the discourses of Javanese centralism, the basis of its authority is estranged.

Represented in this fashionable modernist form, Sukarno's Jakarta therefore characterized the essentially ambivalent nature of postcolonial nation and city building. What we have in that city is the combination of different claims to transcendent values, such as "modernist architecture" and the "linggam-yoni" monument. The political negotiation of Sukarno's Jakarta takes two contradictory, yet mutually constitutive identifications: the relative unproblematic identification with, and also rejection of, for want of a better word, "modernity."

Chapter 3: Recreating Origins

The Birth of "Tradition" in the Architecture of the New Order

Though stripped of almost all his powers towards the end of 1960, Indonesia's first president, Sukarno, continued to express concern about the slow progress of the National Monument in Independence Square. Visiting the site, he addressed the engineers in charge of the projects and asked them to give the Monument priority. "You know, all other works will be resumed one day or another, but this one I fear, if not completed as soon as possible, never will be" (as cited in Leclerc 1993: 47). Sukarno already had a sense that new monuments would be built by the succeeding regime. He was also aware that what came after him would, in one way or another, be a symbolic commentary on his own, now "old" regime.

Perhaps Sukarno was right. Immediately after he was dislodged from power, a commemorative monument at the "Lubang Buaya" (Crocodile Well), located on the Southern outskirts of Jakarta, was quickly built to recall the terror of the 1965 events and the establishment of Suharto's regime. The memorial bears a frieze representing events before and after the coup. Jakarta historian Abeyasekere (1987) reports:

> "Before" appears as a time of chaos, with men and women angrily gesticulating and debating. Then Suharto takes control – the symbol of reason and harmony. "After" shows people quietly going about their business, under the protective eye of the military.
>
> (Abeyasekere 1987)

Not long after, Nugroho Notosusanto, the then Minister of Education and Culture, was instructed by President Suharto to revise school history lessons, emphasizing the instability in the rule of the country's founder, President Sukarno, in the 1950s (Leigh 1991: 29). Under Suharto's New Order, Indonesia was about to receive a government that emphasized "stability."

To achieve this stability, President Suharto explicitly linked the new socio-political order to the goal of economic development. This "development" strategy along capitalist lines was initiated both to "stabilize" the economy and restore some sense of order within social life. Political life was taken away from the population at large, and was both controlled by, and reserved for, the circle of the President. A peculiarly Indonesian form of leadership known as "Pancasila Democracy" was created and installed. All these restructurings of the social, political and economic imagination of the country were made to secure the power of the "new" state. As the governing elites felt their way towards more capitalist modes of exploitation, and related themselves to a more exclusive and authoritarian political order, they increasingly replicated many ideas of the repressive Dutch colonial state.

In the urban realm, a peculiar way of thinking about architecture emerged, one that has, in fact, continued to the present. The "global image," the source of Sukarno's energy, was reversed, or turned upside down. Sukarno had recommended the nation to "look at New York and Moscow, look at any state capital" so that Jakarta could look like them. Contemporary Indonesian architects, however, working within the social field of the New Order, on the contrary suggest that "we pay attention to the effect of global image so that the outlook of our cities will not be the same as cities such as New York, L.A., and Washington" (Budihardjo 1998).[1] A new paradigm has emerged that suggests the embracing of the "inevitable" technological modernization under the condition that "the roots of cultural heritage ('akar warisan budaya') have to be strong" (Budihardjo 1998).

This chapter, emanating from the "cultural break" represented in Chapter 2, continues the argument posed in Chapter 1: the old colonial imagining of "tradition" informs the pursuit of "identity" that pervades architects working within the political culture of the New Order. It continues the connection between architectural discourses and political imaginings by tracing the endeavour of the New Order to articulate the culture constructed since the final phase of Dutch colonialism. I argue therefore that the sign of "tradition," central to the legitimation of the New Order's authority, is both enabled as well as haunted by its earlier colonial construction. The validity of this argument can be evaluated by reflecting on the political history of "Indies architecture" discussed in the first chapter.

FOR THE SAKE OF THE FUTURE: REFIGURING TRADITION

In 1975, a decade after the initiation of his "developmental" policy, President Suharto declared in the opening remarks of his "Beautiful Indonesia in the Miniature Park":

> Economic development alone is not enough. Life will not have a beautiful and deep meaning with material sufficiency alone, however abundant that sufficiency might become. On the contrary, the pursuit of material things on its own will make life cruel and painful . . . One's life, therefore, will be calm and complete only when it is accompanied by spiritual welfare. The direction and guidance towards that spiritual

welfare is, in fact, already in our possession; it lies in our beautiful and noble national cultural inheritance . . .

(As cited in Pemberton 1994: 244)

What this suggests is that, about a decade into the reign of Suharto's New Order, Indonesia was beginning to undergo its first experience of insecurity in its political cultures. This was the result of a curious combination of developments. First, the oil-boom in the 1970s and early 1980s presented all kinds of opportunity for the state to centralize its political and economic power.[2] Second, the riots of January 1974 brought forward issues of class conflict as well as national unity.[3] With the unprecedented growth of economic and social inequalities, the area of commonality – previously paraded under the rhetoric of "Revolution" – became increasingly difficult to sustain (Anderson 1990: 183–190). As a result, the social imaginary of "Indonesia" had to be recreated in such a way that social and cultural stability, within the continuing policy of "development," could still be emphasized. Third, the conviction was gaining ground among the older generation of the elite that established values were rapidly disappearing, particularly in certain elite youth circles (Anderson 1990).

Suharto and his advisers were especially troubled by their realization that a gap – as much cultural as political – had arisen between the generation that shared the aims and experience of the Revolution of 1945–9 and those who did not, except perhaps in the most superficial way (Anderson 1990: 184). This situation was considered dangerous since the country would soon be taken over, ideally through cultural inheritance, by a new generation who had grown up in the space where their parents' journeys had ended (Anderson 1990: 188). This younger generation was considered to be losing faith in the common goals and purpose, crucial for the creation of a "modern Indonesia." Thus, the President proclaimed that the present danger was an "indication of an estrangement of the younger generation, precisely from the history of the national struggle and the national identity . . . The consequence is that they tend to orient themselves towards an alien culture, not their own" (as cited in Anderson 1990: 184). A particular version of the past was therefore to be summoned, in the name of "tradition," to restore the trajectory of the nation. According to the "Revolutionary" generation of the New Order, "stability" could only be achieved by safeguarding their version of nationalism. This also involved "traditionalizing" what was considered national heritage.

Anderson (1990: 183) reported that in 1972 the Indonesian armed forces staged a seminar, the aims of which were put into practice soon after, entitled "drawing society closer to the armed forces." At this event, the President proclaimed that while scientific knowledge could be acquired from abroad, "the source of leadership, character and determination as a people building its future must continue to be drawn from the history of our own struggle and our own identity" (as cited in Anderson 1990: 184). To his own generation, including the fathers, the president stated:

We need to arm ourselves with the philosophy of devoted service to state and nation
taught by [the eighteenth century Javanese King] Mangkunegoro I in his 'Tridarma.' The
first 'darma' is 'rumongso handuweni' – to feel that one has a share of something which
is the property or interest of the state and nation. From this feeling there arises the
second 'darma' – 'wajib melu hangrukebi' – meaning to share responsibility for
defending and sustaining this common property or interest. To carry out this first and
second 'darma,' a third is needed, in other words, 'mulat sariro hangrosowani,' meaning
to have the courage constantly to examine ourselves to see how far we have really acted
to defend the common property or interest.

(As cited in Anderson 1990: 184)

The President was aiming to invest in the state what was considered the
"common" traditional property which subjects of the nation have to be conscious of, defend, and act upon. Ideally, the state was to be given a cultural substance, presumably inherited, and thus conveying a sense of origin and
"traditions." The nation's cultural property, once traditionalized, would stabilize
the trajectory that is properly set out – in the manner of a cultural bequest – for
the development of the younger generation.

COLLECTING TRADITION: "BEAUTIFUL INDONESIA"

The idea of cultural inheritance was put into official practice in the form of the
"Beautiful Indonesia in Miniature Park," the largest, and perhaps the only, self-
proclaimed "monument" of the New Order.[4] Initiated in 1971 by Mrs Suharto,
inspired by a visit to Disneyland, the project was marked from the start by waves
of student protests and critical comments in the metropolitan press. It was considered a waste of money. But for the first lady, the value of the project could
not be quantified. "Beautiful Indonesia" was not merely a theme park, it was
also a museum, claiming to hold "authentic" features of Indonesia's past; it was
also seen as a repository of cultural traditions for future generations. The first
lady therefore was very determined about the project:

Whatever happens, I won't retreat an inch! This project must go through! Its
implementation won't retreat a single step! For this project is not a prestige project –
some of its purposes are to be of service to the people. The timing of its construction is
also just right – so long as I am alive. For someone's conception cannot possibly be
carried out by someone else, only by the conceiver herself – unless I am summoned by
God in the meantime!

(As cited in Anderson 1990: 177)

Thus was built in 1980 an idealized symbolic space of the nation on the outskirts
of Jakarta, far away from the cluster of Sukarno's "monuments" (Figure 3.1).
Just as Sukarno had constructed an idea of national unity under the abstraction
of a National Monument, the New Order chose to collect the immense heterogeneity of "indigenous" art and culture from all regions of the state and

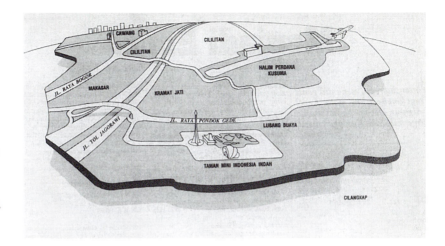

Figure 3.1
MINIATURE PARK 1975:
THE AUTHENTIC, THE
BEAUTIFUL, AND THE
NATIONAL SELF
Source: *Tempo*, June 22,
1991

represent them as part of national cultural "traditions." At the center of the park, indeed, an 8.4 hectare artificial lake represents, in miniature, the archipelago of Indonesia (Figure 3.2).

In its insistence on a certain notion of the authentic, the depiction of the archipelago's cultural traditions bears a likeness to colonial museums of ethnography. In the vast national display, particular importance is given to 27 (including East Timor) "authentic" houses, each occupying one hectare of land and together composing a web that skirts the artificial lake. Together, they purport to represent the cultural richness of each of the country's administrative provinces. As a whole, this series of houses portrays the nation itself as a colorful "traditional" village within which all members supposedly live harmoniously together. Not unlike full-color advertisements for tourists, what has been concealed in the phantasmagoria of "Beautiful Indonesia in the Miniature," is the complex social and historical production of the images themselves. Moreover, as identity is marked and fixed upon the idea of having a physical place within the territory of the nation, traces of "non-indigenous" (su as Indonesian-Chinese) are refigured by "excluding" them from the national belonging of the park. From this park, social attitudes are moulded and national identity is formed which, in "depict[ing] our people, makes us proud to be Indonesians" (as cited in Pemberton 1994a: 244).

"Beautiful Indonesia" served its nationalistic and pedagogic function by producing educated "touristic" subjects who know no better. Here, the display of replicas constitutes the subjects of the nation as passive consumers seeking cultural "authenticity." In his account of "Beautiful Indonesia," Pemberton (1994) suggests that to make the material collections of the complex authentic, an infantile subject in search of "original" knowledge is required.[5] The Department of Culture and Education is reported to have provided a story book account of a visit to "Beautiful Indonesia" (known popularly as Mini) in which the protagonist, a central Javanese child named Mustafa, discovers the "originality" of the collections of Indonesian cultures. Mustafa and his student group

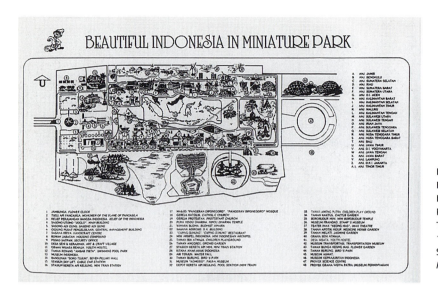

Figure 3.2
REPRESENTING THE
NATION: TERRITORY,
PLACE AND IDENTITY IN
THE MINIATURE PARK,
1975
Source: *Taman Mini
Indonesia Indah*

are convinced that "to see those regional houses in their original ('asli') settings [is to] go to Mini; whatever you desire will be fulfilled!" (As cited in Pemberton 1994a: 244)

"Built to endure for hundreds of years,"[6] these "traditional" houses were, however, constructed merely as a symbol, standing for all houses of the type. They were designed not for detailed observation but were rather made to be consumed within one general sweeping gaze. An overall impression was provided that, "somewhere" in Indonesia, there exists the everlasting authentic culture of "our" nation (Figure 3.3). The director of the Regional Housing Center, whose staffs were assigned the task of compiling information on regional house types, was quite clear about the difference between the original and the copies. Referring to these replicas of the regional houses, the construction of which needs "sophisticated western building materials," the director nevertheless pointed out realistically, "[t]he building of the houses would . . . at least give a point of reference for comparison with the 'pure' traditional form in the future development of domestic architecture in Indonesia" (Sumintardja 1972: 11–12).

These houses cannot be taken as authentic as Mrs Suharto wanted them to be. The collapsing of the difference between the original and the copies into an undifferentiated image of the whole nation shows a consensus of representation that demands the effacement of the social and historical specificity of each structure. The nation demands only the *symbolic* presence of local traditions. As Anderson (1990: 182) indicates in his account of Beautiful Indonesia, these "traditional" houses are replicas without origins, made to represent a sweeping impression of "Indonesianness."[7] The nation demands timeless categories of past, present and future. It also requires no spatial and categorical differentiation between what is replica and what is authentic. The nation simply *is*.

Figure 3.3
NATIONAL REPLICA: THE
INDONESIAN-NESS OF
"TRADITIONAL HOUSES"
Source: *Taman Mini
Indonesia Indah*

After the erasure of the temporal and spatial differentiation of the "national heritage," the nation begins its project of "development." As Mrs Suharto suggested, the *symbolic* presence of the local traditions marks a larger trajectory for the future of the nation:

> As all of us can witness, here we can find the traditional houses and other buildings which are found in our country from one end to the other, and which constitute the heritage of our invaluable national culture. We feel it necessary to preserve this cultural heritage of ours in order to prevent its possible extermination as a result of the demand for the development of modern society . . . All this will serve to increase our love for our country and motherland – a *sine qua non* for a strong growth of our nation in future.
>
> (Mrs Suharto as cited in *Indonesia Magazine* 1975: 28–9)

Here, the traditional houses of the region were to be preserved. Their presence symbolized their agreement to blend with, if not to bless, the "development" of the nation–state. The iconography of traditional houses and museums aims to produce subjects looking for ideal images that fit not only with cultural memories of the "past" but the dream state of the "developing" present.

Indeed, the image of "tradition" in the "Beautiful Indonesia" park is complemented by the representation of national "development." Also in the same park is a series of museums (of stamps, sports, technology, transportation, and so on), imax theater, representative religious buildings, a shopping center and recreational facilities, all designed in "contemporary" architectural styles. Surrounding the complex of "traditional" houses, these "non-traditional" buildings have increased in number, consonant with the course of the seemingly unlimited possibilities of national development. Thus, the site of the park has expanded, with the addition of new institutions and facilities, and radiating from the center of the "traditional" complex. The "core" of the nation represented in the "traditional" house guarantees and legitimates the expansion of the modern institutions of "development" itself.

Looking at the whole complex together from the privileged gaze of the cable car, a visitor might indeed feel that the setting of the park is organized around a tension between the centrifugal forces of "modernization" and the centripetal pull of "tradition." It suggests that the material progress of "development" is always safe-guarded by, and somehow bound to, the "tradition," which is eternally preserved "there," in the center, and thus symbolically within "us."

However, "Beautiful Indonesia in Miniature Park" is not merely a representation of the New Order's "development" that outstripped Sukarno's "nation-building." It is also an attempt of the New Order to erase histories that do not fit with its establishment. John Pemberton (1994a) has written about the emergence of Beautiful Indonesia as an effort of the New Order to secure the cultural and political legitimacy of its rule. Pemberton indicates that the Miniature Park seeks first to displace the violence of the New Order's origin (of the mass killings of the Indonesian people in 1965–6). Second, to create a new center, replacing the (colonial Dutch protected) "ancient" Javanese royal court in Central Java, with its own, presumably higher and more authentic authority in the capital city of Jakarta. In this sense, Beautiful Indonesia represents the insecurity of the New Order and the anxiety of the ruling regime that its authority is lacking "authenticity" in comparison to the previous governments. The technique of representation in Beautiful Indonesia suppresses such histories. In "modernizing" the country, the New Order Indonesia attempts to produce a new ahistorical generation, a uniformity of behaviour and customs, opinions and rules, which have the effect of strengthening rather than weakening its own version of "traditional" symbolism.

THE BUILDING RESEARCH INSTITUTE: COMPILING TRADITION

Perhaps because of the realization of the Beautiful Indonesia project, "traditional building" has become a prominent and visible subject of inquiry in Indonesia. The neglected Building Research Institute in Bandung, established in the mid-1950s to find appropriate methods to improve housing conditions in the country, has been revived, its officials compiling data and inventories of traditional building and construction. This was both for conservation reasons and also to stimulate and inform the design of contemporary architecture in Indonesia. Indonesian architectural historian, Iwan Sudradjat (1991: 100) reported that, in the mid-1970s, various universities and research institutions supported the programme and, by the 1980s, a nation-wide research project was established and financed by the Ministry of Education and Cultural Affairs. The aim is "to collect data and information on traditional architecture in order to make an inventory and documentation of local cultures that form the constituent parts of national culture" (as cited in Sudradjat 1991: 101).

In the course of six years, eighteen provinces were documented and the results published by the Department of Culture and Education in Jakarta between 1981 and 1986.[8] Reviewing them, Sudradjat (1991: 101) reports, "so strong was the bias of this project towards the idea of unity that the structure of all final reports was rigidly standardized, leaving only limited freedom for each research team to organise and present their data and analysis."

This standardization may simply be caused by the requirement of the publications that seeks to make visible the differences in the material presented. However, it may also be caused by the demand of the "scientific" method used for the representational conventions of architecture. Within this order, schematic architectural drawings conveniently exposed the logical structure of the building under the scientific but also poetic gaze of architectural knowledge and imagination. In this way, the socio-cultural order as well as other intangible values were abstracted to fit into the rational logocentricity of the discipline.

However, the substantial funds invested in this project suggested that the state had its own, non-scientific interest, which takes us deeper and closer to the political cultures of the New Order. Not unlike the replication of "traditional" buildings displayed in the Beautiful Indonesia in Miniature Park, the research and the accompanying reports were conducted less to convey the "authenticity" of "traditional" buildings per se, but rather to make each of them fit within the context of a trans-regional national culture. What has been crucial in this process are the replica of the tradition and not the tradition itself. The incommensurability of the diverse ethno-geographic cultural representations is "rationalized," or better nationalized, and transformed into a series of replicated images. These, carefully co-ordinated, are meant to speak, each in its own way, of the nation as a whole.

INDONESIAN CLASSICAL ARCHITECTURE: EXPERIMENTING WITH TRADITION

In quite another locus, attempts have been carried out, though with a different purpose, by a handful of architect–educators, to find appropriate norms and forms of an "Indonesian architecture." In an experiment known as "Unity in Diversity (citing the official state ideology) in Indonesian architecture,"[9] Josef Prijotomo (1987), an architectural theorist trained in both Indonesia and the United States in the 1980s, with a group of architectural students in Surabaya, has assessed the position of "Indonesian classical architecture," which "can be seen as the source or root of architectural discourse in Indonesia whose status is parallel to Greek and Roman architecture which has been the root of architectural discourse in Europe" (Prijotomo 1987: 16). Here, the term "Indonesian classical architecture" deserves further attention. For Prijotomo and others, one of the most important efforts to create an "Indonesian architecture" ("arsitektur yang Indonesiawi") has been to learn from what he terms "Indonesian classical architecture." His use of this term tells of his efforts to link the development of today's architecture in urban Indonesia with that of the vernacular architectures as they are represented in many other places in the islands of Indonesia.

The three terms, "Indonesia," "classical," and "architecture" are, of course, all modern inventions either constructed or mobilized from elsewhere to provide a certain dynamic to the local stock of buildings. The term "Indonesia" connotes a unique entity that is considered to be different from other national representations. It also provides a framework within which the diverse regional cultures scattered all over the archipelago might be represented in a shared translocal platform. "Classical" is a term coined from mainstream European architectural historiography in which Greek architecture has been constituted as the foundational ancestor of Western architecture. The term is consciously chosen in order to bring "Indonesian architecture" to the same historical platform as those of its Western counterparts. The term "architecture," with its Greek etymology, is used to differentiate itself from "bangunan" (building); architecture is seen as a unique field whose aesthetic and artistic component has placed it beyond the realm of mere "building." This trinity of "Indonesian Classical Architecture" thus brings together the material cultures of Indonesia with the national desire to be part of a global venture of architecture.

To achieve this, under a strictly architectural operation, all symbolic cultures of each region and their socio-historical specificity are dislodged and surgically removed from their regional body. What is left on the operating table are the mere elevations of building types to be analysed, rationally and scientifically, according to a technique developed by European architectural theorist, Demetri Porphyrios. Each group of students selected a subnational regional architecture of interest to them and analysed it according to the assumption of what has been the part of "building" (apparently the earliest stage of an architecture) and what components allow it to be conceived as "architecture" (the higher stage of building). This differentiation has been followed by an effort to trace the evolution or development of the building form, from what was understood as a mere building into its more elaborated form of "architecture."

Prijotomo is convinced that the visual and architectural training of his laboratory will provide students with alternative design strategies where references and ideas are not found in Western architectural glossy magazines but rather, within the very space of the national. This attempt to modernize tradition is, while contributing to the production of tasteful images for Indonesia, also symptomatic of the late nationalist imagining of modern Indonesia. What becomes a matter of concern is the "development" of architecture that is *symbolically* based on the image of "traditions." In this formulation, "development" is far from eroding the sign of "tradition." Instead, the former has been undertaken entirely within the continuous creation of the latter, though in the present form of replica.

The centrality of a "traditional" image to the New Order's construction of identity might be further illustrated by the following anecdote. Outside the studio of Prijotomo and his students, in the Indonesian heartland of things "authentic," the governor of Central Java was also thinking up his own idea about how to represent "tradition." He once proclaimed, in a matter-of-fact way, that the identity of the Javanese house lies in the "atap Joglo" (the typical "pendapa" roof form of the houses of Javanese elites – see Chapter 1).[10]

Following this declaration, the Central Java regional assembly was reported as having become obsessed with finding an "operational standard" for Javanese houses. It was later revealed that the governor had been disturbed by a recently built local hospital, erected in his domain, which had adopted a replica of a Greek temple facade for its entrance hall.

> [W]e have Joglo architecture which is more beautiful, why use foreign architecture? . . . Is it appropriate for this foreign architecture to be juxtaposed with the existing statue of our national hero . . . In essence, no matter how much it would cost [to replace the Greek facade with a Joglo one] I will be the one responsible, because it is very important for the pride of the nation.
>
> (As cited in *Tempo*, September 1, 1984: 18)

Thus ended the fateful Greek appearance in that hospital: the entrance hall was demolished to give way to a "Joglo" pavilion. Along with this decision, the governor also instructed all future government buildings in Central Java to be built with "atap Joglo."

INSTITUTE OF TECHNOLOGY AT BANDUNG: NEGATING TRADITION

If, in this Central Java debacle, Indonesian architects seemed to have no power to reject the authority of "Joglo," except by voicing their disagreement, other public projects reveal the nature of their own cultural and professional practices. In the early 1990s, the Institute of Technology at Bandung, the first campus built in Indonesia under the Dutch colonial regime, was extended to accommodate the nation's investment in high technology.[11] New laboratories were built next to the existing buildings designed by the Dutch architect, Henri Maclaine Pont, highly respected in the Indonesian architectural profession (Figures 3.4 and 1.6; see also Chapter 1). Here, no doubt, the postcolonial architects of Indonesia found themselves, like it or not, confronting both a colonial architectural legacy as well as their "Indonesian" realm. In drawing up the new master plan for the Institute, they faced, in one way or another, issues of culture, temporality, history, and identity. Architecturally, how to contextualize the old buildings of the Dutch with the new ones of the postcolonial era; politically, to ask what the colonial and postcolonial could have done to each other.

A solution, nevertheless, finally appeared when the architects and planners divided the campus and its extension into three thematic zones (Figure 3.5). The first is the "konservasi–historis" (historic conservation) zone which contains the original architecture of Maclaine Pont. Second is the "transisi" (transitional) zone where the new buildings are designed with a new interpretation of the "historic" architecture of Maclaine Pont (Figure 3.6). According to the architects, the principal building design of this zone is contextual. "The exterior of the new buildings in the 'transitional' zone has to be architecturally oriented to the

Figure 3.4
COLONIAL REPLICA: THE
INSTITUTE OF
TECHNOLOGY AT
BANDUNG (ITB), 1990
Source: Dr Iwan
Sudradjat

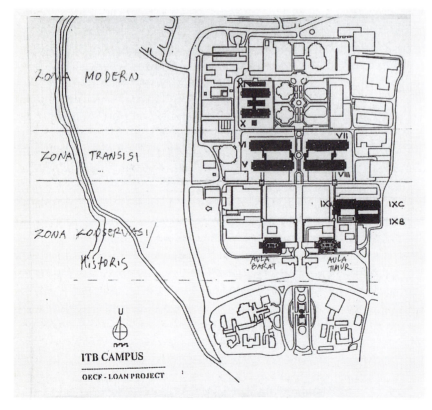

Figure 3.5
STAGING HISTORY: THE
EXTENSION OF THE ITB
CAMPUS, 1990
Source: Dr Iwan
Sudradjat

Figure 3.6
TRIBUTE TO THE
MASTER: "ZONA
TRANSISI"
Source: Dr Iwan
Sudradjat

'historic' East and West Hall; the interior, however, can be 'modern,' understood as related to the new functional requirements."[12]

Third is the "modern" zone in which ties to the historic–conservation zone are minimal (Figure 3.7). If the buildings of the "transisi" zone are bound to the colonial architectural heritage in the form of the roof and the verandah, those in the "modern" zone are conceptually free and, stylistically, are discontinuous from the other two zones. What is curious here is not merely the design vocabulary of the building but also the way in which the words "modern," "transisi," and "konservasi–historis" have been used to describe the buildings. I shall return to this below.

The serial enumeration of these three zones is strictly architectural but it is characteristically political as well. Central to the logic of the zoning system is an attempt to construct a version of postcolonial architectural history, if not a miniaturized version of the history of the nation itself. The internal differentiation between zones, and the principle of relationships between buildings, are less bound by their building function than by a desire to search for an appropriate history, a proper beginning. However, the architects were also quite clear that the floor plan of the buildings, including the interiors, is basically functional and subject to adaptation to new functional requirements. The treatment of the exterior, which provides the zoning system, is however symptomatic of the political cultures of the New Order, searching for an appropriate form to represent its postcolonial present.

Here, the representation of the new buildings in the "transitional" zone seems to work hard to assimilate the "konservasi–historis" architecture into their own substance. It transcodes its elements, foregrounding all the echoes and

Figure 3.7
SOMEWHERE BEYOND
THE POMO: "ZONA
MODERN"
Source: Dr Iwan
Sudradjat

analogies, and borrows stylistic figures in order to overcome them. The repetition of the strong elements of the buildings in the "konservasi–historis" zone simultaneously melts away its supposedly weaker elements. The selected images of these buildings also function as a tenuous reference, the last stubborn "colonial" referent in the process of a wholesale dissolution. Both the buildings of the "konservasi–historis" and the "transitional" zones seem to be absorbed, if not displaced, by the final zone of the "modern."

What we have in the "modern" zone is a building of "international postmodern style," which seems to tell the viewers of the buildings of the other zones that it is the postcolonial time and space that matters. The only continuity between the building of the "transisi" zone and that in the "modern" one is the red color on parts of the building in these two zones. The series of red gutters hanging around the "minangkabau" roof of the "transisi" building seems to cross reference the series of free standing red columns at the entrance of the "modern" building. In this "modern" building, the red gutters are turned upside down and seemingly stand as a series of sculptures that commemorate the "structure" of the colonial past. The "modern," in its own self-sufficient style occupies the ultimate narrative of "progress" from colonial histories. In this narrative of "development" the "modern" incorporates – rather than being displaced by – the colonial legacy.

The striking architectural language used in the "modern" zone for its technology laboratory seems to represent the commitment of Indonesia to a vision of an ahistorical Utopian future based on technocratic ideals (Shiraishi 1996). This vision conforms to the vision of the then State Minister for Research and Technology, also President Suharto's golden boy, B.J. Habibie, who believed that the state of Indonesia could only be developed through a cultivation of science and technology, and not by the understanding of the country's cultures and histories. A decision was perhaps made that the architectural representation of the "modern" zone was not to be marked by a historical signature which was, rather, put into the past and labelled "konservasi–historis."[13] These terms connote preservation and containment of the past in order to achieve stability ("stabilitas"), which, under the New Order, were the prerequisite for economic development ("pembangunan").

Here, the vocabulary of architecture coincides with the language used to explain the building's design concepts. The words used to define the different zones of the campus are all from a constructed local language. The notions of "konservasi–historis," "transisi," and "modern" are phonologically-adapted foreign terms, representative of the globalization of "modern" Indonesia.[14] They tell the buildings' viewers that it is the postcolonial time that is the real matter of concern.

Built into the logic of zoning to mark a different time and space of post-colonial Indonesia is also the *erasure* of histories, including the violence of colonialism and the ironies of postcolonial culture. The "Indonesia" of the Institute of Technology at Bandung was constructed upon a peculiar sense of temporality, a sense of time that considered its colonial "origins" an irrelevant framework. Yet, since the buildings of the "modern," as represented in the final zone of the campus, gains its meaning through the architectural languages of the neighboring zones, the "modern" remains dependent upon the existence of its others. Located at the main entrance of the campus, the "Indies architecture" of Henri Maclaine Pont could still be regarded as the source of architectural reference from which emanates the vocabulary of the subsequent architectural style of the campus. The very fact that the "modern" attempts to negate the Indies architecture is proof of its dependence on it.

This contradiction is also played out in the site planning of the campus. The site plan of the extension of the Bandung Institute is based on the site planning of the colonial "historis–konservasi" zone. In this sense, the appearance of the new buildings, their narrative of progress and the erasure of colonial histories, seem to contradict the new layout plan which is, in the end, still based on the colonial master plan.

THE UNIVERSITY OF INDONESIA: REALIZING TRADITION

If the extension of Bandung's campus shows us a way of framing histories, of negating, or better, incorporating the colonial legacy by transforming it under the name of the "modern," the recently built campus of the University of Indonesia provides us with an expression of what a "modern Indonesian architecture" could possibly be. Situated on the outskirts of Jakarta, on a vast "empty" site (Figure 3.8), free from historic buildings, the campus was designed with a consciousness that "[t]his is the only campus in the country that bears the name of the nation. This campus has . . . been a motivation in the search for a

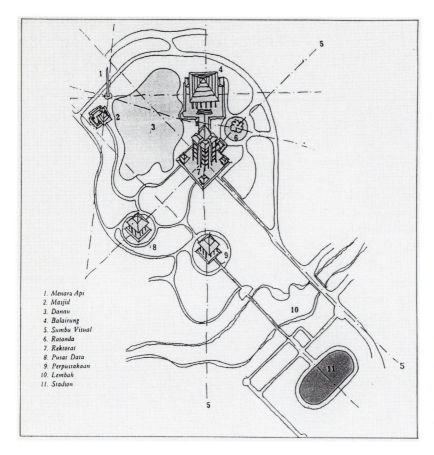

1. Menara Api
2. Masjid
3. Danau
4. Balairung
5. Sumbu Visual
6. Rotonda
7. Rektorat
8. Pusat Data
9. Perpustakaan
10. Lembah
11. Stadion

Figure 3.8
NATIONAL
ARCHITECTURE: THE
UNIVERSITY OF
INDONESIA (UI), c1980
Source: Wiwiek Usmi,
Asri, 53, 1987

modern national style."[15] To achieve this, the typological characteristics of as many local buildings as possible have been collected, reviewed and selected (Figure 3.9). From this exercise, the buildings' masses, elevations, floor plans, patterns and roof shape were born.[16] The architectural reference here is consciously "lokal" (local), presumably drawn from the stock of the national cultural heritage.

The Rectorate tower (Figure 3.10), perhaps the most important and authoritative building of the campus, is thus made up from the house plan of the Javanese nobility. The pagoda-like stacked roofs of its tower are cross referenced to the Hindu-Balinese temple stratified according to the hierarchy of the human head, body and legs. The Javanese spatial conception of center and periphery is adopted to organize the site plan of the departmental complex. What we have here is a mobilization of the cosmological concepts of the Indonesian "classical" architectural heritage to generate a national spatial and architectural form. The appeal to national heritage thus appears to efface pasts and futures together. Several origins are simultaneously presented as in a "national" form, collapsing at once the distance between what represents and what is represented.

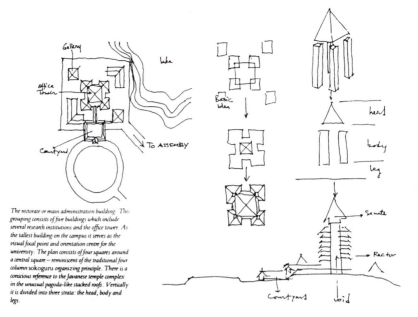

Figure 3.9
JAVANESE CENTRALISM:
THE CONCEPTUAL
DESIGN OF THE
UNIVERSITY OF
INDONESIA
Source: *Mimar*, 12, 42,
March 1992

The rectorate or main administration building. This grouping consists of five buildings which include several research institutions and the office tower. As the tallest building on the campus it serves as the visual focal point and orientation centre for the university. The plan consists of four squares around a central square – reminiscent of the traditional four column sokoguru organizing principle. There is a conscious reference to the Javanese temple complex in the unusual pagoda-like stacked roofs. Vertically it is divided into three strata: the head, body and legs.

Figure 3.10
REPRESENTING
AUTHORITY: THE
RECTORATE TOWER OF
THE UNIVERSITY OF
INDONESIA
Source: *Indonesia
Property Report*, 1, 2, 3rd
Quarter, 1995

Unlike the architectural statement of the Institute of Technology at Bandung, there is no conceptual usage of the word "modern" to describe the University of Indonesia. Instead, the words "lokal" (local), "tradisional" (traditional) and "daerah" (regional) are apparently adequate to convey the national message of the campus. Though I suspect that the word "modern" was used in Bandung for the purpose of putting the 'historic" into the past. For the

University of Indonesia, there is no time differentiation. Everyone is supposed to agree that what has been expressed is from the "lokal" stock. Nothing is to be put in the past. The "lokal" is there within the archipelago of Indonesia which, by definition, is here, in the campus that bears the name of the nation. It is a ready, convenient, and unquestioned repertoire to express what is, after all, the "traditional" property of the nation.

Not unlike the extension of the Institute of Technology at Bandung, the University of Indonesia, while experimenting with "lokal" building elements, has emptied them out of their historical constructions. What is even more important in the National University is a claim to cultural authenticity, of self-sufficiency of the nationalist project. The architectural problem and solution here is principally that of knowing what to incorporate to embody the traditionality of the nation.

BANDUNG–JAKARTA/COLONIAL–POSTCOLONIAL: DISPLACING/ REPLACING TRADITION

Despite this rigorous attempt to represent a sense of cultural completeness of the "shared traditional values" outside the colonial presence, what is striking about the University of Indonesia is its architectural strategy that resembles the colonial buildings of the "konservasi–historis" zone of the Institute of Techno-logy at Bandung (Figure 3.3). These buildings, built under the Dutch colonial regime in 1920, at that time called the Bandoeng Technische Hoogeschool, were also designed by Maclaine Pont to expose a broadly based indigenous architec-tural expression (see Chapter 1). The attempt to create an all-encompassing image of "Indonesia" in the 1990s was already the underlining logic of Maclaine Pont's design for the Bandoeng Technische Hoogeschool in 1920.

What we have in the University of Indonesia is a reappearance, in postcolo-nial times, of an architectural paradigm of the late Dutch colonial regime; a reproduction of a "traditional" architecture that in Bandung is to be tran-scended. What the University of Indonesia represents, therefore, is a recovering of a tradition in architecture which, in the Institute of Technology of Bandung, is subjected to displacement. For while the Institute of Technology at Bandung retraced its colonial origins by overcoming its traditionality, the University of Indonesia arrived at its own conclusion by reinscribing a cultural continuity of traditional "Indonesia."

Bringing together these two campuses, we find a fundamental split in modern Indonesia, a contradictory identity that, on the one hand, gives rise to the coloniality of "Indonesian architecture," and on the other hand, a denial of its colonial origin. We could, of course, read these two campuses through post-modern architectural discourses, grounding their representations on stylistics of pastiche, and cultural citations from all civilizations. Such a reading would necessarily highlight not just a form of postcolonial constructions of national and transnational identity, but also of the late colonial architectural legacy which foreshadowed the cultural framework of the New Order's architects.

When Benedict Anderson (1991) argued that the genealogy of the official nationalism of the (de)colonized worlds of Asia and Africa could be traced to the imaginings of the colonial state, he was really arguing that nationality lies in its capacity to foster its citizens, by means of representations, to collectively imagine a range of things. In this sense, what should be officially recalled to foster a sense of national identity also implies a social consensus as to what should be ignored, or overlooked.

That Maclaine Pont's East and West Hall of the Bandung Institute of Technology was labelled "konservasi–historis" and the new buildings of the "transisi" zone retained traces of its architectural style, tells us what is to be put into the past and what is allowed to be represented in the present. The architectural legacy of the Bandung Institute of Technology was thus to be remembered only by its few surviving architectural elements represented in the buildings of the "transisi" zone. The political culture of Dutch colonialism, its construction of "indigenous" culture and the representation of "Indonesia" which underlie the Institute of Technology at Bandung, have to be suppressed in order to conceal the making of an official "authentic" nationalism of post-colonial Indonesia.

This "authentic" postcolonial Indonesia emerged in the representation of the University of Indonesia. The design of this campus makes visible familiar or authoritative colloquial images of indigenous traditional buildings. What has become important is the mobilization of architectural images, considered to be indigenous to the national community, that would convey a sense of the New Order's "Indonesian architecture."

In this sense, the task of designing the University of Indonesia under the ideological environment of the New Order's official nationalism, is more how to Indonesianize an otherwise derailed "modern Indonesia." Opened by the Head of State, with the Javanese spatial conception behind the design of the campus, the University of Indonesia represents a cultural inheritance central to the New Order's ideology of "development" and "stability" grounded upon "traditional rituals."

This desire for culture is not merely a means of normalizing students' political activities.[17] It is also a representation of the regime's anxiety that its rule is lacking "authenticity." This sense of anxiety and feeling of inadequacy is generated by the political significance of colonial constructions of an "authentic" Indonesia. The Indonesia of the New Order is thus founded on a contradiction that, in relating itself to colonial representations, it nonetheless considered its colonial "origins" as irrelevant. To anaesthetize the pain of this contradiction, a continuous attempt to recover its own "tradition" becomes an important part of the political cultures of the regime. As Pemberton indicates, "this haunting sense of incompleteness so pervasive in New Order cultural discourse has the effect then, of motivating an almost endless production of offerings, a constant rearticulation of things cultural, in an attempt to make up for what may have been left out in the process of recovering 'tradition'" (Pemberton 1994: 11).

Thus, when the architectural paradigm of the colonial Bandoeng Technische Hoogeschool reappears in the postcolonial University of Indonesia, what has been foregrounded is an obsessive recovery of "tradition" represented as being outside colonial legacies. The colonial trace of Bandoeng Technische Hoogeschool that reaffirmed a sense that there is an authentic "Indonesian architecture" has, under the New Order, been safely put into the past, and labelled "historis."

The postcolonial University of Indonesia and the colonial Bandoeng Technische Hoogeschool both emerged in particular socio-economic and political contexts, yet their architectural histories were intertwined. The converging architectural paradigm of the two schools can only be understood by interweaving the late colonial commitment to "social modernity" with the postcolonial devotion to "development," guided by traditional rituals. What is produced by this interaction is a representation of social control and a reproduction of culture in which architecture plays a crucial role.

INDONESIAN ARCHITECTURAL CULTURE: DEBATING TRADITION

How far and to what degree architects under the New Order relate themselves to the continuing representation of official nationalism is an open question. Their roles as "specific intellectuals," working in the postcolonial social environment of technocracy, might situate them as professionals of artistic integrity outside the socio-political realm (see Chapter 7). Yet as they are also constituted under specific constraints of power, they participate in the construction of a rationality that would ultimately produce what is known as "Indonesian architecture."

In assembling the typological characteristics of "lokal" building forms, their architectural strategies call to mind the postmodernist recollection of histories the effect of which is an effacement of history itself. But "Indonesian architecture" as demonstrated by these two campuses is not simply a citation of postmodern forms (Jameson 1991). For what the designers long to recover is an architecture of cultural reproduction of what was and is already "there," an expression of cultural images that are inherently foreign to post-modern consumerist epistemology. What we have is perhaps more a standard political imagination of nationalism: the ahistorical recollection of "cultural traditions" that serves to restore a proper trajectory of the nation.

Yet, as I have tried to show, since the object of architectural desire – "Indonesian architecture" – was founded under colonial conditions, it is an object that is fundamentally split. For despite being a sign of the "indigenous," it is also haunted by its colonial construction. It has therefore to be continually reproduced to recover the sense of an authentic "tradition" – by displacing its "origins," as in the case of Institute of Technology at Bandung, and reciting it in the form of the University of Indonesia.

This persistent denial and affirmation of an "Indonesian architecture," in and outside the colonial legacy, no doubt motivates the further obsessive recovery of "tradition" needed for the establishment of the architectural discipline in the country. It is not surprising to see that the favorite debate in architecture since the early 1980s is "*Towards* an Indonesian Architecture," a debate that takes for granted an unquestioned framework of nationality. Sanctioned by an official nationalism that denies its colonial legacy, this notion of "towards" is an important one; it suggests a future-oriented trajectory of "becoming" and "arrival," instead of an inquiry into the genealogy of a past "Indonesian architecture."

Since 1980, the debate on how to achieve such an "Indonesian architecture" has flourished. From that year alone, the following national-level congresses have all shared that theme: "Traditional Architecture" (Jakarta, December 1981); "Towards Indonesian Architecture" (Yogyakarta, December 1984); "The Role of Cultural Identity in Architecture" (Jakarta, September 1984); "Indonesian Traditional Architecture" (January 1986). Despite the attempt to define and conceptualize its identity, "Indonesian architecture," however, has found itself to be a force field saturated with conflict and contestation. Sudradjat (1991) reports:

> The lack of clarity in vocabulary, a confusion of terms, and the widespread use of banal expressions stood in the way of a clear definition of national architectural style and identity. Even the terminology used itself often became the object of contention. The division of opinion . . . led to the formulation of different conceptions, which are signalled in whimsical terms such as 'Arsitektur Nusantara' (Indonesian archipelago architecture), 'Arsitektur Tepat Guna' (properly functional architecture), 'Arsitektur Pancasila' (architecture of Pancasila-national ideology), and 'Arsitektur Tropis Indonesia' (Indonesian Tropical Architecture). The term 'Arsitektur Indonesia,' which was obviously borrowed from van Romondt (a well-known Dutch professor of architecture), has gained widespread acceptance, despite the myriad of meanings and interpretations which over time differ according to the context and individual viewpoints.
>
> (Sudradjat 1991: 198)

What is crucial in Sudradjat's report is the attempt of the congresses to define, to conceptualize, to formulate, to express what is supposedly already "there," or "here" in the nation, instead of an inquiry into how "Indonesia" and its architecture has been constructed internally and externally through particular power relations.

Departing from the idea that houses and buildings labelled "lokal" and "tradisional" are uniquely "Indonesian,"[18] the main question is how to achieve or promote an "Indonesian architecture." Homi Bhabha (1991: 57) argues that the founding moment of postcolonial consciousness lies in the awareness of cultural "inauthenticity":

> The colonial subject was actually very aware of his of her inauthenticity . . . a form of inauthenticity which was clearly seen to be culturally, politically, and socially constructed, and which then turns to a kind of inward experience, through which most of political and social life is negotiated.
>
> (Bhabha 1991: 57)

Yet, as I have shown throughout this chapter, in the case of postcolonial Indonesia, the issue is posed differently. Rather than putting a general postcolonialist question of "what has made us what we are," the subject for discussion is "how can a national project be promoted"? (Foulcher 1995: 161).[19]

INTERNATIONAL REGIONALISM: DEVELOPING TRADITION

One of the central premises for the condition of "development," which is still insufficiently commented on, is how to develop the "Third World" nation with a particular sensitivity to its own local cultures. As early as the 1960s, along with the hegemonic roots of modernist architecture, opinion already existed that demanded sensitivity towards local differences. Sigfried Giedion (1954), for instance, introduced the idea of regionalism into the history and theory of architecture as an alternative to the modernist "international style" which, at the time, was massively replicated overseas by United States architects.[20] At about the same time research was done, mostly by First World academics, on the importance of "traditional settlements" and "vernacular architecture."[21] It is not surprising then that Indonesian architects of the New Order are starting to ask whether it might be better to develop an architecture of "stability," sensitive towards existing "traditions," instead of continuing to impose the modernist International Style architecture favored by Sukarno (see Chapter 2).

Architectural regionalism was largely a movement intended to give a local inflection to modernism by advocating sensitivity to the indigenous climate and local materials. All this implied that a practitioner, irrespective of location, should analyse a culture's built heritage, the vernacular as well as the high art. For example, George A. Hinds (1965), a prominent architectural professor of the US-sponsored Kentucky Team (1958–62) to restructure the architectural school at Bandung following the withdrawal of Dutch professors, wrote an article during his overseas tenure: "Regional Architecture for a Developing Country." It starts with a question, "How can a contemporary architecture in a newly developing country such as Indonesia be truly Indonesian?" (Hinds 1965: 31). Published for a First World audience in 1965, the editorial introduction to Hinds' article reads:

> By studying the development of a contemporary architecture in an ancient culture newly
> exposed to twentieth century civilization, perhaps we can find a guide toward
> rediscovering a regionalism which seems to have been lost in current American and
> European architecture.

> (Hinds 1965: 31)

Here, the regional cultures of the Third World, among others, have been conceived as "raw" materials for an otherwise sensitive architectural experiment to overcome the supposedly homogenizing forces of capitalism. The Third World built environment, after colonial orientalism, was once again staged as a space of the lost "mythos," a realm from which the logocentricity of architecture in the industrialized countries could reflect on and learn.

Yet the Third World is not merely a space of preservation and contemplation. It is also a space subjected to a version of "development" that suited military dictatorships and the global capitalist economy. Between preservation and development, one finds the productive strategy of architectural regionalism: a transnational development with sensitivity to the local cultural heritage that is inevitably linked to the political context of a territory. As the main interest of architectural regionalism is with the visual aspect and the tectonic expression that conveyed differences of culture, it becomes easier to be incorporated into a nationalist regime that demands an imagining of "traditions" to resolve its identity crises.

In this sense, for the new nation of Indonesia, it seems that architectural regionalism had at least three immediate reasons, of which the last is surely the most important. In the first place, the insistence on the importance of local cultures coincided with the patriotic claims of nationalism of an official kind. Second, the quest for visual difference and an individualistic sense of place converged with the accommodation of cultural tourism that was soon to provide the state with hard cash currency. The third reason takes us deeper and closer to the cultural politics of the nation and nation–state. The display and management of cultural differences, once exposed and properly represented, would reduce the potential threat of social and political disintegration. In this awkward combination the international architectural movement of regionalism found its place in the architectural culture of the New Order of Indonesia.

The capacity of the architecture to encourage a sensitivity towards "tradition" became crucial to the New Order's pursuit of its own traditionality. Thus, since the late 1970s, the discourse of "development" so central to the new regime was carried out with an increasing interest in re-inventing cultural traditions of the pre-colonial past. Suddenly too, architecture in Indonesia found itself associated with the national interest in celebrating, as well as integrating, the fragmented social visions embedded in different norms and forms of the regional vernacular environment.

EPILOGUE

On the other side of the debates and discourses on "Indonesian architecture," is the increasing transnational influence on the architecture of Jakarta and its surrounding area. The *Jakarta Post* ran a headline on the issue of the internationalization of the city with a title "RI (Republic of Indonesia) Enters Post-Mo in Architecture." Largely interviewing architects working in the commercial property sectors, the report quoted a pioneer in Indonesia's real estate business:

> Indonesia is entering the age of the Post-Modern with a combination of other styles . . .
> The lifestyle of Indonesians is similar to Singaporeans, Indians, Europeans, Americans,
> Australians and Arabs. People in these countries achieve material value through trade
> and industrialization. They talk the same language of trade and economics, and

emphasize efficiency and productivity . . . 99 per cent of condominiums and houses are sold to locals, who are not interested in the Indonesian style . . . The local flavor can be maintained in the interior decoration which has a less economic function.

("RI enters PostMo in Architecture" *Jakarta Post* March 16, 1995: 1)

These buildings provided by the business agents are for upper middle class Jakartans, perhaps not more than 20 per cent of the city's population who own houses or apartments largely for speculation and investment. They are represented as voicing the interest of the "private" class, demanding the sign of the "modern," instead of the "traditional;" the "international" as opposed to the "local." As the President of a major real estate company proclaims, "our main concern is providing the finest in infrastructure and facilities rapidly, to immediately create a modern lifestyle for residents."[22] This private sector perhaps represents another sign of the "national." They are literally free to expand as long as there remains a place in which a sign of traditionality could be traced and imagined.

Thus, the chairman of the Association of Indonesian Architects discloses that "between rp.10 and rp.15 trillion will be spent annually during the fifth Five Year Development Plan (Pelita V) on construction. Only 27 percent of the projects will be implemented by the government, the other 73 percent will be handled by the private sector" (*Jakarta Post*, ibid.). This is perhaps an "ideal" proportion of the future modern Indonesia whose development needs both the international signature and the stable image of "tradition." It is a co-ordinate that brings us back to the master plan of the Beautiful Indonesia in Miniature Park, which has prepared the cultural ground for "modern Indonesia."

Part II

Urban Space

Chapter 4: The Violence of Categories

Urban Space and the Making of the National Subject

> Before I came to Jakarta I thought as you do. I dreamed that I would do great things, that I would be equal in mind and body to the opportunities I would find. Perhaps you will be luckier than I was. The wind blows through the provinces whispering that one cannot be fully Indonesian until one has seen Jakarta.
>
> (Pramoedya Ananta Toer 1955)

That the nation not only exists, but is also embodied in the spaces of the city, is something at once obvious and yet often ignored. As an "imagined community" (Anderson 1991) exists only through an array of representations, the nation inevitably has to identify itself with the city and to take concrete form and substance in the "real" spaces of the city.[1] It is this gap between the imagined fullness of (official) nationalism and people's actual lived experiences of the city that practices of representation must negotiate.

Few things bring the negotiation between the city and the nation into more visible relief than the representation of architecture and urban design. Together they profoundly shape the way in which the nation imagines its body – the shape of the people it rules, the legitimacy of its age, and the geography of its domain.[2] Here urban design is understood not simply as a method of representing cities in the postcolonial nation after the end of colonial rule, but is used rather as a technique for turning cities into fields of social, cultural, and national identity production.

It is in this affinity of nation and city, identity and place, that (in the epigraph) the Indonesian writer, Pramoedya Ananta Toer, links "Indonesians" to "Jakarta," and also ultimately questions this relationship. Disillusioned by the promise of the relationship, Toer satirically suggests that the embodiment of the nation, or nation-ness in the spaces of the city, releases an imagination of upward mobility, of becoming "Indonesian," a highly unsettled and contested category, but presumably one with a status that is higher than what was before. This movement through space, from the hierarchically "lower" provinces to the capital of the country, represents a synchronous progression over time by which modernity acquired its meaning as something higher and characteristically urban. In this, and the two chapters that follow, I address the formation and trans-formation of "Indonesian modernity" as it is constituted in urban form and space.

How deep is the affinity between modernity, nation and city? Are they always adequate for one another? If so, at what moment, and due to what mechanism, does the nation become the framework of the city? Or, to further Toer's reflection, what has made cities, such as Jakarta, capable of representing as well as denying, at various levels, the truth of the nation and the version of modernity it produces? More importantly, what are the political implications of the affinity between nation and city for the legitimacy of the state, the production of national subjects, and the imagination of the city dwellers?

In his influential study on the origin and spread of nationalism, Benedict Anderson (1991) argues that nations were not produced by some given social conditions such as language or race, but were imagined into existence. Anderson suggests that major institutional forms, such as capitalism, or a census, map and museum, each in its own mode of representation, allow these imagined communities to take a visible form. What is significant about Anderson's study of nationalism is not merely the importance it attributes to human imagination, and the ways this operates creatively within structures of representations, but that these imaginings were all taking place *in*, and enabled by, the built and spatial environment, particularly that of the city. Yet in his study, Anderson does not regard architectural and urban space as an important component in which an imagined community acquires concrete shape.

This chapter will explore the ways in which the urban structures of the city, as a major institutional form of the nation–state, shape the national imagination. It will dissect selected discourses on urban space in Indonesian history from early independence to the present to show how they relate the nation to the city; how they contribute to the making of national identity; and how, through a variety of urban spaces, people act, or dream of doing "great things," in the materiality of the city which generates, among other things, a variety of social categories. Rather than aiming at an analysis of modernity in its various aspects, this chapter offers a treatment of how and why modernity takes its particular form in the social and political context of postcolonial Indonesia.

In linking the nation to the city, I trace the transformation of the regime in power through changes in urban spaces, changes which consequently also require deep mental change on the part of the general population. I argue that the most powerful results of the changes in the contemporary capital city of Jakarta are posited not on an affinity but rather on a difference with the dis-courses of nation-building generated by the previous nationalist regime of Sukarno. I will begin with an examination of the politics of city building under the first President, Sukarno (1950–65), soon after decolonization, and end with a "journey" through the urban structures built under Suharto's New Order (1966–98). I read the unsettling social and political amnesia generated by the urban structures of Suharto's New Order and argue that the reasons for their existence are traceable in the political memories of the regime they seek to displace. In analysing the urban structure of Suharto's New Order, I attempt to reframe the problem of the formation of national identity. I do this by looking at large scale "modern" projects and visible monumental buildings and analysing the various ways in which the "hardly seen" poor in urban kampung settlements were represented.[3] My aim is also to demonstrate the ways in which the techniques of representing architecture and urban space constitute a version of national identity that generates two profoundly contrasting social categories within the nation, namely, the "underclass" kampung and the "elite-middle class" Indonesians. The potential violence implicit in these two categories was most recently played out in the riots of 1998 that ended the presidency of General Suharto. I therefore begin with the riots themselves.

CATEGORIES OF VIOLENCE: THE RIOTS OF MAY 1998, STUDENTS ON THE PARLIAMENT HOUSE AND YOUTHS ON THE STREETS

In May 1998, after 32 years of ruling Indonesia, General Suharto was forced to resign. His resignation, logically an outcome of year-long economic difficulties in East Asia, was the result of two violent incidents in the capital city of Jakarta. The first was the students' protest, originally against price rises that accompanied the fall in value of the "rupiah," which then led into an expression of fierce political discontent. The students, supported broadly by their families and residents of Jakarta, called for "reformasi" (reform) in which one of the core demands was that President Suharto step down. During the event, four students at Trisakti University, an elite institution for students from privileged families, were killed by elements from the army. The outraged students then marched to the Parliament House and occupied it, strangely unobstructed by the military.

A second, far more violent incident complemented this chain of events. Soon after the shooting, major rioting broke out in about 50 places in metropolitan Jakarta. The main targets were Indonesians of Chinese descent (see Chapter 6). For more than 35 hours, the "underclass" of Jakarta, from which the students distanced themselves, ran amok, burning and looting places that apparently belonged to Chinese Indonesians (Figure 4.1). This took place regardless of the presence of police and military who apparently allowed the riots to occur.

Despite the students' mistrust of elements from the street, these separate violent incidents, one taking place in the Parliament House but watched over by the police and military, the other unfolding in the out-of-control space of the streets, forcefully obliged General Suharto to step down. What is important about these events is not merely the overthrowing of Suharto, and the violence done to the Indonesian Chinese, but the expression of categories: "student protesters" and "underclass rioters." These two overlapping instances immediately appeared as the unspoken framework of events in the Indonesian media, thereby reinforcing the categories of violence that were already in place.

Why are two different bodies of protest constituted in one city: the "stu-

Figure 4.1
"RIOTERS LOOT":
COLLECTIVE VIOLENCE,
MIDDLE CLASS
FASCINATION AND FEAR
Source: *Kompas*, May 16,
1998

dents" (and behind them the national media) and the "massa" (considered by the national media as "perusuh," a term for those who "lost their self control and sense of morality" as a result of the "immediate situation" of the riot)?[4] How are these categories produced? And more particularly, what is the relation of these categories to the ways in which the space of the city is constructed? To try and answer these questions and understand how the connections are made between the city, the nation, and the formation of these divided national subjectivities, we need to return to the regime of power prior to Suharto.

THE CITY, THE SUPREME LEADER AND THE EMBODIMENT OF THE NATIONAL SUBJECT

Soon after its independence from the Dutch in 1950, Indonesia tried to find a political system in which the mass population of the country could interact with each other without having the figure of a supreme leader. By 1960, however, all these experiments had failed (Ricklefs 1993). Social and political unrest had increasingly threatened the nation's unity, and the national economy was in a state of disaster. Sukarno, the first president (1950–65), finally came to the conclusion that the country had to institute a form of leadership that was based on his personal authority. For him, the immediate social and economic crisis was an outcome of the "looseness" of the center. Indonesia should, therefore, "become whole again, that the state becomes whole again." (Sukarno 1957, as cited in Feith and Castles 1970: 88) To arrive at this goal, it appeared important for Sukarno to find a way to communicate with the whole population, and to convince them that he, the leader, is not merely representing "them" as the head of the state, but he actually *is* them:

> My friends and my children, I am no Communist . . . I am not prejudiced. I am no dictator. I am no holy man or reincarnation of God. I am just an ordinary human being like you and you and you . . . Why is it that people ask me to give a speech to them, even when the sun is at its hottest? The answer is this: What *Bung* (brother) Karno says is actually already written in the hearts of the Indonesian people. The people want to hear their own voice but . . . they cannot speak eloquently for themselves . . . (Therefore) when I die . . . do not write on the tombstone: 'Here rests His Most Exalted Excellency Dr. Ir. Raden Sukarno, the first President of the Republic of Indonesia' . . . [but] write . . . 'Here rests Bung Karno, the *Tongue of the Indonesian People*.
>
> (Sukarno 1959: 3, cited in Hanna 1961; emphasis added)

On another occasion, Sukarno stated that:

> In every Seventeenth of August meeting [Independence Day] . . . it is as though I held a dialogue. A dialogue with the people. A two-way conversation between Sukarno-the-man and Sukarno-the-people, a two-way conversation between comrade in arms and comrade in arms. A two-way conversation between two comrades who in reality are one . . . That is why, every time I prepare a Seventeenth of August address I become like a person possessed.
>
> (Sukarno 1963, as cited in Siegel 1998: 23–4)

Sukarno, as the "extension of the tongue of the people" is also "Sukarno the people." This political representation demanded that Sukarno embody the people in himself as a way to communicate with them (Figures 4.2 and 4.3).[5] As a result, "populist politics" was initiated, a policy which demanded the constant

President Sukarno addressing a mass meeting in Semarang, Central Java.

Figure 4.2
MASS SUBJECT:
SUKARNO IN
SEMARANG, 1950s
Source: Willard Hanna,
Bung Karno's Indonesia,
American Universities
Field Staff, Inc., 1961

danger to the stability of the nation (Goodfellow 1995). As a result, the space of the street, the locus of Sukarno's revolution, has been turned into the site of "disturbance." It became a "dangerous" place which, in the name of national security, demanded constant anticipation of the government. With the end of populist politics, Sukarno's revolutionary subject was decapitated and the street, where they used to parade, was criminalized.[7] An illustrative, and perhaps extreme example taken from a later period of the New Order will illuminate the regime's politics of the street.

In 1983–4, when the New Order was in the midst of producing a new generation of "modern" Indonesians, building up elevated highways, constructing office towers, and promoting "dream houses" and shopping malls in every urban center of Indonesia (which I discuss in the following chapters), urbanites were shocked by an event which was eventually discovered to be a state-sponsored operation. During this period, urbanites began to find the corpses of tattooed men known as "gali" on streets.[8] "Gali" were mostly petty criminals and members of gangs. To ensure the winning of the 1982 election, the government hired many of these people. When they were no longer needed, the shooting began. These "gali" were killed and their bodies left in the streets as public spectacle. This state-sponsored operation became known as the case of "Petrus–Penembak Misterius" (mysterious shooter) and "Matius–Mayat Misterius" (mysterious corpse).

There have been many accounts of this "Petrus–Matius" event (Kroef 1985; Anderson 1992; Pemberton 1994: 311–18; Siegel 1998: 103–16); what I want to emphasize here, however, are two points. First is the use of the names of the two Catholic saints – Saint Peter ("Petrus") and Saint Matthew ("Matius") – for the event. These names refer to a powerful presence of Catholic officers and civilians in Indonesia's security apparatus that were sent to "discipline" the Catholic province of East Timor (Anderson 1992). In the course of the "pacification" of East Timor, annexed in 1976, this military apparatus developed all kinds of techniques of violence. These techniques of "social control" were then exported to other places, including the capital city of Jakarta. By the middle of 1980, soon after the "troubled" province of East Timor was considered as having been successfully "pacified," "Petrus" and "Matius" made their appearances on the streets of the urban centers of Java.

Second, this technique of violence was soon integrated into the national pedagogy. To the incident of "Petrus" and "Matius," it was reported that President Suharto, after the operation, was proudly fascinated by the technique that ". . . the corpses were left where they were, just like that." For him "this was for 'shock therapy' (in English)" (as cited in Siegel 1998: 110). This therapy, as James Siegel points out, is meant to shock in order to cure, and is directed not at criminals but at the general populace. The corpses were left in the streets, Suharto continues, "so that the crowds ('orang banyak') would understand that, faced with criminals, there [are] (sic) still some who would act and would control them" (as cited in Siegel 1998: 110).

What is extraordinary in this statement is the way the state makes its appearance on the streets through the dead bodies of those considered as "criminal." Through the display of the murder victims, viewers see the state, and acknowledge its presence. This "theatrical representation of pain" in which the power of the state was inscribed in the visible flesh of the condemned served to discipline and normalize the well-being of the general populace (Foucault 1977).[9] However, the corpses, instead of scaring people away, as Siegel reports, "became attractions not only to newspaper readers but to people on the streets where the bodies were distributed" (Siegel 1998: 110). Through this display of violence towards the underclass, collective identities were constituted. The dead body is the message sent by the state to the "underclass," who are seen as potential criminals, as a way of communicating with them. The message, however, also addresses the upper class, which fears that they are not distinguishable from "criminals." This method of "criminalizing" the street makes the corpses on the street a sign of menace provoking, as a result, as Siegel (1998) indicates, a fear among the general populace not merely towards the "gali," but the possibility of them to be like the "gali". This displacement of the street creates a collective body of the populace whose identity is constructed through a retreat from it.

In his influential study of modern forms of domination, Foucault (1977, 1982) argues that since the eighteenth century, the state in Europe has attained an extraordinary capacity as "both an individualizing and a totalizing form of power" (Foucault 1982: 213). In *Discipline and Punish*, Foucault used the modern prison to explain the development of (Western) society from one based on external "spectacle" to one founded on internal "self-regulation." The panopticon, a space where subjects were always seen by invisible but all-invasive eyes, is a metaphor that illustrated the dispersal of power from the state to a wide variety of actors with reasonable claims to authority. Foucault's scrutiny of the changing field of power relations is important in understanding modern forms of domination. But the theoretical input that allowed him to analyse the shift of governmentality, from "spectacle" to "disciplinary," was based on an unselfconscious idea of history as a "progression" (if not digression) of linear time in which one regime of power gives way to the next, more complex, though not more liberating one. In what I have shown and will be showing, what Foucault theorized, as the "pre-modern" form of power, is in no way the antithesis of the "modern" power of discipline and normalization. The case of Indonesia shows that both the spectacle of punishment and the bio-power of surveillance could coexist in styling the "behavior" of the state and its subject.

THE PROTECTING EYES OF THE FATHER, THE DEATH OF THE STREET, AND THE BIRTH OF THE NATIONAL FAMILY

The politics of regulating the self always carries with it the culture of self-regulation. Power can not be confidently assigned to the state without it being cultivated by the populace. This is particularly so when both the state and the general populace are fascinated by the display of the victim, as described above.

The New Order of Suharto, however, did not legitimize its presence by merely fabricating the threat of internal "others," initiating the danger of the street and providing security measures. Instead, a second point of tension associated with a desire to form a new collective subject that represented "modernity" complicated these techniques of social control through the heavy-handed display of power and spectacle of punishment.

Towards the end of the 1970s, following a decade in power, the ruling regime faced a whole new generation of young Indonesians who did not share the unifying experience of the Revolution of 1945–50, except in a very tangential way (Anderson 1990: Chapter 5). Through the Malari incident (the first student protest in 1974 when, for the first time in Suharto's regime, Jakarta was hit by student demonstrations and urban youth riots),[10] the leader of the New Order was made to realize that this new generation had ironically grown up within the cradle of the national economic development policy of the regime and demanded attention. The Malari riots refocused the policy makers' attention on the importance of not merely bridging the gap between rich and poor, but also facilitating the demands of young Indonesians aspiring to upward mobility. The capital city of Jakarta, once again, and *after* Sukarno, became an important component in the formation of the "modern" Indonesian and this time, under the definition of the New Order regime. As the symbol of the nation, Jakarta, beginning from 1975, faced a challenge of forming national subjects who were both obedient and "modern."

After that, the New Order was reconstructed by evoking an image of itself as the head of a family who benevolently oversees the well-being of its other members. In return, they must remain loyal and self-disciplined. Here, the nation is the family. Suharto summarized his "leadership principles" in the following manner:

> In order to develop *self-discipline* an educational method is needed . . . This method ("Tut Wuri Handayani") is aimed at none other than giving as many opportunities as possible to the Child to develop self-discipline naturally, through his/her own experiences, his/her own understanding, and his/her own efforts. What needs *to be watched* is that the giving of these opportunities should not endanger the Child him/herself or pose threats to others.[11]
>
> (Suharto 1991: 582; emphasis added)

A regime was therefore established that made its appearance by producing a new generation who, as a child (or family) of the New Order, incorporated the cultural and political representation of the state ideology of "development."[12] The notion of "development," broadly similar to modernization theory, informs the political culture of the Suharto regime and replaces the populist politics of Sukarno's "revolution." Since then, the more egalitarian notion of "Bung" (brother), given to Sukarno as President, was replaced by "Pak" (father) for President Suharto, and "Bu" (mother) for the first lady. If Sukarno's image was projected by his profound voice in public or in radio, that of Suharto was portrayed by the "smiling general" who made his appearance on the TV or billboards (Figure 4.4). He is there smiling, supporting, and watching over his children. Yet, people know that he was also capable of killing and also mobilizing fear from behind. This "guiding from behind," the style of the New Order's

Figure 4.4
FATHER OF
DEVELOPMENT:
GENERAL SUHARTO,
1985
Source: *Tempo*, October
19, 1991

leadership, had its sense of authentic Javanese wisdom in which the children of the family are guided from behind on their way to a destined place. The lesson has been that they know their place, do not get lost, or go astray (Figure 4.5).[13]

This task, of preventing national subjects from going astray, was perhaps first practised by the famous Governor of Jakarta, Ali Sadikin, a Sukarno protégé

We are not merely building elevated highways. We have built up the confidence and enthusiasm of the Indonesian contractor services sector in which case they have moved us *a class upward*. We have successfully accomplished a big task, which before was thought to be impossible to be built by our nation.

(Rukmana 1990: 238–9; emphasis added)

As the city completes this project, a new regime of visuality consolidates itself, altering the spatial experiences of commuters and pedestrians alike.[16] Driving through the elevated highways suggests an experience of flying over the top of the city, escaping from its congested roads and leaving behind the "lower" classes who are routed through the crowded street at ground level. From this suspended driveway, the details of the urban fabric of Jakarta's streets and kampung, the poor urban neighborhoods, are transformed into a series of blurred images, giving a sense of detachment from the "worldly" place below. The elevated highway is thus a system of representation that allows some forms and spaces to be visualized and others to be concealed. It is a kind of fluency provided by the city to create a dream-state of upward mobility in order to overcome the contradictions of "development."

The imposition of elevated highways can be seen as a technique for resolving the urban chaos and constructing, at the same time, a status category by adding another layer of modern infrastructure to the existing sea of "unsightly" kampungs and streets which the city seeks to negate. As an infrastructure that helps to construct the identity of the "upper-middle class," the elevated highways also define what is "normal" and "pathological" in the city. They serve as a metaphor for the mobility aspirations of Indonesians with kampung origins.

Figure 4.6
UPWARD MOBILITY:
FLYING OVER THE
KAMPUNG, JAKARTA
1990s
Source: *Tempo*, October 19, 1991

However, this infrastructure is not merely a representation of the dominant class. It also helps to constitute the general populace by way of city buses that occasionally travel on the elevated highways. On these occasions, the relatively poor urbanites are also provided with a similar new experience of the city, but with different political implications. Here urban space is constructed to define and regulate both the privileged and the poor. They are both celebrated and constituted by the urban infrastructure, constructed to assemble crowds for uplifting purposes.

This emphasis on the centrality of vision in architecture and urban space constitutes a phantasmagoria of display of the achievement of the New Order in embracing commodity capitalism. Along with the highway network, it reaches its apogee in the design of department stores, high-rise office towers and real estate housing, all of which are seen to provide a field of vision available for the well-to-do. On the other side, the majority poor that live behind this facade, surrounded by images of a metropolis, are conditioned by the visible proof of "historical progress." From pleasure, alienation and wonder that are derived from spectacle alone a society of consumption is produced.

Looking at one of the largest shopping malls in Indonesia, located in a newly-developed suburban "satellite town," an ex-kampung dweller, displaced to the city's low income housing complex, recalled "only recently have people dared to enter [the nearby shopping mall]; before, we only stayed outside watching the fireworks at the evening of weekends."[17] Gradually, the underclass, like, for instance, Rohiman, a pedicab driver, begins to enjoy the "department store" that mushroomed in his small town. He likes to take his family to these places, "to walk around, see how Cirebon has progressed. It feels good. Everything is so luxurious. You can get anything you want, as long as you have money."[18] Rohiman finally participates in the web of social prestige – as well as the anxiety of falling "backward" by spending as much as five days' income on one visit.

THE PHANTOM OF THE KAMPUNG: MODERN NIGHTMARE AND ELITE HOUSING

The strength of disciplinary power, as Foucault (1977) indicates, lies in its flexibility. Often, the implementation of a normalizing power through the ordering of spaces is not merely applied to the marginal. Instead, the disciplinary technology of space is applied for the self-construction and auto-regulation of the privileged community. My next illustration is concerned with the way in which the kampung, as the periphery of the modern vision, plays its decisive role in accomplishing the identity and self-ordering of the "upper-middle class."

Inseparable from the discourses of elevated highways, real estate housing development constitutes a new identity for the emerging "middle class" by offering them exclusive residential neighborhoods away from the kampung. "Real estate" housing refers to the private sector that runs the residential development in the city. Emerging in the late 1970s, and proliferating since then, real estate housing takes over the "burden" of government to provide housing with registered lands and in conformity with land use and building construction regulations. Its appearance therefore constitutes a contradiction to the kampung that has been built on unregistered lands and for the most part not in accordance with land use and building construction codes (Leaf 1991). Starting on the periphery of Jakarta in the late 1970s, and expanding in the 1980s to the surrounding regions of Bogor, Tangerang and Bekasi, were neighborhoods seeking to represent the "attraction" of living in a new housing environment. Since then, urban dwellers, regardless of their backgrounds, have increasingly found themselves, in one way or the other, represented as "national" modern subjects living in an idealized "home." Targeted at individuals with some potential for upward mobility, housing exhibitions have been intensively staged in the metropolitan city of Jakarta, offering a discursive (re)construction of linguistic order that contrasts the "modern house" with the hierarchically lower living conditions of the kampung.

For instance, the catalogue of the 1995 Ninth Housing and Interior Exhibition consists of 46 advertisers (out of 110 participants); keywords in either Indonesian or English such as "location," and "modern facilities" received the most attention, followed by a focus on the attributes of the built environment and its images.[19] The three dominant factors (Leaf and Dowell 1991) that determine the value of a house in Jakarta have been carefully exploited by the private housing institutions, namely, location (in relation to the elevated highways), availability of urban services (infrastructure), and security of tenure (having a registered title). These qualities are those presumably outside the milieu of the kampung. Statements such as "your dream house with real estate facilities," "live comfortably in a beautiful environment" and "modest house with the aura of real estate," and so on are visible everywhere. As a song performed at the 1990 opening ceremonies of the annual convention of Real Estate Indonesia stated:

> Welcome happiness.
> Now I will receive that which I have waited so long for.
> It will come and touch my soul.
> I have tried to find the peace which before I didn't have.
> For in the house there is the peace of love.
> Sweet house, sweet house, there is peace within you.
> I want your warmth, I want your tranquility.
> The world is full of smiles, the world is full of laughter.
> Flowers will blossom and birds will sing,
> Because everyone loves peace, everyone loves peace.

(As cited in Leaf 1991: 222)

The "sweet house" provides a vital source of energy for the more public arena. From there, connections are made to offices, shopping malls, and fitness centers. With houses located in safe-enclaves and "beautiful environments," advertisements depict kitchen, dining and living spaces with commentaries from "housewives." Their immediate outdoor spaces are represented by images of women and children in an environment characterized by a sense of tranquility, security, cleanliness, and order. From here emerges a gendered space which associates "work" with men (with car), and "living" for women (with children), a classification usually denied by the social and spatial environment of the kampung.

Each "real estate" company inserts a location map depicting the propinquity of its housing project to the center of the city where access to the elevated expressways is emphasized. Their names are in English. These extra-ethnic and supra-local identifications are addressed to transnationally oriented clients, or those who would be on their fringes. As a manager of a real estate housing development argued:

> Today, clients want to be international, because of their extensive travels to Europe and the U.S. They are also highly influenced by television. They aren't too keen on ethnic (Indonesian) architecture . . . They want Mediterranean style, Los Angeles style and Beverly Hills style . . .
>
> ("RI enters Post-mo in architecture," *Jakarta Post*, March 16, 1995: 1)

This process of knowledge and identity construction in "modern" Indonesia, deprived of any identification with the specific cultural space of the nation, assumes a transnational connection to the market place ideologies of the rich and happy "First World" (Leaf 1994: 343–56). Yet, the sublime imagination of transnational conceptual space provided by the real estate housing promoter for its potential consumers is presumably realized through living memories and, not least, knowledge about the kampung as well (Figure 4.7). Though the items promised are varied and prizes are offered in accordance with the values that can be put on the house, they are all constructed around one basic market principle: the promise of an architecture that sets itself against the kampung but with which it exists side-by-side.

In her study of the Indonesian family under the New Order, Saya Shiraishi (1986: 106–7) discusses the emergence of stylistic houses whose logic lies in an increasing separation of Indonesian "family" life from its surrounding social environment. Shiraishi suggests that the stone "Spanish style" house, which became popular from the 1980s, plays out an effect that separates the house from the context of the streets. In the eyes of the inhabitants and also the viewers, the stone house, amusingly termed the style of the "Stone Age," suggests that the surrounding world is dangerous, as violent as during the Stone Age. The walls, turrets, high fence with sharp steel-pointed railings, combined with patrolling dogs, builds up a bulwark of resistance which, in turn, contributes to the fear the inhabitants cultivate in themselves (Figure 4.8).

Along these lines, it is therefore plausible to say that the real estate housing industry attempts to construct a "modern" Indonesia, in relation not merely to "developed" countries but, most importantly, to the surrounding environment, including the context of the streets and the conditions in the kampung. This kampung, located at the periphery of "modern vision," has

Figure 4.7
REAL ESTATE HOUSING AND THE "REALITY" OF THE KAMPUNG
Source: *Kongres 35 Tahun Pendidikan Sarjana Arsitekture di Indonesia, Jakarta: IAI, 1985*

Figure 4.8
HOUSE OF STONE AGE
STYLE
Source: Saya Shiraishi,
Indonesia, 41, 1986

played a decisive role in providing a framework for the city to represent the nation, and its production of "ideal" national subjects. The possibility of escaping from these environments, of entering or leaving the built up area of the city, is connected to people's images of power, status, and the excitement of being located in the extended space of the "city," with parking space and cars, in gated and guarded enclaves in a segregated suburban landscape.

Yet the very conditions which render such an individual-private sphere necessary also prevent its possibility. The individual or the private forms an integral part of the strategic field constituted by the political imagination of the New Order state. The possibility of upward mobility and escape from the "city" exists only in and through the state that seeks to secure obedient subjects who know their place, and who do not get lost in the street and in the crowds. This self-ordering of the "middle class" community provides a good example of how space and its representation operates not merely as a device of domination and exploitation, but as a formative process whereby all those enmeshed within its bounds are involved in its operation. A spatial hierarchical ordering of class is certainly intended in the way the city is planned. But, in these examples, the disciplinary ordering of space is applied primarily to the fixing and surveillance of privilege, under conditions of luxury and liberty.

THE ECOLOGY OF THE "MIDDLE CLASS"

As the New Order went into its twentieth year, accompanied by the transformation of the city following the ups and downs of the economy, the number of children in the national family increased, their presence a sign of Suharto's achievement. At this time it became possible, at least for sociologist H.W. Dick (1990: 63), to declare that "the Indonesian *middle class* has been discovered . . . no one, Indonesian or foreigner, disputed that there was such a thing, or that it was growing in size and political significance" (emphasis added). Moreover, the appearance of this "middle class culture (though never made clear) is most evident in Jakarta, and is becoming the *national culture*" (Mahasin 1990: 138, emphasis added).[20]

Within these developments, the kampung was relegated even further, by the inhabitants themselves, to a lower status in which, as an observer indicated, "for those unprepared to compromise with their middle class status, the sensible strategy is to move out of the kampung" (Dick 1990: 67). In the 1980s, it was reported that in the kampung, "the heads of middle class households exempt themselves (from the obligatory night watch), by the payment of a monetary contribution. And their houses are not watched, because they have fences and can be protected by the police" (Dick 1990: 67–8).

Articles on the rapidly growing world of the "middle class" appeared regularly in the Indonesian mass media in the 1980s. One of the first attempts by a national newspaper to explore this "middle class" world identified this group as those whose:

> education makes it possible for them to develop significant insights and to think acutely. Their income frees them from the constant necessity of seeking their daily rice. Within limits, their income also makes it possible for them to gain access to social infrastructure and power. And their age, on the average, is relatively young.
>
> (*Kompas*, May 11, 1986; reprinted in Tanter and Young (eds) 1990: 169)

By this time the "urban rationality," first made explicit by Sadikin, has gained in appreciation by the increasing numbers of the "middle class." Faced with this phenomenon, experts became more confident in linking the identity of this group with the particular place they live. Sociologist Aswab Mahasin could thus suggest that:

> the upper fraction usually lives in good residential areas of the city, while the lower fraction lives in the kampongs or in the new low-cost housing. The middle fraction lives in between: in good houses of the kampongs or in selected blocks in the low-cost housing complexes where, as members of the select few, they live in brick houses, earn regular salaries and live a good life. To the kampong people, however, all the middle class, including the lower fraction, belongs to the gedongan people: those who live in brick houses, earn regular salaries, are better educated and live a good life. Even if they live in the kampong, they belong to the 'fortunate' few and become informal leaders of some sort.
>
> (Mahasin 1990: 141)

If the urban poor, or the kampung dwellers, have usually been unwilling to accept this affinity of place and identity, they have nevertheless developed an imagination of their own, conceived in "development" terms that "with some stroke of good luck," they too could move a class upward. It is in relation to this force field of the possibility of becoming part of the "new national subject" created by the New Order that the state holds its legitimacy. The disciplining process of the state overlaps with the social imagination of the populace: to be "modern," one should follow order, not go astray, be disciplined and, most importantly, stay away from the street.

In 1995, for instance, on the National Awakening Day, President Suharto launched the National Discipline Campaign which promoted discipline and orderliness for they are "the foundation for a society that is modern and progressive."[21] This time, following the President's proclamation, more than 2,000 military personnel were distributed around the streets of the Jakarta area. The military was to "take action against anyone violating the city's ruling on sanitation and order" and to "install a high sense of discipline among the public."[22] Along with this, 14,000 "volunteers" armed with clubs, were mobilized to help prevent the activities of petty criminals and ensure that pedestrians crossed the street properly so as not to interfere with traffic.[23] In addition to this discipline and order, as if continuing Sadikin's aspiration for a fast track urban environment, gated suburban housing was promoted and the construction of elevated highways accelerated. The creation of these new infrastructures allowed "modernity" to be experienced outdoors, but off the streets, away from the imagined threat of possible "gali."

The idea of the street as a space of menace in Indonesia has its genealogy in Javanese culture. Streets, as Siegel (1986: 117–37) writes, as opposed to the "house," have often been seen as a space of the unpredictable, the locus of disturbances where the mad, the wanderers, and ghosts make appearances. This "tradition" was institutionalized by the New Order so as to overcome Sukarno's street-based populist politics.

Therefore, as the state's rhetoric of national "development" replaced Sukarno's populist politics of "revolution," the political representation of one body was displaced by the production of two different collective bodies, the privileged ("family" of the nation) and the underclass ("on the streets," as potential threat to the nation's well-being). Within this political culture of the nation, the city provides the framework of displacement. To see the affinity between the nation and city during the New Order, it is not enough to think that the transformation of the city, and the production of divided national subjects, result from the political games of the New Order against the previous regime. Instead, the new generation of Indonesians, who often grew up uneasily under the "protective" eyes of the New Order, is also responsible for shaping the techniques of social control. It is in this sense that the state emerges through its material and spatial effects, and by way of the civil society it creates and embodies. Through them, the state registers its power. It is crucial to think of power as not coming just from above, in the manner of Machiavelli, but also from below the nation–state; from the popular imaginations that are then harnessed by the state

to increase its social control. It is therefore important to consider the accommodation made by the state to "fulfill" certain aspirations of the youth who
provide, in turn, the efficiency of self-regulation among "chosen" members of
the society.

CONCLUSION

The representational effect of urban knowledge and design under the New
Order has produced an obedient and productive body of national subjects who
could represent the "modern" nation, *after* Sukarno. This production is inseparable from the attempt of the New Order to overcome the historical memory of
the city under the previous regime. For these "modern" subjects of the Suharto
generation, the building of the elevated highways, the proliferation of large scale
air-conditioned shopping malls, and the creation of gated suburban housing in
the major city of Indonesia constituted a form of modernity which was also
accomplished by a fear of falling towards the category of the "internal other" –
the Indonesian underclass. This fear demands an acceptance of the idea of
upward mobility, away from the kampung and withdrawal from the streets. In
this manner, the street, the locus of the popular politics in the 1960s, was displaced. In their place are the *knowledge* of the street and the spaces of the
underclass, such as the kampung, as a permanent threat. No longer the locus of
political performance, the street was made to embody the forces of criminality.
Here, the police and military performed their roles and the state was given a
space for its existence.

What I have tried to show through an analysis of various urban structures
in the capital city is the construction of an "internal other" by the nation–state
and for the formation of an ideal "middle class" subject of the nation. For the
most part the New Order represented and legitimized its rule in two contrasting
ways: through the production of "modernity," understood as embodied in the
"students" and their "middle class" family, and "criminality," represented in the
form of the "underclass." The very conditions that rendered such a move necessary resulted from an attempt to overcome the one-body-based populist politics
of Sukarno. It is in this sense that Suharto's New Order could not contain within
itself a unified body of the nation. It follows then that the primary concern of the
New Order was neither to side with the "middle class" nor the "underclass" as
such, but rather, to initiate a form of social and political violence which would
eliminate their potentially revolutionary unification. It is within this regime of
power that the city assumes the framework of the nation, producing a
"modern" national subject while making visible conflicting identities and social
status.

By connecting the populist politics of the Sukarno regime with the attempt
of the New Order to overcome it, we are better placed to understand the conditions circumscribing the New Order's construction of national subjects. This
subject formation, while assuming the form of a self-disciplining of the people, is

along the lines of the "leadership principle" of the New Order. Back in the 1960s, Sukarno's sovereignty was based on visualizing the body of the nation in the form of the supreme leader and the city he built. In contrast, the politics of the New Order has implicated a form of political representation in which the state made itself disappear by "guiding from behind" the "development" of the city. Suharto believed that:

> If you are too forceful with someone who is out of sorts, he will only become angrier.
> But if you *face* him with wisdom and *an attitude of respect*, he will be subdued . . .
> There was no question of force being used. It didn't happen because I used threats of any kind. Absolutely not.
>
> (Suharto 1991: 210; emphasis added)

This idea of "face" and "respect" acquired materiality through the way the city was represented. It works not simply through ideological speeches but, more powerfully, through a heterogeneous transformation of urban spaces and the representation of architectural form. This "training of the senses" (Chakrabarty 1998: 295) through material space constituted a frantic search among national subjects for an architecture of the "respectable face"; a culture which simultan-eously also demands the subordination of social classes. The political implication of this is that the state ideology of "development" spreads rapidly into the city through the discourses of professional subjects (architects, planners, the business class, technocrats and so on) who often see themselves as working for a "modernity" that is considered to be beyond the nation–state. The state, for its legitimacy, needed such self-generating and self-sustaining transformation of urban space. It is in this auto-regulation among national subjects, aspiring to move a class upward, that their discourses only culminate in reinforcing the state ideology; it helps to embody and erase the cultural memory of the state. Thus, even in their own "autonomous" eyes and professional subjectivity, these modern national subjects of Suharto unavoidably become part of the New Order. It is this more than anything else that explains why the recent "middle class" revolt has been so ambiguous when pressed hard to move beyond the social field of the New Order. In this context, the modernity of the "middle class," as a category produced under the political environment of the state, is not structurally novel. It remains within the spectrum of political cultures of the New Order. The city too cannot be the "public sphere" as it is ideally imagined by Pramoedya Toer in the epigraph since it is built and remodelled upon the basis of a subordi-nation of social classes and, most significantly, in the wake of the ideological self-image of the nation–state.

It is in this sense that the contemporary development of the capital city of Indonesia was not the determinate product of capitalist development, nor simply the outcome of global cultural flows. These forces are clearly powerful and important, but they do not, in and of themselves, provide a framework for the nation–state to represent itself in the city. To accomplish this task, the political memory of the previous regime plays a decisive role.

Chapter 5: Colonial Replica

Urban Design and Political Cultures

Appeals to the past are among the commonest of strategies in interpretations of the present. What animates such appeals is not only disagreement about what happened in the past and what the past was, but uncertainty about whether the past really is over and concluded, or whether it continues, albeit in different forms, perhaps. This problem animates all sorts of discussions about influence, about blame and judgement, about present actualities and future priorities.

(Said 1993: 3)

In the previous chapter, I have argued that the discourses of urban design in post-colonial Indonesia should be understood within the "logic" of the country's changes of political cultures. The reflections I proposed are concerned with the perennial problem and understanding of the "dependency" thesis whereby the postcolony has been understood as having developed largely according to the norms and forms of the metropole. Accepting the idea that neo-colonial dependency and control between metropole and (post)colony has marked the urban knowledge and city planning in the latter, I argued that neither the domination of the economy nor the culture (by the "west") could in themselves create either the nature or shape of a postcolonial city. Neither seems to be adequate to provide the framework in which the development and characteristics of a postcolonial city could be appropriately measured. In accomplishing this task, the political memory of the previous regimes, such as that of Sukarno, played a decisive historic role.

Along with this, I argued that the urban kampung, which occupies the periphery of the "modern" gaze, carried with it an imposed burden of a "historically feared" object and through which the New Order regime displayed its disciplinary power. Under this condition, it appeared to me necessary to locate the kampung in the perceptions and experiences of the civil society and ask why the kampung has become a convenient framework, or better, benchmark, from which the "state" aims to achieve its hegemonic position. The capacity of the New Order to sustain itself and its ideology of "development," is due in no small

measure to the "support" of those sections of civil society who shared and cultivated the "fear of the kampung" and that was then used and appropriated by
the state. It is in this way that civil society contributes to the making of a particular
political culture that has ruled, more or less unchallenged, for more than three
decades. I believed I had found an answer in identifying, not so much the power
of the state, but some assumptions of the civil society concerning "modernity"
and "upward mobility" that contributed to the pathologization of the kampung
on the one hand and the normalization of state power on the other. This chapter,
while continuing this inquiry into the effects of "culture" that can be seen and
felt in the state, takes a different trajectory and critical approach.

As suggested, my assumption in the previous chapter was that urban
design in the decolonized world could be most fruitfully understood as a result
of, and also as a mechanism that made possible, the local knowledge and specific political cultures of each of the respective countries. Subsequent reflection
however has persuaded me that this view has its own limitation, and that the
imagining of the kampung and the immediate "technique" of urban design that
accompanied it could, in fact, be traced to the colonial past.

This chapter aims, therefore, to bring together the colonial past and the postcolonial present of Indonesia, intertwining them in order to shed further light on the
politics of urban design, and the cultural paradigm on which it is rested. The main
objective in looking at the ways the kampung is represented historically is to grasp
the urban design paradigm of postcolonial Indonesia as well as that of its colonial
past. Caught within the "problems" of the kampung are the making and unmaking
of the country's political cultures represented through issues such as identity, cultural heritage, citizenship, order, progress, and modernity as they are constructed
outside the cultural space of the "West." I examine at some length the spatial discourses of Dutch colonialism. I do so, however, not for the sake of writing a history
of, for example, Indies Town Planning, but rather, in an attempt to shed light on the
spatial discourse on the "city" and the "kampung" that informed Suharto's New
Order. I begin with the discourses of urban design in the social field of Suharto's
New Order, followed by the urban discourses in the Dutch East Indies in the early
twentieth century when modern urban design was first introduced.

JAKARTA IN THE TIME OF SUHARTO: A CONTEXT

In the previous chapter, I have shown how Jakarta, as well as other major cities
of Indonesia under Suharto's developmentalist regime, illustrated the role of
space in forming disciplinary subjects. The urban infrastructure, and the capacity
of the state to arrange things and bodies in public, sought to allow the people to
know, rather than be known as subjects. There are, therefore, certain monuments, museums and parks which glorify the sovereignty of the nation. There are
also practices of disciplinary space for both working and living spaces within and
beyond the boundary of the city. Indeed, during the New Order regime, a wave
of prosperity brought on by the growth of capitalism stimulated the combination

of empirical social studies and coordinated efforts to plan for future needs. Economic growth, commerce, and middle class prestige are all involved in constituting the state's claim to discipline and hierarchical order.

However, in terms of power, unlike in Sukarno's Jakarta (1950–65), there is a shift in focus from the state itself towards the commercial classes themselves, with their particular conceptions of growth and efficiency. Even though the state still claims its authority over space, it is clear that the most remarkable aspects of the urban transformation of Jakarta were carried out by groups of investors and professionals whose common interest was the most profitable development of particular yet large-scale activities such as the construction of modern skyscraper offices, elevated highways and luxury housing. These "private" groups, however, work hand in hand with the aspirations of the state to produce, through the spaces of the city, a "productive," "obedient," and "modern" subject.

However, this important dislocation is not to suggest that nation-wide spatial organization has lost its importance; in fact, one could argue that, if anything, the centrality of control over domestic and nation-wide space has taken on a degree of importance unparalleled even by the history of Dutch colonization. However, space at this time has lost its dominant role as a medium through which order and its change could be represented in a single perspective. The organization of space, unlike in Sukarno's time, now follows another set of considerations in which world-wide economic relations provide the guidelines. Often, under the guidance of the project of "Global Governance" (Smith 2001), as pursued by the World Bank Development Project and private capital investment, the problem of space has been shifted from the correct ordering of a meta-concept to a coherent organization of a series of disparate and multivalent elements of urbanism (Nas 1986, 1995). Despite this fragmentally operated policy, the purpose has been quite total and clear, that is, to produce an obedient and productive body of "middle class" subjects who could represent the modern nation.[1]

The best way to enter this topic, however, is not by looking exclusively at the large scale "modern" projects and visible monuments and monumental buildings (as in the previous chapters), but by looking at the various ways in which the "poor" kampung settlements have been represented and treated (Figure 5.1). This internal other – "the residential area for lower classes in town or city" (Echols and Shadily 1990) – colloquially has been understood in the social field of the New Order as "having no taste, no class" or as a set of "country bumpkins" and "not like a lady or a gentlemen" (Podo and Sullivan 1986).[2] However, in this peripheral position it has played a decisive role in providing a framework for an ordering of space, as well as the production of the spatial identity of "modern" Indonesia and ultimately, a political culture for the country.

REFASHIONING THE KAMPUNG: ARCHITECTURAL INCORPORATION

In 1995, the then mouthpiece of the New Order, *Kompas* newspaper, published a special section praising the architects and urban planners who had improved the

Figure 5.1
URBAN VILLAGE:
SKYSCRAPERS RISE UP
FROM THE SEA OF THE
KAMPUNG, JAKARTA
1990s
Source: Larry Ford,
Geographical Review, 83,
4, 1993

condition of a kampung in Bandarhardjo, Semarang, the capital city of central Java. The article salutes the upgrading ("peremajaan") of the kampung, and especially, the participation of its citizens ("warga") in a process of "development without condemnation." For comparison, the article recalled the circumstances of the previous upgrading process, typically done under the command of the state apparatus:

> A tragedy of life was staged like a mass performance when a series of military armored vehicles and marches of uniformed troops were attacked, like waves of high tides, by the inhabitants ("penduduk") as a response to the demolition of their dwellings. Some of them even tried to burn one of the nearby armored vehicles. The screaming and crying of children and mothers, the scorning and shouting of the inhabitants, were confronted with threats and intimidation by the officials. Physical disputes could not be avoided. For days, the atmosphere at the site resembled a state of emergency.
>
> (*Kompas* 1995)

This memory was contrasted with a totally different working procedure seen as paradigmatic of the professionals. "At the North of Semarang," the story continued, "the counseling process of the Bandarhardjo inhabitants (whose kampung was to be upgraded) was done intensively and enthusiastically under the regional officials formed by local government with the assistance of the Public Works Department and a Development Consultant" (*Kompas* 1995). As a result of this "public" participation, "something pretty and artistic began to emerge in the building, not only physically, but also in the overall process, which is democratic and dynamic since it takes into account the patterns of living characteristic to the people on the site" (*Kompas* 1995).

Unlike the previous one-way approach carried out by state functionaries, the role of the professional is crucial in this collaboration.³ Urban transformation is no longer done through the rhetoric of "nation-building" but on the basis of "the love of the people" and "conforming to the aspirations of the inhabitants." The understanding of the kampung thus shifted from the ulcerous site whose remedy is demolition, to a resourceful site in need of improvement, each according to its own existing potentiality. For the professionals, the upgrading of the kampung is to be carried out by solving "problems" identified scientifically and listed in their notebooks:

> Dense population, decrepit houses, threat of fire, problems of sanitation, bad drainage system, lack of open spaces and social facilities, disordered spaces, lack of pathways and hierarchy of street, unregulated and unclear land ownership and so on.
>
> (As cited in *Kompas* 1995)

After a "dialogue" with the inhabitants, what has thus been built is a low-rise housing complex designed in a local tropical building style. The result, the architect reports, "is not a cheap house, but a house built cheaply with quality materials, sound construction, aesthetic considerations and cultural imagery." Furthermore, "the flat is designed to face the sea so that the occupants can have a good 'view' (in English). Small people ('rakyat kecil') have the right to obtain a good 'view' . . . aesthetics cannot be neglected, because they enable people to be cultured" (as cited in *Kompas* 1995).

A new identification is thus complemented with a new identity previously disallowed by the knowledge of the kampung. "Through architecture," the article explains, "social ranks are elevated. The poor will become trustworthy citizens, enabling them to enter other social classes. With this upward mobility to other classes, it is hoped, their social welfare will develop." In this case, the visual appearance of the exterior is paramount. "Like 'apartments' (in English)," the architect explains, "low rise housing should not look low cost. Their differences lie in the interior (which can be left to the inhabitants). But spaces exposed to the public have to be properly done" (as cited in *Kompas* 1995).

This architectural determinism, constituted to match the nearby elite private housing estate, has its memory in the "West." The article reports that the architect, who was also once an urban designer in Europe and America, will re-order the other kampungs following the principles of European town planning so that it can represent itself as a "new" town. "The building and the facilities will be arranged according to the concept of 'garden city' in England. The present situation has been filthy ('kumuh') and unorganized. Lots will be formed as an 'urban village' (in English) composed of an appropriate zoning" (as cited in *Kompas* 1995).

However, it would be misleading to say that all design memories are derived from the "West." The professionals of the Bandarhardjo housing complex are aware of the local cultural heritage, at least from an architectural point of view. The traditional motifs of old Semarang buildings, used in the design repertoire of the housing, function as important cultural signs that do not bend to the functionalist architectural paradigm of the "West." Recalling a local architectural memory and placing it in the present also collapses the distinction between identity and identification of here and there, modern and traditional, local and beyond. The mind of the professional does more than remember – it is a memory that is put into practice and ultimately into the politics of identification.

The design of Bandarhardjo's housing complex, the attention given to its inhabitants, and the knowledge used to rationalize the process are the miniaturized version of the creation of modern Indonesia. What is significant in the upgrading of the Bandarhardjo kampung is the emphasis not only on the measurement of health and order but, more importantly, on the class-status of the house and the centrality of vision through which the house is valued. When the architects proposed a "garden city" for upgrading and beautifying the image of the kampung, what happens is a designing of a façade, one that faces the beholder and conveys an illusion of upward mobility.

The display of the idealized class position from the outside, leaving the inside with what their own class has really produced, is the form that modern Indonesia takes. The exterior of the upgraded kampung at Semarang is similar to the way the capital city of Jakarta seeks to represent itself. Not unlike the elevated highways, which provide an elevated vision of a blurred cityscape, the "upgraded" kampung is displayed in a manner that suggests order, clarity, systematized infrastructure and imagery that are all aesthetically and culturally sound (Figure 5.2). The vision of the architect coincides with the look of the neighborhood and both ways of seeing become important as the gaze of the nation–state.

The emphasis on the centrality of vision in urban design constitutes a phantasmagoria of display of the achievement of Suharto's New Order in embracing commodity capitalism. The capital city not only provides a fantasy of a Utopian metropolis but each part of the modern sector become "evidence" of historical progress. The transformation seems to provide a field of vision comfortable for the well-to-do. However, it is meant to incorporate the whole range of Indonesian society. They therefore have an effect on the subjectivity of the wide spectrum of people who are aspiring for upward mobility.

PROGRESS AND ITS DISCONTENT: THE KAMPUNG IN THE COLONIAL MODERN AGE

The memories of architectural and urban planning discourses exemplified by the Bandarharjo project can be traced back to the first few decades of the twentieth century when Dutch colonialism was experiencing a "new age." Under the new Ethical Policy, Dutch architects, urban planners, and social reformers played the role of "specific intellectuals" who were neither geniuses of their epoch nor typical of their culture.[4] Yet they embodied and articulated, in contradictory ways, an essential dimension of "social modernity" that eventually shaped postcolonial Indonesia and predicated, in one version, the project at Bandarhardjo.[5] The "specific intellectuals" of the Bandarhardjo project that worked

Figure 5.2
KAMPUNG
IMPROVEMENT UNDER
SUHARTO AND THE
WORLD BANK 1980s:
BEFORE AND AFTER
Source: *Architecture and Community*, Islamic
Publications Ltd

independently as "development consultants," could perhaps find the origin of their ideas among a group of Dutch technicians and social reformers who identified the urban "problems" of the kampung in the Indies. Here, they also faced the inseparable questions of how to deal with, and represent the kampung.

The opening of the twentieth century was also the age of the new colonial "ethical" policy. Furnivall has named it the age of "expansion, efficiency, and welfare" (as cited in Shiraishi 1990: 27). The watchword of the new era was "progress." "The words signifying progress – such as 'vooruitgang' (advance), 'opheffing' (uplifting), 'ontwikkeling' (development), and 'opvoeding' (upbringing) – embellished the language of the day together with 'bevordering van welvaart' (promotion of welfare)" (Shiraishi 1990: 27).[6] "Progress" here was understood as a movement towards Western modernity, an evolution taking place under Dutch guardianship who also at the same time had their eyes opened to what were considered to be "indigenous" cultural traditions. However, among the inhabitants of the Indies, a sense of direction towards "modernity," symbolized by "Western" education and the introduction of electric trams in Batavia, was felt to be more powerful and attractive. Short stories of the time reveal a fascination for urban life styles (Tickell 1981). Images of asphalt roads, cinemas, gas street lights and trains were repeatedly featured, and often at length. This infatuation with "Western" technologies, the prime symbols of modernity, was often juxtaposed with images of misery and poverty of the urban masses. In Mas Marco's (1890–1932) stories (which centered on the urban life of Surabaya and Semarang), these conflicting images of the city provide the framework for political activism.

The effects of the age of progress could no longer be limited to the circle of the educated, the elite and aristocracy. Enabled by the proliferation of vernacular newspapers (Adam 1995), the urban masses living in the enclave of the kampung were also already able to participate and, in their own way, became part of the "age in motion" (Shiraishi 1990). In the late 1920s, the vernacular press, along with its campaign to influence the kampung communities, was widespread. According to Frederick (1983, 1989), historian of Surabaya, newspapers becomes a new entertainment and a means for social dialogue in the kampung of Surabaya. Frederick indicates that newspapers read aloud created considerable interest, with those who listened often participating in the debate after the reading was finished. The world of the kampung was no longer confined within the compound but expanded to the outside world; the kampung inhabitants were now able to see issues that could affect their community. Their own kampung problems were now seen in a much broader setting.

Along with the experiences of everyday life going on in and out of the kampung, the inequalities of colonial social structures were revealed. Office workers and urban proletariat, who frequently came into contact with Europeans, Eurasians and Chinese during the day, were increasingly embittered by what they perceived as the privileges these groups enjoyed. Resistance to colonial authority took the form of many small gestures, like buying illegal salt from vendors, and later, hanging pictures of national leaders such as Kemal Atatürk, Gandhi, and Sukarno in their living rooms (Frederick 1983: 364; 1989: 26).

As early as the 1920s, according to Frederick, the general discontent of kampung dwellers began to be felt outside the boundaries of the kampung, especially in the various places of the city where they worked. The kampung dwellers, ranging from the harbor coolie workers to railroad clerks, working outside the isolated kampung, protested against their conditions of living and working. Strikes and protests of significance occurred in 1920, 1921, 1923 and 1925–6 (Frederick 1983). Through matters concerning issues of employment in the city, the kampung became a place identified with problems and unrest. A measure of urban design was called for to overcome the strong outburst of the kampung's disobedience.

Within this contestation over space, disputes over socio-political justice and health conditions, the kampung was incorporated into the order of the municipality. In 1920, a municipal authority announced that "there was no part, no matter how small and no matter where it lay, of the territory within the boundaries of the city, that did not belong to the jurisdiction of the city" (as cited in Cobban 1988: 275). Since then, all land within the city boundaries was subjected to the terms outlined by the municipalities.

This development prompted the municipality to manage the kampung for the sake of its own well-being. Said to be aimed at improving the welfare of the mass population, the municipality measured the living condition of the kampung and qualified its characteristics:

> The housing of a large part of the urban masses is considered extremely poor, especially with regard to the layout of the kampung and construction of kampung dwellings. This leads to difficult access to the dwellings, poor drainage and a lack of sewage disposal, street lighting and water systems. Moreover, this situation is made worse by the growing density of kampung housing.
>
> (As cited in Nas 1986: 91)

These "miserable hovels, scarcely deserving to be called human dwellings," according to the two earliest reports on the housing and living conditions in the kampung areas of Semarang, Central Java, resulted in the first colonial "kampung improvement" project. It was understood to be urgent and "there was no time for delay" (as cited in Wertheim 1987: 541).

The changing relationship between the "city" and the "kampung" then became part of the larger issue contained in what became known as the Kampung Question.[7] It included kampung improvement and public housing, matters that became a concern to all cities in the Indies. And more importantly, a space was opened up for the identification and construction of an identity for the kampung.

RESTORING THE KAMPUNG, IMPROVING THE FACADE

Around 1938, and within this politicized context, the kampung becomes visible, not only as an insanitary space with the danger of fire hazards, but most importantly, as a *living* space of the Indonesian that could be "improved" and incorporated into the urban knowledge of the city. In a well-known report of "25 years of Decentralization in Netherlands Indies, 1905–1930," twenty two municipalities (especially those with kampungs) were reported as undergoing a process of "improvement."[8] Saturated with the keyword "improvement," none of these reports seem to suggest any possibility of kampung removal as a logical solution to the "unhealthy" situation:

> Road improvement, cemetery improvement, bazaar improvement and city improvement, i.e. improvement of squares, small parks, sluices, bridges. Improvement in this context primarily means physical improvements to make everything more orderly and above all more healthy.
>
> (Polle and Hofstee 1986: 117)

This technical surgery to improve the physical environment to obtain a healthier and more disciplined and orderly-looking landscape was conducted with political as well as economic concern. If the removal of the kampung was not an option at the time when the labor of Indonesians was needed to sustain late colonial rule, then pacification through the "improvement" of the Indonesian built environment was a much preferred alternative.

Colonial kampung improvement however carried with it a remarkable ambivalence, which could be understood through the logic of the "ethical policy": the double movement of modernizing and preserving indigenous heritage. On the one hand, it sought to transform the social environment of the Indonesian so as to appreciate "western" visions, knowledge and skill and thus contribute to the efficiency and maintenance of colonial rule. On the other, it suggested respect for what was thought of as the integrity of Indonesian life by improving, not removing, its kampung. Under this "ethical" policy, the insanitary condition of the kampung was not only threatening the public health of the city; it also threatened the idealized indigenous values believed to be imbedded in the area. The restoration of a "normal" appearance and the provision of the technical needs of hygiene, sanitation, and drainage were called upon to provoke a *sensibility* of "modern" living and a *sense* of order in the kampung. The improvement was done on the principle of a "visual ideal" in such a way that the overflowing of the unhealthy kampung-appearance into the European space could be suppressed. This surgery of the appearance of the kampung was believed to be able to help exorcise the threat of anti-colonialism (Figure 5.3).

The "ethical" respect towards "indigenous" civilization on one hand and the force of technocracy in the Indies on the other could perhaps be best understood in the town planning concepts of Thomas Karsten, the most influential figure in the history of town planning in the Netherlands Indies. Karsten's work exemplified not only the politics of the Ethical Policy but also the most advanced type of urban restructuring of the colony: the transformation of the racial segregation of space to a spatial order based on class. Although his works are genuinely political, analysis along these lines is curiously unexplored.[9]

Thomas Karsten was a most important member of the Stadsvormingscommissie (City Planning Commission) in the Dutch East Indies (1915–40). Most of

Figure 5.3
KAMPUNG
IMPROVEMENT UNDER
THE DUTCH, 1930s:
BEFORE AND AFTER
Source: C.N. van der
Heiden, *Planning
Perspectives*, 5, 1990

his ideas are compiled in the "Explanatory Memorandum on Town Planning in Java" (1938).[10] The significance of Karsten's analysis lies in his critical assessment of "the basic roots of the specific urban problems in a colonial society" (Wertheim 1987: 542) as a result of the previous racial policies dominating in the Netherland Indies. His treatment of colonial urbanism was thus based on seeing the colonial city as what Wertheim (1987) has called "an arena of conflict."[11] Here, town planning became a device that helps to pacify the confrontation between and within different racial groups experiencing the "age in motion."

SOCIAL STATUS AND ENVIRONMENT: THOMAS KARSTEN AND COLONIAL URBAN PLANNING

The basic problem of colonial cities, according to Thomas Karsten (1958), was the conflict between different social groups, manifested most strongly in the fundamental dualism of urban society in the Indies and its stratification from social, economic, legal, and technological points of view. In Karsten's view, the urban area of the Netherlands Indies in the 1920s comprises of "a non-Native and a Native group, the former powerful, rich, alive, and pushing, but small in numerical size, and the latter subservient, poor, and slow to develop, but with a strength in its massive size and its roots in tradition" (Karsten 1958: 66).

Between these two groups were the "in-between" groups of the Eurasians and Chinese. Together, all these four groups, far from living together peacefully, constituted rather a "scene of conflict." According to colonial census categories, each of these groups had its own relative autonomy of socio-cultural practices that were largely in conflict with the others. From the perspective of a Dutch observer, "they live, work and build in completely different ways, and in those respects, have dissimilar needs, potentialities, and ideals: to some extent they even have dissimilar legal institutions" (as cited in Nas 1986: 94).

At the turn of the twentieth century, these communities, particularly the "colonial middle" such as the Arabs and Chinese, brought ideals from their "homeland" which largely questioned the authority of Western power. The Arab communities brought a modernist notion of Islam from the Middle East, challenging both the traditionality of existing Islamic practices as well as Western ideals. Chinese immigrants arriving in Batavia in the early twentieth century brought new forms of political ideas, as a result of the Chinese Revolution of 1911, and posed a challenge to the colonial "ethical" policy that turned against them.[12] These "non-European" communities grew in size and were increasingly in contact with one another, resulting in competition and conflicts as well as heightening each others' sense of social justice and anti-colonial consciousness.[13]

To create an orderly situation and resolve conflicts of special interests among groups, the authorities responsible for the colonial situation were urged by the reformist–pacifists to take measures to prevent a greater, and potentially more dangerous, urban development. Karsten thus indicated that "here in the Indies . . . the authorities responsible for the colonial situation need to take effective steps to avert the great dangers to urban development inherent in the colonial situation . . ." (Karsten 1958: 71). Karsten believed that:

> management and planning by the government are essential to East Indian planning, if it
> wishes to carry out its administrative role to the full. Even if this task is difficult it must
> be realized that planning in a material sense must be striven for as it is also a condition
> for social and internal order.
>
> (As cited in Bogaers and Ruijter 1986: 79)

For a successful process of town planning which, by definition, was to develop a peculiar political order in the Indies, the conflicting interests of these groups, constituted on the bases of colonial racial census categories, had to be overcome.

It was under this analysis that Karsten decided to use the zoning system, widely known as one of the basic modern urban planning paradigms,[14] to restore a "normal" social environment of the Indies. The zoning system was used to replace the racially-organized colonial space with a spatial order based on the function of spaces and building types. Here, the commercial or working areas are regrouped away from the residential kampung area; the recreational from the governmental area, thus blurring the spatial organization based on race. Furthermore, the kampung, in which the majority of Indonesians lived, was to be "improved" to fit the residential category requirement. With this, new spatial categories based on economic class were introduced.

This zoning system itself was partly enabled by the increasing dependence of the colonial city on the labor services provided by the kampung. Here, the kampung was no longer a self-enclosed space in which working and living intertwined, but it became a "jumping stone" for upward mobility where inhabitants tended to come and go more frequently. Indeed, the kampungs of the 1920s were already internally divided along class lines. A coolie laborer, working in the nearby "city" and living in a boarding house, might find himself to be in the same kampung as the middle class elite who owned a substantial home but couldn't afford a house on the road. Both subjects, however felt a need to be incorporated into a "modern" urban existence.

With the improvement of the kampung, Karsten believed, the social attitude of the inhabitants would also change. The run down kampung, when properly improved, could constitute the well-being of living, if not the working spirit of the inhabitants. The perfection of the character of the kampung inhabitants would ultimately be achieved under a proper "milieu" of the physical upgrading of the kampung.

It is in these ventures of technical, economic and cultural "progress" of early twentieth-century colonial urban development and along with the professional attempts to upgrade the kampung, that the kampung was given the "pre-capitalist" meaning of "traditional," "indigenous," "popular," "informal," "illegal," "semi-permanent," or "transitional." All these categories emerged as a further development of the transformation of a colonial spatial category, from one based on a racial classification of the kampung (such as "Arab," "Melayu," "Chinese") into one based on socio-economic position. The kampung then begins to be placed within a stage of "development" and is largely understood as a space for a lower class subject who remains in "transition" to a middle class one.

Working in the Indies, Karsten could perhaps see that the notion of "progress," the catchword of the time, began to be invested with economic power in which private enterprise, entrepreneurship outside the structure of colonial government, increasingly gained respect from the kampung inhabitants themselves. The improvement of the infrastructure and the physical appearance of the built environment could no longer be merely invested with technical meaning but was already to be infused with signs of "progress," a new age and a new mode of consumption. The division into districts would be on the basis of social position (with its implication of economic well-being) in which only those who could pay would get "better" housing (Abeyasekere 1987: 121). Accordingly, the visibility of a socio-economic gap, as it was represented in the racial ordering of space, between the European, Chinese and the Indonesian was covered under a social identity of upper, middle and lower class.

As early as the 1930s, according to Prijotomo, the kampung of the better income Indonesian had already tried to represent itself in terms of the architectural signs of the Western-oriented "street" where "modernity" was displayed. "Mostly of private houses, these (kampung) buildings provide a very striking facade. Designed by the Indonesian and inhabited by Indonesian people, the facades are hardly Indonesian at all; they are Western neo-classical!" (Prijotomo 1988). One could interpret Prijotomo's discovery as evidence that the architectural signs of "western" modernity displayed along the street of the European enclave had been appropriated into the vocabulary of the indigenous environment. However, it could also indicate that the kampung was a space of "transition," on its way to becoming "modern" street housing.

Things were clearer for the colonial technicians. The urban "problems" encountered in the kampung were immediately seen as a mechanism of a "universal development process" through which the colony has to go although at a pace in accordance to its particular condition (Nas 1986: 93). For them, colonial crises were settled by assuming the specificity of the indigenous conditions whose developmental pace was quite different but the path nevertheless remained certain.

KAMPUNG IMPROVEMENT: "CULTURE" AND THE POLITICS OF THE SOCIAL MILIEU

The idea of zoning lies in the belief that the built environment could function like culture and representation, enabling its inhabitants to be transformed in a particular way. Rabinow (1989: 126–38) argues that "zoning" comes from the concept of "milieu" which was probably first used, most effectively, in biology. Milieu connotes interaction and transformation,[15] a conditioning environment in which the activity of an organism takes place and adapts according to the setting of the milieu. As such, the "milieu" can be seen as a concept invented to transform cultures. Within this genre, Karsten (1958) indicated that the disheartening condition of the urban scene not only signals the character of the town's society but, more importantly:

> Children brought up in a disorderly and unpleasant home learn to be untidy and indifferent, and in the same way a people forced to live in disorderly and unfriendly towns will be encouraged in a tendency towards social discontent and unruliness. Hence the degree of aesthetic harmony and beauty in the Indies town, though above all important from the idealistic point of view, also has a very concrete, in fact, almost a political significance from the realistic point of view.

> (Karsten 1958: 55)

As a social-democrat, Karsten's town planning is as much professional and technical as it is political. Without a proper milieu, a society could not be changed and the "scene of conflict" could not be resolved. Town planning has to be measured according to certain standards of hygiene and aesthetics, while economically it has to protect the "weak." Thus the first target of town planning in the Indies is the re-fashioning of the "milieu" of a kampung, understood as possessing its own internal characteristics that had to be cultivated in the course of its improvement.

For Karsten, the kampung is still a world of its own, a space with its own characteristics. He believed that "kampung improvement" would change the outlook of the kampung, but it should not create a new pattern for it. Here Karsten seems to share the ambiguity of colonial "ethical policy" which was a combination of progressive and conservative measures. His understanding of the kampung is ambivalent. On the one hand, he insisted that the milieu of the kampung should be improved, but on the other, he also believed that some substantial part of the kampung should be preserved by virtue of its "traditional" integrity. This ambivalence was most strongly played out in his attempt to bridge the urban kampung tradition with those of the modern requirements of traffic and public health:

> [I]t is highly important, above all for cultural reasons and reasons of social psychology, to base modern solutions on the traditional ones wherever possible, particularly in the native residential sections and in the smaller towns where Western influence is less strong.
>
> (Karsten 1958: 70)

For Karsten, "as long as such guidance and planning are in keeping with Native traditions," (Karsten 1958: 70) then the inhabitants will cooperate positively. In this aspect of preserving the kampung heritage and modernizing its infrastructure and facade, a "cultural identity" of the indigenous was curiously created by the benevolent colonial regime. Here, the question of the insanitary condition of the kampung was not about the culture of its inhabitants but rather that the unhealthy environment could threaten the idealized indigenous values believed to be embedded in the kampung.

The improvement of the people's welfare, the application of Western science and technology and the cultivation of Javanese cultures based on the idea of "opvoeding" (upbringing) are all parts of the Dutch ethical ideas. The concept of "opvoeding," when brought into Javanese culture in the realm of civilization, played a role similar to that of "milieu." A proper milieu should allow the Javanese to reincarnate themselves into a new person akin to the modern age.[16] The spatial and town planning discourse seemingly shared the idea that the new Javanese have to be provided with a proper milieu in which they could be transformed into a new person. Here, indigenous "civilization" was believed to be embedded in the kampung, but it had to be safeguarded through the improvement of the infrastructure.[17]

Logically, the kampung improvement of Karsten was focused on the provision of a modern infrastructure and the upgrading of the appearance of a kampung, but leaving intact the socio-economic milieu. Through the physical transformation of the built environment, the social and the economic circumstances of the inhabitants were expected to follow suit. For the colonial authority, to "improve" the kampung is not to negate its idealized past but rather to re-create or repair it in such a way that an indigenous "kampung heritage" could be drawn into the proper present. Under the gaze of the colonial vision, the kampung became known as a site in which integral Indonesian values and their changes are located. As such, it became a place the colonial state intended to protect from the onslaughts of modernity and cosmopolitanism that had, by the 1920s, already greatly influenced their "sophisticated" anti-colonial elite.

MEMORIES OF DISTANCE: COLONIAL TRANSMIGRATION AND THE EXTENDED "CULTURAL" MILIEU

While Karsten was seeking a town planning solution to the potential danger of overpopulation and increasing poverty of the native urban population in the Indies by improving their kampung milieu, the colonial government had, for some time, been experimenting with a resettlement programme known as "kolonisasi."

The census taken in 1905 by the Dutch colonial government showed that 30 million people were living in Java and Madura, with only seven-and-a-half million in the other islands of the Indies. Presented as part of the Ethical Policy to improve the welfare of the ordinary farmer in Java, the programme of "kolonisasi" was to offer a transfer of populations from the overpopulated Java to the Outer Islands, identified as "underpopulated" (Hardjono 1977: 16). Officially represented as strictly an issue of demography, the resettlement programme was justified and a style of governing the "underpopulated" communities of the Indies was invented. Parallel to this knowledge construction, the poor, unemployed population of Java – the desirable target for resettlements – was identified as the "surplus people." The Dutch government assumed that, by moving them to the Outer Islands, it would not only lead to improved social and economic conditions but would also reduce a (potential) source of social and political unrest in Java. Along with this was a strictly economic reason, namely the expansion of colonial plantations that needed labor, particularly from Java (Hardjono 1977: 16–17).

Here town planning coincided with the spatial planning of the Indies;[18] both found themselves to be working along the power of the colonial "ethical" state which conceived that the modern "progress" of the Indies was best conceived within the civilization of Java. However, if town planning discourses were measured on the standard of hygiene and visual order, the resettlement policy, from the start, relied heavily on a demographic, labor-oriented approach. Both, in reality, were social, economic and, most importantly, political concepts.

The management of the inner and outer islands of Java was practiced differently but they also shared a similar assumption, particularly about the effect of the "milieu." These two ways of organizing the population shared the idea that the social environment could change human behavior. For Karsten, the predominance of "milieu" – social environmental factors, keeping the possibility of human improvement – was to maintain the basic characteristic of the kampung. Town planning measures were then applied to the infrastructure and appearance to enhance the basic quality of the kampung milieu itself. Through the provision of infrastructure for "kampung improvement," Karsten believed, the quality of life in the kampung could eventually be upgraded by the inhabitants themselves and consequently the social position of the indigenous people improved. The important assumption for Karsten was the belief that the kampung milieu possessed its own individual character that could become productive provided it was supported by a sensitive town planning technique.

As for the logic of "kolonialisasi," by representing the conquered Outer Islands in terms of a myth of emptiness, this "untamed" and supposedly no-man's land of the Outer Islands provided an opportunity for the poor and unemployed Javanese to prove their "inherited" skill and socio-cultural leadership without any obstruction (Figure 5.4). The government provided only the land and some basic tools, but they were essentially on their own to cultivate what were supposedly "their" cultures.[19] The state just needed to provide some infrastructure, while the community of the settlers performed the agricultural skills of their ancestors. Javanese social institutions, village organization, leadership patterns, place names and traditions, were all recreated to enable the Javanese to imagine him/herself "at home" while remaining in the new land (Otten 1986: 16). As Wertheim reports, "as the willingness to move to 'the land beyond' had not yet developed very greatly at the time, the Dutch tried to make settlement attractive by reshaping conditions as nearly as possible to resemble those in the homeland" (as cited in Otten 1986: 16). With this "simulation" of Javanese rural social institutions, it was expected that the Javanese settlers would introduce familiar agricultural as well as cultural systems to the Outer Islands and thus to the familiarity and convenience of the Dutch colonial control mechanism. Far from being condemned to his past, the transmigrant would perhaps be the most dramatic expression of the effect of the environment on the individual and *en masse*. Along with the Outer Islands, the transmigrant was thus subjected to Dutch colonization in and through an imagined "Java".[20]

Although the colonial state was extremely anxious to increase the number of Javanese every year in the Outer Islands, it nevertheless attempted to have a rigid selection made. A set of rules, called the "ten commandments of colonization" was devised:

I   Select real "tanis"; non-farmers are a burden for a colony and endanger its success.
II   Select physically-strong people; only they can stand the hardships of pioneering.
III   Select young people; by taking them, one reduces future population increase in Java.

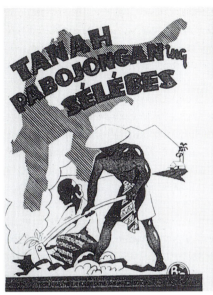

Figure 5.4
DISTANCE AND
CIVILIZATION: POSTERS
PROMOTING DUTCH
"KOLONIALISASI"
PROJECT, 1930S
Source: Karl Pelzer,
*Pioneer Settlement in the
Asiatic Tropics*, American
Geographical Society,
1948

IV   Select families; families are the foundation of peace and order in the colonies.

V   Don't select families with many young children; the working members of the family cannot carry that burden at the start.

VI   Don't select former plantation laborers; in 90 per cent of all cases they are the cause of discontent in the colonies.

VII   Don't allow so-called "colonization marriages"; they are a source of unrest in colonies.

VIII   Don't accept expectant mothers; the pioneer settler needs the full help of the wife during the first year.

IX   Don't accept bachelors; sooner or later they will become involved with somebody else's wife.

X   Allow 'desas' or 'kampongs' to migrate as a whole; in such a case the first nine commandments may be ignored."[21]

(as cited in Pelzer 1948: 210)

In this sense, the milieu and the external environment of the new settlement provided less a radical transformation of the Javanese themselves than a way of preserving them as a unique version of a kampung community known as "Java." In the Outer Islands, the unemployed, poor and "pathological" Javanese were turned into the enlightened, civilized and "normal" population. The (potential) urban wanderers found themselves, in one way or another, to be farmers, the "proper" cultivators. They were not only relocated because of the "problems" they created in Java but because they supposedly acted as agents of a colonial civilizing mission. The Javanese were distributed in separate communities, but all were equipped with tools and land, the veritable step of departure for a "civilization." With land and tools came status and trustworthiness, lineages and heritages that would define the family tradition of the new settlement. "Kolonisasi" became an institution, while working for the profit of colonial capitalism authorized the new settlers to ultimately assume a role of ancestors and keepers of what the Dutch imagined Javanese civilization to be.

The policy of Dutch colonial resettlement was never organized merely around the idea of simply distancing the poor, the unemployed, and the "undesirable" population of Java from taking part in urbanization; it served another purpose. Part of the Ethical Policy was to provide a basic setting imagined as an ideal condition for the Javanese to explore and cultivate their cultural heritage, ranging from matters of agriculture to patterns of leadership. Aside from demographic, political and economic considerations, the purpose of colonial resettlement is to put into practice the politics of the colonial state on re-vitalizing, and thus conserving, the glorious, nostalgic portrait of an autonomous village community of Java. Here transmigrants are expected to be a role model by trying to re-identify themselves as a new force of independent, if not authentic, Javanese farmers. Redemption for the poor and unemployed meant effacing personal histories, and replacing them with an organized collective identification with the benevolent colonial state on the subject of Java.

The resettlement area becomes a site not only for revising one's own past, but a new beginning of it under the guidance of the colonial state. The faults of urbanization in Java were put into the past by a return to the supposed roots of Javanese civilization, patterned onto the Outer Islands. This meant reconstructing earlier stages in history but under the rational experiment managed in the name of colonization with ethical principles.

Yet the Dutch politics of pacification carried out through the introduction of Javanese institutional cultures in colonization settlements made any sort of integration impossible. Not only did it fail to incorporate the "others" of the Outer Islands under a system of colonial control, but the politics of enclaves produced only resentment and even open hostility to the indigenous people of the various colonization areas. As one of the observers of the transmigration programmes points out,

> . . . integration with local communities was hindered by socio-cultural barriers that had been erected by the deliberate encouragement of traditional provincial ways of life. The village community in a colonisation area remained a static agrarian community, living cut off from the society of the settlement area.
>
> (As cited in Hardjono 1977: 21)

The establishment of an enclave for Javanese settlers to avoid conflicts marks the many dilemmas which circumscribed this experiment, and one in particular: the moment when the new settlers come into contact with the indigenous of the settlement areas. For the latter, pressed by the coming of the Javanese, who were under the protective authority of the Dutch colonial apparatus, losing space meant the extinction of a living culture. Hunting and cultivating the crops, the "tribes" and the "coolies" proved to be the unwritten witnesses not only of encounters, but of two cultural traditions which forbade communication and understanding and not unfrequently, entailed a fatal collision.

50 YEARS LATER: THE POSTCOLONIAL PRESENT

At the end of 1983, not long after Sadikin, the famous Governor of Jakarta, was relieved of his official burdens, a newspaper reported that a mass marriage ceremony was being held in Trenggalek, East Java:

> The men and women have reached the canopy after many ups and downs and not a few hair-raising experiences (in the city). They were first forcibly rounded up by the authorities and put into barracks, then transported to Trenggalek and put into special training centers for vagrants and given several weeks training in basic skills, plus religious and social education to prevent them from doing things that could be troublesome to the government.
>
> (As cited in Otten 1986: 70)

After pairing the people off, the "happy" couples were transported to a new land in which their "miserable" pasts in the city were to be forgotten and a new life in the Outer Islands was to begin. Trenggalek, their new place, was reported to be the transit center for transporting migrants to Irian Jaya (West Papua), the resettlement area said "to have every disadvantage existing elsewhere in the archipelago" (Hardjono 1977: 13).

"Hunting" for transmigrants is probably an appropriate term to describe the postcolonial state politics of national spatial planning. Not only are the kind of people to be transmigrated unproblematically classified, but the target for the number of families to be resettled within a specific time is also fixed at the highest level of the central state bureaucracy (Otten 1986: 44, 67, 69, 72). The lower officials are encouraged, if not pressed, to fill the quotas, either for their own advancement in the bureaucratic hierarchy or to get rid of their enemies. As an activist-researcher points out, "they used [the pressure from the state] as a pretext to send villagers [and urbanites] away who were considered to be 'less desirable' people: the non-conformists, the trouble makers or the old and sick" (as cited in Otten 1986: 69).

Meanwhile, the transport of the "less desirable" people was complemented by the control of the population through the marriage requirement organized under the state Department of Social Affairs (Otten 1986: 71).[22] The married couple is presumably an ideal unit to promote family values and culture of the state. The transmigrants who are selected are "the poorest of the poor," a nuisance to the (capital) city and to the island of Java. Through the transmigration project, known officially as "transmigrasi," they are given a new chance to "develop" in a far away land but along the lines of a version of culture ideal to the nation–state.

The ideal of a new life with the hope of making a decent living in the Outer Islands was organized to catch the imagination of the poor. Imagining the idealized form of livelihood, some of the candidates for "transmigrasi" are indeed trying to fulfill the requirement for the resettlement as much as possible in order to obtain the basic components of a decent life in Javanese society. For instance, as a team of researchers points out:

> It is clear that in terms of land ownership, house ownership, land cultivation and property ownership, these transmigrants came from sections of the Javanese/Balinese community that were poorer than the average . . . Being poor as they were, most household heads registered to migrate in the hope of obtaining land, for land is of prime value to Javanese and Balinese villagers.
>
> (As cited in Otten 1986: 74–5)

With this "local knowledge" the "transmigrasi" ultimately provides a stage to consolidate national boundaries in which the surplus population of Java is to be spread to all parts of the archipelago, marking the constitution of One Indonesian Family under the hegemony of Java.

Under this knowledge the city authorities, in their effort to modernize the city, find clues to send unskilled and unprepared people from the "degraded" kampung away from the city. At least starting from 1985, a city like Jakarta was able to make official that "excess urbanization" could be overcome by raids against "beggars, vagrants and prostitutes." Calling the raids against the urban poor a "public order operation," those "undesirable" people without proper I.D. cards issued by the city would be "requested" to return to their home villages or otherwise participate in the national programme of "transmigrasi" (Otten 1986: 69). Promises of a "better off" life with land waiting in "tanah sebrang," the land beyond Java, are for the "surplus people" who are "obstacles" for (national) development.

However, even after this experimentation, this mode of disciplining the city through a strategy of population movement has apparently been unable to solve the overpopulation of the urban center. The privileging of Java over its Outer Islands reproduced the cycle of migration to Java rather than from Java. Through this awareness, in the late 1980s, the government began to promote a concept of regional development in which the Outer Islands, rather than Java, become a prominent site for capitalist development, or better, exploitation. Under this new vision, potential transmigrants are no longer classified as the Javanese "surplus people," but are redefined into "human resources," or "workers from the central region" (Otten 1986: 137).

At this turn, the poor and unemployed communities are reformed to take part in the "development" of the Outer Islands according to the norms and forms outlined by the authority in Java. Here the Outer Islands, with all their resources, are expected to provide new fields of employment. To open up the area, industrious and disciplined transmigrants from overcrowded Java are needed.

> For those wishing to take part, don't think it is enough just to apply. All participants are trained and given extension, including education about the credit system and farming techniques over a period of between one and three years. During that period the suitability of the candidate is evaluated (by) the Plantations Office.
>
> (As cited in Otten 1986: 142)

The training of the transmigrants from Java is also coupled with the disciplining of the people in the Outer Islands. To accommodate the "human resources" from the overpopulated island of Java, the population of the Outer Islands has to remain stable and numerically less. The fertility rate of the local regional population has to remain low otherwise "development" will not enter the Outer Islands (Otten 1986: 145). The state believes that regional development is not possible without immigration and thus "transmigrasi" becomes the key to "develop" the Outer Islands, economically, socially and culturally. Along with the "development package," the top military and government figures also promote the "civilizing" mission of the "transmigrasi." Referring to an "undeveloped" area of the Outer Islands, a Christian military man thus proclaims to a foreign newspaper:

> We try to pull these primitive people towards civilization. But even attempts to clothe them encountered greatest difficulties. We want to stop their wandering existence, we want them to settle permanently, to practice agriculture and cattle-breeding and to go to church. But this takes time, for primitive people are suspicious.
>
> (As cited in Otten 1986: 169)

"Transmigrasi" is then understood by the Indonesian Ministry as "probably the only way of getting stone age, primitive and backward people into the mainstream of Indonesian development" (as cited in Otten 1986: 169). Stages of development are thus portrayed as a natural phenomenon, and with the help of the "transmigrasi", all communities under the nation–state are envisioned as progressing. Regional economic exploitation and profits go hand in hand with the civilizing mission to achieve one nation. As part of the result, the "traditional" long-houses founded in the Outer Island were suggested to be destroyed because they are considered to be cradles of "communism," and symbols of low morals and sex orgies (Otten 1986: 191). The Army Chief of the time was very clear about the "transmigrasi" and the raising of national resilience. "On the whole, the movement of the people in the framework of the 'transmigrasi' program has helped to disseminate knowledge and understanding of state ideology, political attitudes and cultural values to the relatively 'naive' local residents" (as cited in Otten 1986: 188).

Under the military regime of Suharto's New Order, "transmigrasi" was not merely a resettlement of population from overpopulated to under-populated parts of the nation. Neither was it merely an experiment that sought to erase the past of the "undesirable people" and the "uncivilized" ones and replace them with a particular narrative of progress, work, land, settlement, family ownership and patriarchy. It was also control of the new settlement areas (such as East Timor) and their populations understood to be less loyal to the regime (Otten 1986: 203–212). Under "territorial management," enemies of the state were constructed and the morality of the state imposed.

On a larger canvas, the memory of Dutch colonization was replaced with a selective postcolonial state's preoccupation with national integration, capitalist exploitation and the (capital) city's performance. The fantasy of spatial planning in the city as well as in the far away land coincided with the imagination of the nation–state with its grand, singular narrative of identity, progress and development.

CONCLUSION

What I have tried to show in this chapter is that the technique of regulating the postcolonial city and nation through the practices of urban design and planning is far from a new invention. Instead it is "inherited" from Indonesian's colonial past. Some of the urban schemes I have presented can be traced back to the first few decades of the twentieth century when Dutch colonialism was experiencing a "new age." During this time, the urban center of colonial Indonesia had repetitively been the locus of riots and various anti-colonial movements – encouraging, as a result, the development of techniques of organizing urban spaces into the repertoire of the colonial state. Under the new Ethical Policy, the specific components of bio-power therefore entered the colony and it was marked by the arrival of Dutch architects, urban planners, and social reformers (Doorn 1982). Embodying an essential dimension of social modernity, these "specific intellectuals" (Rabinow 1989), not unlike the post-colonial "development consultants," identified the urban kampung "problems" of the Dutch East Indies and the inseparable questions of how to deal with, and represent them. This chapter has shown the ways in which these intellectuals, while producing the relatively autonomous "culture" of their professions, in no way stand outside the stretch of the political imagination of the repressive state. What is remarkable about urban design and planning, at least in the case of Indonesia, is how much it is *culturally* shaped. While urban design in turn becomes a cultural symbol of the modern nation, it leaves behind its problematic of knowledge making and the socio-political construction of culture and reality.

The forces of "neo-colonialism" seem to work not only upon architecture and urban planning, but on the wider social, cultural and economic relations which it subsumes.[23] Edward Said (1993: 3) indicates that "it is not what happened in the past and what the past really was" that is at stake, "but uncertainty about whether the past really is over and concluded, or whether it continues, albeit in different forms . . ." These pages suggest just how true this is. They narrate the various ways of disciplining the non-modern elements of the city only to discover that they are, indeed, the founding conditions for a "modern" nation. They demonstrate how the achievement of the "national" was a replaying of a colonial mode of governance. As such, postcolonial nation-building is ambivalent. While it may offer viable means to transgress the limits of colonial domination, the imagining of its integrity and autonomy is often contradictorily embedded in the form of colonial representation.

Chapter 6: Custodians of (Trans)nationality

Urban Conflict, Middle Class Prestige, and the Chinese

> We must wake up from the world of our parents. But what can be demanded of a new generation, if its parents never dream at all.
>
> (Walter Benjamin, as cited in Buck-Morss 1995: 26)

A central theme of this book has been the ways in which architecture and urban space are represented, appropriated or equally nationalized and aestheticized in order to "develop" the nation. As such, it suggests that architecture and space not only aim to represent the aspirations of the societies that produce them; they are also an effort to shape such aspirations and social attitudes. Yet, the extent to which these discourses of buildings and spaces, nation and cities are actually absorbed as messages poses for us the unsettling question that marks out the problem-field of the book. This chapter, through sketches of illustrative materials, attempts to reflect on this issue of subject formation by shifting the focus of observation from discourses of the self-proclaimed professionals of space to the provocative practitioners of urban space.

In the previous chapters, I have traced the construction of an "internal other" of the city – the kampung in the formation of collective subjectivity in postcolonial Indonesia – by considering the "rational" bases of urban design. I have also shown that the technique of regulating the "city," in the framework of the "nation," is far from a new invention. Instead it is "inherited" from Indonesia's colonial past. However, the "modeling" of the colonial past in the practice of postcolonial urban design that I have presented so far, works basically by the logic of "rationality" of the discipline rather than by "copying" colonialism in any simple manner. The new form of colonialism emerged (perhaps only) through the inevitable, but particular, relation urban design has with the social and political environment of which it is a part. However, urban design, in its relation to the nation and the city, also opens up a range of "new" experiences within the metropolitan society. This chapter asks how successful urban design accommodates these new experiences, and translates the problematic ideal of the nation into the practice of identity formation. To what extent are discourses of urban design absorbed, appropriated and contested by their participants and recipients?

To those groups who run the state, particularly through their control of space, how much does urban design offer a sense of being able to promote an "official nationalism" and buttress the stability of the ruling regime? To the professionals who control disciplinary knowledge, how much does this provide a sense of skill in managing the techniques of visualizing architectural spectacles and "resolving" urban problems? To private developers, how much does this offer a sense of command and profitable contribution to the "development" of the nation and the city? To the consuming upper-middle class public, how much does this provide a sense of cosmopolitanism? To the working class, kampung dwellers and rural audiences, how much does this offer a sense of participation in the wheel of fortune, the experiments of life, and the unpredictable fate of "development"?

This series of questions, framed to consider the reception of architecture and urban planning discourse, cannot be answered in any determined way. Nevertheless, it is important to think about the contribution of the field of power such as architecture and urban design in addressing, if not helping to change, the social and political environment. I will begin this chapter first with sketches of some provocative "everyday," but unruly practices of urban dwellers to accommodate "new" experiences that do not seem to conform with the problematic ideal of Karsten's zoning and the disciplined city of the military order. Second, at the risk of being ahistorical, I present a series of "perceptions" of the city through which a trace of identity formation could be conceived. Thirdly, through the experience of the present, I conjoin the class-based urban planning of Thomas Karsten with the contemporary issues of social inequality in order to shed light on the relations between class and race in the formation of national identity. How much does urban design contribute to providing a postcolonial "national" city that cuts across class, ethnic and racial boundaries? Or (if excused from being a spatial determinist) was it the "planning" of the city that (unintentionally) allowed – or encouraged – the consciousness of anti-colonialism back in the 1920s, and the urban conflict of the 1990s? Finally, this chapter asks what kind of urban culture (beyond that anticipated by architects and urban planners) has been produced in the contemporary metropolitan society that contributes to, as well as shapes, the political cultures of the state? The purpose of exposing and linking all these disparate practices together and imagining the city in one chapter is, besides probing the question of reception and subject formation, to retrieve Wertheim's (1987) suggestion of seeing the city as the "arena of conflict."

SPATIAL PRACTICES: THE DISCURSIVE, THE UNRULY AND THE APPROPRIATION OF THE KAMPUNG AND THE CITY

Heir to the colonial perception of spaces, the postcolonial nation–state attempts to cleanse the city from the sign of "underdevelopment." I have shown in Chapter 4 that the setting up of modern structures, such as elevated highways, real estate housing and high-rise buildings to ensure fluidity of the global and national economies is carried out by repressing the mobility, if not the threat of the kampung. The housing estate, the elevated highways and the office towers are all patrolled by private and public security guards watching and marking the imagined frontier separating the private and the public, the city and the kampung. These representatives of modern structures, while protected by groups of police officers, are at the same time securing the military regime whose livelihood is based on maintaining insecurity.

Yet if these modern structures represent the repressive power of the New Order, they are also new ways of mediating the mutual yet conflictual relationship of the "city" and the "kampung," the contradiction of the formal and informal economies. While the elevated highways, high-rise towers and real estate housing might be seen as an outcome of the city's desire to become a metropolis under the guidance of the military state, they also deploy the power imposed on and carried by them. As a co-ordinating system inserted into the heterogenous spaces of the city, these modern structures also, at the same time, produce the contradiction the city tries to suppress.

This contradiction is thrown into relief by the ways in which the kampung represents itself in the space of the city, at the feet of the skyscrapers, the gate of the shopping mall and in the intersections of motor vehicles. The immense pool of cheap surplus labor provided by the kampung sustains the economy of the formal sector of the city (Figure 6.1). "Informal" canteens, for instance, lap the feet of skyscrapers, or scatter in the remaining kampung areas behind the concrete office towers erected to conceal them. They provide office and construction workers not only with an affordable place to eat but "temporary" and convenient housing as well. Hidden behind the towers, the kampung appropriates the contradictions of the formal sector that does not provide many of its employees with sufficient income for "formal" food and lodging. Marginalized yet essential, the persisting kampung sustains the formal sector that operates in and through the high-rise building.

This contradiction can also be seen in the elevated highways which, despite their image of mobility, suffer from the perennial problem of "traffic jams." The "traffic jam," perhaps one of the most popular memories and widely shared experience of Jakarta, is a persisting "problem" that always seems to exceed any proposed solution (Figure 6.2). As two columnists write:

> For all these years, no matter how often the authorities launch their orderly-traffic
> campaigns, no matter how many new rules and regulations are introduced and no
> matter how many new roads are built or enlarged, Jakarta's traffic snarls continue to
> grow worse, almost by the day . . . Appeals are made for commuters to use buses,
> instead of private cars, to commute to or from work. All to no avail, for reasons that
> must be obvious to anyone who has ever boarded a bus in Jakarta during peak hours . . .
> So zones of restricted traffic are introduced around the city's busiest business areas – the
> so-called 'three-in-one' zones where, during morning peak hours, cars are prohibited

from entering unless they carry at least two passengers besides the driver. In response, hordes of 'jockeys,' street urchins who appear along the streets from seemingly nowhere, offer their services as momentary passengers to motorists intent on beating the law.

(*Jakarta Post*, January 8, 1995: 1)

Here the urban excess is constituted both by the elite and the popular, each in his/her own way using the highway to fulfill his or her own demands. The drivers mostly work in the formal sector of the city, using the highways and appropriating the excess of the nearby kampung youngsters who, in turn, gain extra "income" as passengers. The urban excess is constituted mutually by both the kampung youngsters and the riders in private cars who would have taken public transportation if not for its inefficiency. In this way the highways are not only a device for social control but also a medium through which subjects of different interests articulate themselves.

The contradiction I try to expose here is not simply one between an ultimate function of capitalism or the exclusive power of the state. Instead of looking at urban discourses as an ideology of the powerful imposed on the powerless, I am proposing a reading of the city based on their mutual relationships in which power works at all levels. The structure of domination contains its own

Figure 6.1
INVERTED MODERNITY:
THE "CITY" AS SEEN
FROM A KAMPUNG
Source: Herve Dangla,
Belantara Jakarta, French
Cultural Center, Jakarta

Figure 6.2
JAKARTA 2005: WHERE
HAVE ALL THE
KAMPUNGS GONE?
Source: B.N. Marbun SH,
Sinar Harapan, 2, 24,
1983

ambivalences and contradictions through which the one dominated inscribes its own agency. The form the city takes, such as the elevated highways, high-rise towers and real estate housing are devices for social control as much as the medium through which different meanings and values are in dispute. The main question remains whether the pressures of the various users of urban space could constitute a culture of the city shared by both the state and the civil society, and that brings up questions about the place of class, race and sex in national identity.

SPATIAL IMAGINING: THE NATION, THE CITY AND THE REVISION OF OLD IDENTITIES

In his study of the Southeast Asian urban tradition, Richard O'Connor (1995) has argued that urbanism has to be seen as a supra-local and supra-ethnic order that must make it conspicuously "foreign." City dwellers of the region are at least bi-cultural in the sense that they retain some features of their local–regional culture while participating in the urban culture for other concerns. As a supra-local space, the city is subjected to the response of different groups, each according to its own political and socio-cultural milieu. Therefore, the norms and forms of a postcolonial city, while constituted by supra-national forces, are marked by inter-pretive disputes between different meanings and values of the city's inhabitants.

In this sense, the city, particularly in the postcolonial context, is a site of contestation between many modernities that move between particular language games: local, national, and transnational and specific, often place-bound issues of class, gender and race.

Given these multiplicities of experiences, to get a coherent account of what Indonesians of diverse backgrounds think about their cities, as a way to conceive their subject formation, may well be a futile quest. Yet it is possible to isolate an account of historical characteristics which will permit us to make sense of how, in particular situations, certain practices and intentions emerged, though they may well have gone beyond the conscious intentions of the actors. At the risk of being ahistorical in order to arrive at an articulated perception of the city by its inhabitants over time, in the following I present a series of expressions of actors engaged in her or his own specific action that shows the ways the city is imagined.

In 1952, in order to foster a sense of supra-local national identity, Mohammad Hatta, the first vice president, provided for the Indonesian people a vision of what a city is. Known as a member of one of the "westernized" elites, the former vice president was addressing the problem of unity and integrity, both of which are needed for the formation of the new nation. The city provides such an imagining:

> If there is anything to fear from bad influences, it will possibly be in the large cities which are very much influenced by the way of life of foreigners, especially Westerners. In these places, most of our people just become imitators. As usual, the easiest thing to imitate is the shallow, the superficial. Those people do not penetrate to the inside, to the kernel of the foreign culture concerned. The reason for all this is that most of our cities did not arise from our own society but rather as appendages of a foreign economy. These cities are not centers of the creative activity of our own people but primarily distribution centers for foreign goods. They emerged before a spirit and soul capable of receiving the core of the foreign culture concerned was ready . . . As I have said, the Indonesian city was built from without and became a center of foreign power. It is not a place where handicrafts or national economic activities have developed but is primarily a center for the distribution of foreign produced goods. That is why our cities are not capable of filtering the foreign cultures that come here . . . Now that we are consciously building up our culture, the center of this culture-building will be in the cities, too. Let us clean them out and fill them with the national spirit. We must be cautious and selective in the face of foreign cultures. Take the core and throw away the peel! It is the core that we must hold on to and use to enrich our culture, not the skin . . . Let us actively study the science, which has been brought to us by westerners and develop and spread it as widely as possible through our society . . . For more than three hundred years we were dominated by the Dutch, and this did not destroy our culture.[1]

> (Mohammad Hatta 1952, as reprinted in Feith and Castles 1970: 289–91)

Taken together there are two themes here: first, that the postcolonial city tends to be parasitic since it is, by nature, not developed from within the indigenous culture. Second, the city is a critical space in which a genuine culture of "our" own could be developed. The city here is urged to indigenize itself, to become a space in which a national culture could be built. Hatta's speech reveals that he is not so much criticizing the city and its "westernizing" forces, as he is considering the value of the "modernization" of the "indigenous" population. For Hatta, if the city has any merit, it is by viewing it as a critical device to transform the culture of "feudal" Indonesia. By re-centering the city into the domain of "our" society, the space of the "foreign" could finally "enrich our culture . . . our society." Hatta's statement appears to consolidate a collectivity of "modern" Indonesia as "indigenous" *vis-à-vis* the "foreign" as it is encapsulated in the form of big cities. The reference to handicraft and national economies recon-structs an "indigenous" form of expression, presumably outside the economic system of the West. What is important here is that national identity is con-structed in and through the trope of the "city" which is seen as "foreign" and "raw," needing to be civilized by a more national form of representation. By doing so, the indigenous culture itself is modernized through the spreading of science and technology.

From Hatta, we can see the construction of inside and outside. The city was not merely western in origin, but is instrumental in forging an "inside," namely, a national consciousness. It enabled a new culture-building that a pre-modern city of Indonesia could not possibly do. Here, the postcolonial city appears to be a space of exile, in which "nationality" arises.[2] In this sense, after decolonization, the postcolonial city performs this sense of exile from which nationality is imagined. The "culture of the city," while transnational in orientation, curiously plays the decisive role in providing the framework of a new consciousness, such as that of the "nation."

In the 1980s, Ayip Rosidi, a writer, provides a similar, though more per-sonal, ambivalent feeling about the city that catches Hatta's message. For Rosidi, the alienating city of Jakarta gives him a second life that he could never obtain in his place of "origin":

> I felt that I'd been placed in a sickening cage, that I'd lost my roots, that I stood right in the middle of an international city's whirling confusion, a city that opened itself to every current and never flinched away, a bustling activity without direction or purpose, a city of lies and tricks.

> (Cited in Abeyasekere 1987: 195)

Yet, he was no longer comfortable with his home village and had to return again to the capital city, as he then wrote:

> I love you Jakarta
> Because you are the city of my second birth.

> (ibid.)

First Jakarta is represented as a foreign space, "completely different from that of the country," a space from which Western culture is imported and the earlier village mentality forgotten. Despite its foreign-ness, Jakarta has been adopted as a "mother city" from which a completely new self is born. What is remarkable is not the rejection of the city as such but quite the contrary, an acceptance of its capacity to rethink the writer's relationship to its own rural "past" identity. Yet, after the city, the "(rural) comes to represent the reality of the Indonesian people." This transposition of space from rural to city enables both a forgetting of rural origins as well as a remembrance of them. The city here is far from obliterating the rural, but it enables the imagining or re-emphasizing of the common people that are presumably living in rural areas. The city represented as "foreign" thus enables the production of a new individuality and, by definition, an imagining of the old collective rural and also vernacular-indigenous identity.

In a similar way, a Sumatran in 1954 expressed his view of the city in terms of what one was in the "rural":

> Because we in the cities believe we 'have to go along with the spirit of the times,' we have deviated further and further from the simplicity of life, materially and spiritually, of the 'rural areas.' We can no longer clothe ourselves with the products of the rural weaving industry because we are afraid we will be regarded as a 'peasant.' We have gone over to 'import' in order to appear 'modern.' We are no longer satisfied if we don't have the refrigerator, a shining car . . . We are restless if for once we cannot go to the cinema, in order to 'divert' ourselves. We feel lonely, if the radio does not accompany us . . .
>
> (As cited in Kroef 1954: 170)

As for Ratmi, a woman factory worker in the time of the New Order seeking to take refuge from the poverty and overpopulation of rural Java, the "city" and the "rural" form a circle of oppression. While Ratmi is "reborn" in the city, she also finds herself trapped in a vicious circle of poverty and patriarchy:

> I forced myself to leave my home and village, my family and everything else there was to leave . . . because I think of my parents, . . . the fate of my brothers and sisters . . . I want to lighten the burden of my parents . . . they continued hurling their advice at me with their tears; but I didn't pay much attention . . . [they said] I am a woman and will be far from my parents and relatives; I should be careful and I must be submissive . . . city after city I passed by, *without regret* that I was being carried away from my family.
>
> (Cited in Tiwon 1996: 66–7; emphasis added)

Ratmi found herself in a factory whose exploitative practices led her to initiate a labor movement which ultimately failed. Ejected from the factory compound, she returned to the family as a divorced woman and with an ungrateful son. Since then she has been no longer accepted by her "community" because she is considered "too independent, too head-strong, and too outspoken" (Tiwon 1996: 70).

Ali Sadikin, the well-known ex-Governor of Jakarta, has his own way of imagining the city. For him, the urban kampung within the city is *a version* of the "rural" since it has been a place in which "villagers" largely found themselves when first migrating to the "city." The images of social relations in the milieu of the urban kampung thus called up the 'traditional," smoothly working, relatively harmonious, self-enclosed "village" of "rural" origin that cherished communalism. The urban kampung is believed to encapsulate the spirit of mutual assistance of the authentic, indigenous "village" communities. Sadikin recalled his paradigmatic intention of transforming the "city" by means of cultivating its kampung:

> From the very beginning, I was interested in the problem of how to 'urbanize' the poor
> kampung in the city and how to 'ruralize' the urban societies that have become
> individualistic and lost their collective spirit. One way is to bring back the norms of
> 'gotong royong' (mutual assistance), that is my will to help each other and defend the
> 'nilai-nilai kemanusiaan' (human values) in everyday life.

(Sadikin 1992: 60)

Recapitulating all of these accounts, there are two remarkable points to note in these imaginings of the city. The first is that all share one common condition: they all speak from a "place of origin" which was then remembered, negotiated and negated. In other words, the construction of the city as a site of things "foreign" goes hand in hand with the idea of an "indigenous" space in which social relations are depicted as different. While the social relations of "rural" communities, in their capacity as the "other" space of the supra-local "city," provide memories of unpleasant "authenticity," the city too does not provide any comfort of familiarity for them. This leads to a second remarkable "consensual" articulation: there is a "standard" conception that the city is transformative, fascinatingly alienating, but equally unpleasant. To arrive at this "standard" perception of the postcolonial city, it is necessary to bring together the arguments already posed in the previous two chapters.

RACE, CLASS AND NATIONALISM

In Chapter 5, I argue that the introduction of the "science of the city" to the Indies by Thomas Karsten in the first quarter of the twentieth century changed a situation of residential segregation based on race into one based on social class. This urban planning concept, however, all through the remaining Dutch presence, remained overshadowed by the colonial spatial order based on ethnic communities. It was only after the transfer of sovereignty in 1949 that the ethnic composition institutionalized by the Dutch through the census, along with its spatial organization in the city, underwent a remarkable change. The thrust of nationalism, based on supra-ethnic identification, demands a representation that suppresses differences. In practice, Sukarno's anti-Western policies drove most Eurasians (referred to as Indos or Indo-Europeans) away and only very few ever returned to Indonesia. The "foreign-oriental" (as the Chinese are referred to), while continuing to play a significant role in the economy, under both Sukarno's regime and the subsequent New Order, has been allowed much less opportunity to develop his or her cultural life. Since Independence, various governmental measures have attempted to curtail public representations carrying strong Chinese influences (Krausse 1988: 175). Nationalism has, since then, provided a new way of imagining communities and these have determined public representations.

In postcolonial years, though there have been some kampung clusters consisting of ethnic concentrations, the influx of migrants has no longer lead to the formation of well-defined ethnic groups in the city. Groups of migrants to Jakarta, for instance, choose their location more on the basis of employment opportunities and occupational status. In his study of the ethnic profile of post-colonial Jakarta, Krausse (1988) points out that:

> The old downtown district continues to have a sizeable segment of the city's Chinese community . . . the extended Chinese families frequently share the same living space, or combine residence with place of work . . . A team of Javanese 'becak' (pedicab) drivers in Kebon Kacang, concentrations of Sundanese factory workers in Angke, groups of Madurese food-vendors in Tanah Abang and Sulawesi fishermen in coastal settlements.
>
> (Krausse 1988: 183)

Krausse's study (perhaps still the only work that provides a link between ethnicity and place in the postcolonial city of Indonesia) concludes that the concentration of population in Jakarta, unlike in its colonial past, was not merely based upon ethnicity but more on occupation. The spatial mobility of Jakarta's dwellers therefore depends mainly on socio-economic status and this has resulted in a more rapid assimilation of ethnic groups. This is perhaps the optimistic view shared by Thomas Karsten, that class formation would help soften old racial antagonisms.

Taking such an optimistic view, there seems to be a good reason to agree with Krausse's observation. Indeed Terry McGee (1994), a guru of Southeast Asian urban studies, in his article on the future of the Indonesian city, indicates that:

> Indonesians now live in three main types of housing. The wealthy mostly occupied single-family houses in large developments on the edge of the cities, or high-rise apartments in the city core. The middle class, which now comprise a majority of the urban population, lived in smaller houses in suburbs scattered throughout the periphery of cities, and in upgraded 'kampung'-style houses within city boundaries. For the urban poor, the majority now live in legalised and upgraded squatter settlements, or in low-rise, walk-up, low-income housing.
>
> (McGee 1994: xi)

This hope is also shared by intellectuals who find class formation the way to resolve racial conflict. "A multi-ethnic capitalist class is . . . in active formation, economically and politically. Although this class remains far from anything near hegemonic over Indonesian life, its very formation has helped soften old racial antagonisms."[3] This view, along with McGee's outline of the future of the Indonesian city, is as optimistic as Karsten's. All seem to share the idea that the "future" stratification of Indonesian society, in terms of the types of housing people occupy, is seen as a natural outcome of a well-planned development, consequently accepted by all strata of the population and supposedly without any friction. This account, however, when examined across the memories of the nation–state and the racial tensions implicated upon class relations in Indonesian "plural societies," has a special poignancy about it. It gives us pause to reflect on the processes of spatial segregation generated by economic and political disparities; on the urban riots that recently exploded into anti-Chinese violence in many urban centers of Indonesia; and on the ways the nation–state attempts to mend (and to manipulate) the increasing gaps between different social groups.

In Chapter 4, I have shown how the practices of architecture and urban design have constructed a profoundly standardized conception of (trans)forming identities – constructing as a result, a kind of collective "national" subjectivity which takes in the idea of upward mobility. My argument is that the important economic interest and the powerful imagery of the First World could not, or did not of themselves, create the framework of a "new" identity of the New Order modern Indonesia. In accomplishing this task, the fear of falling towards its internal other, the hardly seen but intimately felt object of the kampung played a decisive role. The enormous change in the city under the developmentalist regime of Suharto has encouraged, as a result, a formation of status-conscious subjects who are "afraid of falling." By emphasizing the significance of the kampung, I reframe the problem of the formation of collective subjectivities from one based on the "West" to one founded within the internal space of the post-colony.

Now, if the argument posed in Chapter 4 has any validity, two general considerations suggest themselves. The first involves the relationship between the acceptance of the ideological aspects of "modernization" closely related to the formation of national identity and the negation (or better transformation) of the social environment of the kampung. The second concerns the limit of "modernization" itself as to what extent these discourses of upward mobility towards "modernity," represented in the built environment, may be absorbed or tolerated by Indonesian subjects of various backgrounds and not less by the ruling regime itself.

The best way to think about this concern is perhaps in relation to the recent riots, which provide a less optimistic picture of Karsten's plan and McGee's prediction. In the middle of May 1998, after a year-long economic crisis Suharto was forced to step down, following the killing of four student protesters and savage riots in the city. What began as a campus-based protest mush-roomed to include kampung dwellers, academics, professionals, activists, journalists and many others whose voices had been stifled under Suharto's New Order regime. The rioting still demands explanation, but one peculiar though not at all new phenomenon remains, that is, the physical and symbolic attacks on the Indonesian Chinese. After the riots, Indonesians are reported as being shocked by the dislike expressed towards the ethnic Chinese "which really has reached its peak."[4] They are also disturbed by the difficult question that if the riots were not entirely spontaneous, they were co-ordinated by powerful elements at the top, or why the city dwellers, from the lower to upper middle class, did not oppose the violence against the Chinese. An Indonesian secretary in her twenties represents this anxiety:

> Some people think the looting was maneuvered by someone or another, but I don't think so. At the big malls, maybe, but not at these small shops. The trouble is that for so long these people have seen on TV, on the news, in the soap opera, how much luxury some people have. Now with the economy the way it is, they have nothing. There is such a gap and they have been patient for so long.
>
> (As cited in Siegel 1999: 82)

The secretary saw what happened in the streets with mixed feelings. She is neither the victim of the violence nor an actor in the riots. Though aware, and even critical, of the riots, she and other Indonesians, who feel safe, nonetheless did not stand in the way of the damage and violence done to the Indonesian Chinese. She, like other middle class Indonesians, found herself in the position of observer, standing outside the event, participating perhaps in the call for "reformasi" but nevertheless sharing in a particular aspect of the political culture of the New Order: the construction of Indonesian "Chinese" as a nationally bounded "foreigner." This perennial "problem" of ethnic tension and conflict, historically shaped by early Indonesian nationalism and rooted in Dutch colonial strategy of "divide and rule," has now taken a new dimension within the social field of national "development" and the growth of the "middle class" in Indonesia.[5]

In his study of the Indonesian riots during May 13 and 14, 1998, in Jakarta, James Siegel (1999) shows the "mentalitet" of the Indonesian middle class and arrives at four important points pertinent to this chapter. First, the Indonesian middle class has been produced entirely within the cradle of the Suharto regime, and their protest against the regime was limited to the social field of that class. Second, the identity of the middle class is formed by its ambivalence towards the underclass (who are "Indonesian," but of lower class) and the Indonesian Chinese (who are considered "non-Indonesian" but understood as sharing cultures belonging to the same class). Third, this ambivalence was turned into a locatable identity (the middle class as different from both the underclass and the Chinese) when the underclass riot against the Indonesian Chinese took place. Fourth, though it was clear that the Chinese owners of small shops were not wealthy and their long history in the archipelago and consequent intermarriage made them indistinguishable from other Indonesians,[6] the attacks were nonetheless carried out through an abstraction of the Chinese as "outsiders" and through an association of them with "wealth."[7]

Siegel's study enables an understanding of the popular political imaginations as they are then appropriated by the powerful elements at the top. In what follows, I utilize Siegel's insights to illustrate the ways in which the popular imagination is shaping as well as being shaped by the transformation of the capital city of Jakarta. To arrive at this, a perspective from the state is needed. In a recent valuable study, anthropologist Larry Chavis Jr. (1997) has shown that Suharto's government, in the midst of its "development" agenda, attempted to mend social frustration and tension created by the display of excessive wealth in the city. Chavis explores the ways in which the government tries to "nationalize" the overwhelming representations of "modern" Indonesia that also implicated the ethnic Chinese. I appropriate what is basically Chavis's account and, along with Siegel's, put it into the "problematic" field of this chapter, that is to see city as the "arena of conflict" and the site in which (national) identity is formed and transformed.

Instead of centering on the role of the state, I emphasize here the conflicting aspirations of Indonesian "nationalists" and the Indonesian Chinese in modernizing the urban center. The Indonesian Chinese, as another "internal other" of modern Indonesia, while contributing to the formation of an idealized national identity, also reveals its limitation. To pose my argument, I will continue the story of the real-estate housing (Chapter 4) as an illustrative case. This will allow a conclusion that responds to the question I posed, namely, to what extent are the discourses of "modernity" under Suharto's regime tolerated and in what ways does the city represent their limitations.

CHANGING CITYSCAPES, THE POLITICS OF NAMING AND THE QUESTION OF CHINESE CITIZENSHIP

As metropolitan Jakarta of the 1990s expanded to incorporate its neighbors, creating clusters of what are to be "self-sufficient" pools of suburbia, "baptized" in global "English" phrases and installed with expensive hospitals, country clubs, schools, and vast areas of mall space, a curious decree was issued by the government. Approaching the 50th anniversary of Indonesia's independence (August 17, 1995), the Ministry of Education and Culture ruled that the names of all housing estates, apartment buildings, office blocks and shopping malls be represented in Bahasa Indonesia, the national language.[8] A lawyer, supporting the government agencies, described the matter in this way:

> In the business world today, one feels an increasing use of foreign terms while they are available in Bahasa Indonesia. For instance, instead of using 'real estate,' one could use 'kompleks perumahan,' 'puri,' 'wisma,' and so on. Using Indonesian terms should be required in the world of education and business . . . To straighten up the order of language, force and harsh sanction should be applied to those who disobey. If still stubborn, the violator should please leave the Indonesian soil, because as a citizen we

are required to follow the instruction of the government, including here the use of
Bahasa Indonesia as the language of everyday life.

(*Gatra*, June 17, 1995: 8)[9]

Compliance with the instruction was soon followed. Despite causing considerable costs, developers changed the names of their projects, from English into Bahasa Indonesia. Lippo Village became "Lippo Karawaci," Sentul Highland became "Bukit Sentul," Citra Garden became "Perumahan Citra" and so on. A major developer declared, "by using Indonesian names, it also shows that we, in the business sector, have a strong commitment to society, to be the pioneers in promoting the spirit of nationalism."[10]

Behind this event, trivial in itself and of very uncertain use, lay a long and far from trivial story. Questions concerning name dropping and changing; of foreign terms and Bahasa Indonesia; of citizenship and national loyalty; of business and commitment to society; and, most critical of all, the sense on the part of government agencies that un-Indonesian components have become increasingly visible in the city, are all caught up in what is considered to be a perennial problem for Indonesians of Chinese descent. The above "dialogue" between an indigenous professional and an Indonesian Chinese businessman was marked by a division and, ultimately, a resolution of what a "modern Indonesia," should be, i.e. what it ought to look like at a time of a growing gap between the rich and the poor, and most importantly, a decreasing gap between the indigenous "lawyer" and his Indonesian Chinese "businessman."

Indonesians of Chinese origin today constitute about three per cent of the country's two hundred million population, yet they are perceived as dominating the country's economy.[11] The resurgence of the private sector, initiated by the New Order government since the late 1960s to foster inward investment by foreign and domestic capital for the "development" of the country, has led to the domination of ethnic Chinese business enterprises (Winters 1996). This has become even more controversial with the enormous physical transformation of the city, in which land ownership is reported to be largely but not exclusively concentrated in the hands of a few super-rich Indonesians of Chinese descent.

About 60,000 hectares of land for housing, located on the outskirts of Jakarta, is said to be controlled by ten large developers, mainly of ethnic Chinese background.[12] The Minister of Housing was disturbed not only by the scale of private land ownership but also by the fact that these developers tend to sell lands merely to speculators or otherwise, to build luxurious houses for the middle to upper class Jakartan.[13] This practice far from conforms to the ideal of the privatization of the housing industry which, according to the Minister of Housing, "should be to create housing areas occupied by various groups of mixed professions, economic levels, and social status, based on togetherness and mutual aid."[14] But in the consuming eyes of capitalist modernity, cheap houses do not make profits and "could be an eyesore for the modern, prestigiously designed compounds."[15] To promote image and social prestige, many of the satellite towns were given foreign (for example, English) names and phrases, a representation of exclusivity for the upwardly mobile class.

The cultural orientation of these developers is neither rural nor "national." One might argue that they merely represent the other side of nationality, namely, a desire to pursue material progress like their "overseas" counterparts (Chatterjee 1996). Yet, when we look across the history of the Indonesians of Chinese descent who control a major portion of the housing industry, their temporal and spatial imagination of Indonesia could hardly be other than supra-local.[16] In 1967, after the collapse of the Indonesian Communist Party, accused of having close political ties with China, the New Order of Indonesia banned the public representations of Chinese cultural events. Aiming to build Indonesian official nationalism to foster assimilation with the indigenous people, Chinese schools were shut down and the use of Chinese characters in public was made taboo.[17] The logical outcome of these developments is that the private business initiative of this group makes the reproduction of the Euro-American suburb, with its common transnational living style, its most defining feature. The source of inspiration for this and other models of representation for their housing industries are supra-national. The prime barometer of the developers is "standar internasional." For the dream of Ciputra (Figure 6.3), the largest real estate developer of Indonesia, who is also of Chinese descent:

> [It is] the world [that] inspires us, to bring forth innovations, as our dedication to man's livelihood. All the beauty and harmony in this world are the sources of inspiration to create and innovate special designs that will enable people to enjoy a more colorful and joyous life. Ciputra's group philosophy is to create a better life and environment for man's livelihood. The belief is that as long as the Group produces creative and quality products, it will prove its dedication and contribution to the society.
>
> (Advertisement page of Ciputra, *Far Eastern Economic Review*, May 22, 1997: 51)[18]

Yet, as this idea of the "world" city becomes ever more luminous and more absorbing in the sprawl of modern urban life, it becomes increasingly significant as the cultural aspiration of only one particular class, the members of which may or may not be particularly comfortable with it. "English," as used to represent the aspirations of "modern Indonesia," connotes an international flavor in which only the emerging middle class (Chinese as well as non-Chinese) has a chance to really make use of it. It therefore connotes an essential class difference in Indonesia,[19] as, indeed, it does in most (Anglophonic) postcolonial societies. The problem however, is not merely the widening income gap between the haves and the have-nots, but that the long history of the society's resentment of the Chinese transposes the staging of whatever is "foreign" (such as the English language) into a symbolic representation of Chinese domination over Indonesian society.

These attitudes have therefore extended into anti-Chinese riots that have

The Good Life Starts Now

Ciputra's dream of developing Bumi Serpong Damai (BSD) into a Self-Contained City (Kota Mandiri) has been realized. The city, located in the southern part of the Tangerang Regency, West Java, now looks amazingly complete, even though only the first phase of the project has been finished. This is because all supporting facilities needed for such a large new city have already been made available. When fully completed, it will cover 6,000 ha of land and be the home of 600,000 people. BSD is much more than just a collection of residences, it will include a CBD, shopping centres, sporting and recreational facilities, Hospital and educational facilities.

Figure 6.3
AMNESIC UTOPIA:
PROMOTION FOR THE
SELF-CONTAINED CITY OF
BUMI SERPONG DAMAI
(BSD)
Source: *Indonesia
Property Report*, 1, 2, 3rd
Quarter, 1995

become increasingly common since the 1980s.[20] In 1984, weeks before the commemoration of Independence Day, the commander of the armed forces called on the nation to stop using the term "pribumi" (indigenous) and "non-pribumi" (for the Chinese).[21] In part, this idea of assimilation is intended to make invisible the ethnic component of social–economic tension (between the indigenous middle class and their Chinese counterparts; and between them and their underclass counterparts). Following this, many Indonesians of Chinese descent dropped their Chinese names either to promote assimilation or to avoid discrimination and to "publicly" represent themselves as national subjects. Yet the policy of "assimilation" only provides occasion for more practices of discrimination. Chinese entry to the public schools and state universities is strictly limited if not prohibited. Entry to the civil service and military is discouraged, if not prevented. Until recently, the identity cards that all Indonesians must carry when they reach 17-years-old contained a code that could identify the holder as of Chinese descent. As a replacement, thanks to the innovation of technology, in 1995, a separate file on this ethnic minority was suggested for storing on a new system's database (Heryanto 1998).

This politics of containment, where subjectivity is constructed without the subject involved being immediately aware of the practice, could also be illustrated in the event immediately following the May 1998 riots. Here urban space is "invisibly" used to make visible the category of "Chinese." The Jakarta police, in their efforts to accelerate the revival of the collapsing national economy, issued a new decree to Chinese shop owners, providing a 24–hours security coverage to all reopened shops in the districts where most shops were destroyed during the riots. The good will of the police was first enthusiastically applauded by the shop owners who were then, however, disappointed by the following decree. "But," the chief police said, "if my men are on duty for 24 hours in business districts such as Glodok, Mangga Dua and other economic centers, they will need places for rest, for prayer, and for a bath, and they also need to eat. Therefore, I request [as a deal] that these facilities be provided by the shop owners."[22]

The silence that followed this decree showed that Chinese shop owners were perfectly clear that this deal, while showing the attempt of government to restore their livelihood, carried with it a dangerous condition with which they will once again be stigmatized, based on their protected spaces, as "exclusive." This "culture" of exclusivity, as they were told, is the main reason why they were the main targets during the riots (Figures 6.4 and 6.5). The presence of the police in a designated area, funded privately, not only signifies the danger of the place but also the marking of an identity. These spatial politics, even when they appear to be well-intended, continue the practice of "visualizing" the Chinese as an exclusive category.

The concern of the police to "protect" the Chinese thus overlaps with the aesthetic and moral reaction by the municipality to "foreign names" appearing in the cityscape as offenses against the regime of nationalism. They both work to simultaneously mask and reveal "Chinese identities" in Indonesia. By containing them under an "Indonesian" name, a sense of national integration is supposedly felt, social inequity blurred, and discrimination concealed. By isolating them with an exclusive "protection," the Indonesian Chinese are made a visible target for the ills of nation-building. The campaign against "foreign" representation is, in a strange way, also a protection against the exposure of the "real" conditions of its existence.

Figure 6.4
BULWARK OF
RESISTANCE: POLICE,
WORKERS, AND THE SITE
OF ANTI-CHINESE
VIOLENCE IN SUMATRA,
1990s
Source: *Far Eastern
Economic Review*

Figure 6.5
MODERN ARCHITECTURE:
INDONESIAN "CHINESE"
ENTRANCE WAYS, 1990s
Source: *Far Eastern
Economic Review*

The "covering up" of Chinese cultural existence, while parallel to the wrapping up of the excessive display of the wealth of "development" in the city, also works like the overcoming of the kampung by the elevated highways. The Chinese and the kampung each in its own way marks the contradiction and the limit of the making of a "national" identity.

BROKEN MODERNITY, URBAN RIOTS AND NATIONAL–CULTURAL RENEWAL

In the 1950s, the situationists argued that "the visual aspect of cities counts only in relation to the psychological effects which it will be able to produce" (Constant 1993: 315). Goenawan Mohamad (1994), a contemporary Indonesian writer and poet, has indicated the "psychological effects" which the capital city of Indonesia produced during the heyday of national development. In his account of Jakarta, Mohamad points out that, despite the aspiration of the middle class towards upward mobility away from "their place of origin," the modern sector of Jakarta remains an uncomfortable place to live. Mohamad was worrying about the mentalities of the urban middle class whom he knew would remain uncomfortable with the city even though they benefited equally from it. While the city offers many things that catch and hold people – "it doesn't shape us . . . we merely accommodate the demands of this city without ever assimilating it." Mohamad indicates that a person who lives in Jakarta is "a type of person who does not love his place of origin enough to stay there, but yet cannot tie his heart to his new place." (ibid.)

Writing critically about the Indonesian middle class in 1984, at the time when Jakarta was witnessing the emergence of the middle class, the privatization of the housing industry and the globalization of the city's social life, Mohamad was concerned about the city as it is tied into a chain of commodities. This city, personifying the middle class he is depicting, demands accommodation from "people like us" who "buy and sell everything – our things, our bodies, our spirits." (ibid.) Jakarta does not seem to offer any meaningful sense of connection; there is nothing that must be retained and must not be lost. "Nothing." It is like "a foreign town with no one to take care of you." (ibid.) The city is alienating and it cannot stand alone, it is neither controlled by the "Dutch-style fortress" nor by the spirit of the ancient Javanese "Mataram Kingdom," but by "something else, something stronger – the economic and political forces around it" that made "us all foreigners here." (ibid.)

The psychological effect of the city on Indonesians, described anxiously and reflectively by Mohamad, underlies the explosion of Jakarta during the May riot, which represents a crude and vulgar way of exorcising the source of shock: the "foreign-ness" of the city, which should be kept in place (Figure 6.6). The desire of the Indonesian middle class towards the capital city of the nation comes from sources that they cannot anticipate. There therefore emerges the possibility of them being owned by commodities and foreigners rather than they owning them. This practice of "national" discourse takes the form of destroying, instead of constructing, the cities from which emerged the "ideal."

This different way of embodying the "nation" in the spaces of the city is transposed in the context of riots against the Chinese. Siegel's (1986) reading of the earlier riot in the city of Solo indicated that the event stemmed from a vision among the rioting youth that their future had already been marked by their

Figure 6.6
SOCIETY OF SPECTACLE:
A VIEW FROM THE
FLYOVER
Source: *Tempo*, October
12, 1998

Chinese counterparts. The possibility of future Indonesians seeing themselves as more like Indonesian "Chinese" because they produced and consumed commodities distributed by them, rather than having an identity of their own, has to be disavowed. The foreignness of Jakarta comes as a result of not following the proper process of nation-building. Here the city embodies a series of identities constructed initially for the Indonesian Chinese: "money, exclusivity, and transnationality."[23] Like the Chinese, Jakarta represents the forefront of the international commodity. It is charged for not deserving its wealth, for not holding it properly, and in the correct manner. The "wealth" of the Indonesian Chinese, like the wealth of Jakarta, is not rightful and "they" are not "assimilable." Siegel (1986) writes that the stoning, looting and burning of Chinese shops is therefore an act of making the Chinese know that they do not deserve the wealth that really belongs to the nation. By breaking the identification with the Chinese, the displaced hierarchical order that "they [the Chinese] outperform us" is symbolically revised.[24]

However, there is another peculiar dimension of the riots that takes us further into the ways identities are constituted through the symbolic and physical violence of the city. Through the riots, the rioters showed that they are not like the Indonesian Chinese. In this sense, as Siegel (1986, 1999) indicates, riots against the Chinese were not only meant to teach them to behave in the nation, but to demonstrate that Indonesians are morally unlike them.[25] In a strange way, as Siegel points out, the riots against the Chinese became a message sent by the rioters, less to the Chinese than to themselves, that "we" are not like "them." In the violence against the city, identities were formed and also transformed. The riots against the city produced "recognizable" identities for the Indonesian middle class, their Chinese parallel, and the underclass counterparts (Figure 6.7). Through the expression of violence in the form of a destruction of the city, identities such as "underclass," "middle class" and "Chinese" were constituted in practice. In this sense, the "spontaneous" May riots from "below" against the state and the concomitant symbolic and physical violence against the "Chinese" curiously replicated the state violence, as exemplified in the "public" killings of the "gali" (see Chapter 4). They both produced not merely a disciplined self as a result, but also a marking of identities and identification: "we" are not like

Figure 6.7
"US" AND 'THEM":
SECURING SAFETY
THROUGH A SIGN
Source: *Far Eastern Economic Review*,
January 9, 1997, p. 14

"them," "we" are not like "gali," "we" are not like "Chinese," "we" are not like the rioting "massa" and we don't like Jakarta.

THE OTHER AND THE ALMOST THE SAME: THE MAKING OF A CULTURE OF FEAR

Since Suharto consolidated his power in 1967, the Indonesian Chinese have been excluded from politics and have been made to represent themselves in the garb of economic success and hardship. As Chinese cultural practices have been extruded as mere "difference," this social group is susceptible to extra-national signification and being made an unimaginable community of the nation. They are largely visualized through a series of narrowly bounded abstractions by which their cultural signs and identities are fixed to "money," their sense of community reduced to "exclusivity," and in the optic of the nationalist, their loyalty disappointingly "transnational."

This stigmatization of Chinese "modern" culture, I argue, overlaps with the values of the significant numbers of today's Indonesian middle class of *non*-Chinese background. As both Indonesian Chinese and non-Chinese Indonesian middle classes are products of the New Order's developmental policy, their identities have become "almost the same." The abstract identity of "money," "exclusivity," and "transnationality" has increasingly become a surplus value of national development shared in the "dream" of (the upwardly mobile) Indonesians. The "dream" however, turns into a "nightmare" as the embodiment of these "modern" values finally confronts, retroactively, the spectre of "nationalism." The modernity that is generated so far in the city of Jakarta is considered to embody unscrupulous elements of the nation. Identification with it then has to be disavowed (Siegel 1986). The recent riots represent therefore the complexity of both identification and the disavowal of the kampung (from where Indonesian middle classes came) and the Chinese (with whom they uncomfortably see their future).

By bringing the previous two chapters together, I have examined in this chapter the ways in which particular urban spaces have been represented in the period of the New Order Indonesia (1966–98). I explored the ways in which techniques of representing architecture and urban space, while making visible mutual as well as conflictual identities and social status, have contributed to a formation of a culture of fear in the urban spaces of Indonesia. This "national" culture of fear is not merely a feeling of fright towards the police state, but a sense of fear in regards to "other" groups with whom they live side-by-side: the majority of the poor kampung inhabitants and the minority Indonesians of Chinese descent.

To date, the prevailing works of "postcolonial studies," which conceive transnational flows of culture and power, have put much emphasis on the relations between the "East" and the "West," the "colonizer" and "colonized", the metropole and the colony. What has been overlooked in these studies is the substantial role played by historical subjects who are not quite the "other" but also, not entirely the "same," subjects such as the Chinese, and who live side-by-side in constituting the identities of postcolonial subjects. The political and economic power of the "West" is well known and obviously of fundamental importance. Modernity and "western" technological innovation clearly had a powerful impact in providing a vocabulary for postcolonial subjects to fantasize their identities. However, neither of these "Others" could, or did, create in themselves the kind of framework to imagine a position needed for postcolonial identity formation and transformations. In accomplishing this specific historical role, those who are "almost the same" have played a significant role.

Part III

(Trans)national Imaginings

Chapter 7: Professional and National Dreams

The Political Imaginings of Indonesian Architects

I am an engineer. In my profession I take deep pride, but without vainglory; to it I owe solemn obligations that I am eager to fulfill. As an engineer, I will participate in none but honest enterprise. To him that has engaged my services, as employer or client, I will give the utmost of performance and fidelity. When needed, my skill and knowledge shall be given without reservation for the public good. From special capacity springs the obligation to use it well in the service of humanity; and I accept the challenge that this implies. To my fellows I pledge, in the same full measure I ask of them, integrity and fair dealing, tolerance and respect, and devotion to the standards and the dignity of our profession; with the consciousness, always, that our special expertise carries with it the obligation to serve humanity with complete sincerity.

("Faith of the Engineer," *Prospectus of the Institute of Technology at Bandung,* 1950)

Considerable scholarly work has recently been devoted to the relationship between architectural representation, nationalism, and questions of national identity in postcolonial nation–states.[1] In this research, however, little attention has so far been paid to the formation of architectural cultures in such states and their significance for these issues. In this and the following chapter, I attempt to invert my analysis, from the one based largely on exploring the socio-cultural milieu within which architects work to the "political" imaginings of the architects themselves. I begin with Indonesia and in the following chapter turn to the neighboring countries of Southeast Asia, to focus as much as possible on the "thinking" of the architects, to understand them as products of creative imagination, and then show them as part of the socio-cultural milieu within which they work. Questions that circumscribe these chapters are: how does architecture, as a profession, respond to the cultural framework of the nation–state within which it is embedded? What are the social, cultural, and political conditions that have influenced the forms of architectural knowledge and practice in such places and the way they have developed? What pressures have existed from either international, regional or local institutions to rethink their practices in relation to local requirements, or to address the construction of distinct "national" or "regional" cultural identities? And what social, political, economic or cultural outcomes do members of the architectural community see as emerging from existing or alternative architectural cultures?

At its twenty-fifth anniversary in 1985, about three decades after the "Revolutionary" declaration of the "Faith of the Engineer" (as represented in the epigraph), the Association of Indonesian Architects proclaimed that "since 1974, when the political climate moved toward *stability*, the professional organization has begun to clarify its existence" (*Arsitek Indonesia* 1985: 9; emphasis added). A special issue of the professional journal was published to commemorate the event and to affirm that the identity of the Indonesian architect–engineers has been secured in the New Order's declaration of "stability" in culture, and the economic and political sphere.[2] Harnessing the documentary system of the state apparatus, the profession represents itself, teleologically, as the triumphal progress of a professional class whose members, from the beginning, have almost exclusively devoted their time to the ideal of professionalism. The narrative texts are filled with names, dates, places, and decrees, all of them highlighted in bold type suggesting that readers should, at least, remember these important constituencies whether or not they read the report.

For those who do read the text, however, it becomes clear from the archive that the professional association was consciously distancing itself from any political engagement. Yet, in its quest for professional autonomy, the institution also demands a sufficiently stable condition in a country where all kinds of market relationships can be found, from highly oligopolistic arrangements to a system of relatively free competition. The only way of hoping to realize "professionalism" is to secure it under the stability of the New Order. Thus the document starts by describing that:

> The development of politics in Indonesia in 1959 (a year after the Institute of Technology at Bandung produced its first architectural–engineers) has enabled the formation of an architectural professional association (IAI). . . (however) for almost 15 years since its formation, the path of the professional organization was never clear. The political situation in Indonesia at that time was not supportive, if not indeed constraining the 'normal growth' of the organization. The mind-set ('alam pikiran') of all Indonesians at that time was oriented towards an 'image' of the National Grand Effort ('Usaha Besar National') to struggle for its political aspiration through a command system by mobilising the national resources known as 'Funds and Forces.' At that time, all organizations, be they trade, professional or student, were forced to choose a political affiliation. Criteria for the right to live were based on the power of the masses rather than on moral issues. Thus the IAI, as a new organization with different aspirations, had no chance at all to develop because it is grounded on the principles of non-affiliation to any kind of political ideology.

> (*Arsitek Indonesia*, February 1985: 9)

When we think of the architects who wrote this, as individuals who not only specialize in a particular field of knowledge but who are also members of a particular social and cultural order, we begin to understand that their quest for professional autonomy is in itself a comment on the social conditions within which they operate. Descended from "western" architectural traditions, in themselves known as a somewhat esoteric practice, the knowledge and practice of architecture in Indonesia is largely confined to a very limited urban minority. This was perhaps felt for the first time, even though sporadically, under Sukarno's postcolonial nation-building regime (see Chapter 2). Yet, this professional class constitutes an important part of "nation-building," especially in its relation to the ideology of "development" of the New Order. As we learn from the twenty-fifth anniversary report, it was only in the period of the New Order that the profession was able to form a tradition that was detached from socio-political inquiry. In this chapter, I shall show the ways in which a professional quest of cultural autonomy generated various imaginations as a response to the cultural order of the nation–state.

In this chapter, I will examine the formation of a particular architectural culture through a discursive reading of some of the inaugural lectures delivered since the formation of the Indonesian school of architecture, papers presented at the national architectural congresses as well as articles published in architectural journals and newspapers. In doing this, I want to demonstrate how issues raised in their representation of "professional identity" have not been sufficently understood as a cultural effort of the postcolonial Indonesian to construct a version of reality within which they are shaped. Although very few of these imaginings have, for various economic, political or strategic reasons, been translated into explicit programmes and practices, the public representation of the architects, both as practitioners and academics, has nonetheless provided a cultural space in which they could think of themselves less as technicians subservient to a political regime and more as "autonomous" intellectuals. This would enable us to conceive their agency and trajectory as inseparable from the socio-political circumstances in which they participate. The examples used throughout this chapter are intended less to show the socio-economic bases of architectural thought in postcolonial Indonesia than to ask why the making of a place for architecture has been conceived in "national" – rather than in other – forms. It also provides an analysis from the perspective of the "Indonesian subject" even though this is all male, and from the particular "middle class" social background that enables them to become "architects."

I define these architects then, primarily in terms of their postcolonial subjectivity. Historically produced, within certain limits as well as reluctantly, by the Dutch colonial authority at the turn of the century to fulfill technocratic functions in a colonial regime, these professionals are thus formed as ambivalent subjects who are the same as in the "West" but "not quite."[3] Living between their ethno-regional identities and the (neo)colonial structures following decolonization, this newly specialized elite functions technologically in terms of western knowledge even though spiritually, they may be more comfortable with their traditional, local and regional milieu. Caught up in simultaneous identities of being both "foreign" and "indigenous," the effect of a (post)colonial ambivalence is to construct a third "national" space of Indonesia that is believed to be developing. This represents the spirit of these intellectuals who seek to "modernize" their traditionalist regional cultures without being completely subsumed under the idea of Western modernity that they have criticized. What I am also interested in seeing are the ways they perceive their profession and themselves in terms of categories such as "foreign" and the "national," "modern," and "traditional," terms that are also mobilized by the nation–state in its attempts to forge a national culture. This identification constitutes a link between architecture, as a discipline, and the ideology of the nation(–state).

The chapter is organized in three parts, each representing particular instances of the (inter)national order within which architecture is articulated. The first part, the professional imagination of the new society, represents the intellectual thought that is closest to the realm of politics. The second part, after 1966, represents the growing interdependence between the professional identity and the vision of the nation–state in which the architect is accepted as a non-political being. The last part represents recent (architectural) attempts to achieve a particular autonomy which is, on the one hand, not quite subsumed within the framework of "society" and the "state" but, on the other, still works within a notion of "national" responsibility.

Despite their different intellectual imaginations, I argue that these professionals largely work within the trope of the "national" which gives them a critical position in relation to the state. However, I also argue that this "national" framework has been understood to be outside political (and colonial) constructions. It is also through this framework beyond colonial legacies and political constructions that Indonesian architectural culture insufficiently sees itself as a critical political agency.

VAN ROMONDT: ARCHITECTURE AND THE NEW SOCIETY

The idea that postcolonial Indonesia should produce an architecture appropriate to its social and cultural "traditions" and philosophies, a culture of architecture that reflected the conditions of nation-building and even responds to the phases of "development" of the nation-building process itself, has been a constant agenda, if not a common-place, in architectural debate since the establishment of the first architectural school in 1950. A discipline that was first tailored by the Building Engineering Department of the Technische Hoogeschool at Delft, Holland, and in its intellectual origins shared the assumption that architecture and epoch are in some ways fundamentally related, could hardly refuse the belief that an "Indonesian architecture" should both possess and also express its own distinctive character. This search for a new paradigm and a recreated role for the discipline were based on a fundamental insight that architecture is far from autonomous; instead it "grows and develops especially within its *own* culture" (Prawirohardjo and Sularto 1984).

Perhaps the most dramatically formulated concerns surrounding "Indonesian architecture" are to be found in the inaugural lecture of Vincent van Romondt, a Dutch professor popular with his Indonesian students and faculty, delivered in 1954,[4] just a year before the withdrawal of all Dutch professors from Indonesian higher institutions following the rise of the radical Indonesian nationalist movement. Unlike much of his earlier interest, which was exclusively in Indonesian vernacular architecture, and possibly because of the change in the political climate, the lecture is a rigorous attempt to think of Indonesian architecture in the terms and needs of a new, "modern" nation.

There are at least two closely-related issues at stake in van Romondt's lecture; the first is the possibility of an Indonesian architecture and of a national culture; the second, the ways in which these two phenomena might be related. For van Romondt, the search for an Indonesian architecture is also the search for a national culture that, once determined, would logically provide a platform on which an Indonesian architecture could stand. A new tradition has to be formed through the construction of a national culture that, clearly enough for him, has to be different from the West.

The "Indonesia" of van Romondt's understanding is undergoing a transitional epoch and is thus in need of a "new" cultural framework. In this respect, he is worried and ambiguous about what the Dutch have left to the Indonesians. This is especially the case with the city ("kota"), an urban space where culture and architecture were represented, merged and were in conflict:

> They have to ask themselves, if the life of the 'kota', as a result of industrialization (sic), will lead to different kinds of building form (namely an 'Indonesian' one). Will the emergence of the row-housing and flat in many 'kota' have a future? Theaters, concert halls, museums and exhibition spaces only have very few people attending. Does Indonesia really need these sorts of facilities and do they conform to Indonesian life?
>
> (van Romondt 1954: 18)

On the other side, van Romondt understands the exigency of "kota," as opposed to "desa" (rural), as a space where (high) culture is cultivated and acts of governance are displayed. The "kota," represented by many "foreign" building types and living styles, is seen as simultaneously both alienating and inspiring to the "Indonesian."

In van Romondt's opinion, the post-colonial "kota", in the hands of the "Indonesian," has to find its own architectural forms which "are in accordance with the aspiration of their home country ('tjita-tjita tanah air')" (van Romondt 1954: 18). Constantly reminding Indonesian architects of their responsibility in defining Indonesian culture, van Romondt nevertheless provides the members of this community with what he believes to be the path necessary for the construction of an "Indonesian architecture."

The important task in creating "Indonesia," according to van Romondt, is to construct a time and space peculiar and distinctive enough to be "Indonesia." Here, van Romondt locates "Indonesia" simultaneously inside and outside the world. He displaces Indonesia from the time and space of colonial modernity and simultaneously replaces it with quite another form of modernity, namely, that of "the spiritual will of a nation." This calls for an imagined community which goes beyond the Indonesian's own heterogeneous past, is spatially located "here! in 'Nusantara' " (van Romondt 1954: 21) and encompasses temporally the future in which the nation should stand.

Rupturing the singular time and space of the West, van Romondt's "Indonesia" was presumably formed through its own genealogy outside the legacies of colonialism. This "new" Indonesia was uncoupled from, and juxta-posed with, the West whose cultural legacy was understood as undergoing a major crisis:

> Cultural crises, which hit the West more than half a century ago, are deeply felt here and indeed have taken a more horrible form. Indonesia has been used to following the ruling West. Though the West has gone (formally), the ruling elites have not been able to 'develop' Indonesian culture. . . In essence, Indonesian culture has long been stagnant and people feel satisfied by following foreign culture which has created conditions as if Indonesia is developing. . . In these circumstances, the issue is not merely about searching for new (architectural) forms, but more essentially of finding a new culture. Like the call of revolution which is not yet over as there are still difficult tasks remaining to be done to fill 'kemerdekaan' (independence). The field has been opened, now it is the planting that is at stake.
>
> (van Romondt 1954: 15)

The erasure of colonial cultures is to be done by turning "Indonesia" into an order of "Indonesian modernity," an order that suggests its own "authenticity" with no universal significance to the conception of Western modernity. The "Indonesia" of van Romondt should no longer follow the West; instead it must be able to find its own norms and forms of representation to go through a trans-ition into the world community of nations.[5]

Van Romondt's critical view of Western cultural hegemony is combined with a progressive anti-traditional stance. This situates him along the lines of a nationalist architect in search of "Indonesia" that yet transcends both sub-national and transnational cultures through which a national architecture can be built. To guide an appropriate architectural form, a new cultural framework is thus needed; a framework which is neither "foreign" nor "indigenous"; neither of the pre-colonial past nor the product of Western cultural hegemony. It could perhaps be a combination of both that would be culturally appropriate for the newly born nation–state. It was an ambiguous position towards the surplus of Western signs in the "kota" and the decay of the traditional order that have justified van Romondt as a nationalist – a man who sees the nation as an enter-prise. For such men, as Anderson (1990: 166) aptly indicates, "defining what is national can be a complex project of juxtapositions and separations between the 'foreign' and the 'indigenous'.''

Working in and for the (post)colony, van Romondt nevertheless feels that the task of constructing an Indonesian national culture remains one for the ''indigenous'' architectural elites who are seen as fully responsible for the shape of postcolonial ''Indonesian architecture;'' who have to face the heterogeneity of their own communities that have not been easily formed under a single umbrella of ''Indonesian architecture.'' Van Romondt indicated that:

> It is with the [Indonesian] architects to give it [the new cultural norm] a form. An honest one. . . For they have to be responsible for what those forms convey. They have to search for what is now glorifying the heart of Indonesia. . . Indonesian architects should enter through the main gate into their Indonesian realm. . . I can only bring you to the gate, which we [van Romondt and other 'foreign' professors teaching in Bandung] do not enter.
>
> (van Romondt 1954: 24, 17)

Van Romondt's vision is discussed here not as the ''origins'' of an institutionalized consciousness of Indonesian architecture, but to suggest that the construction of difference between ''foreign'' and ''indigenous,'' ''modern'' and ''traditional,'' and the intertwined relationships between them have been crucial to the (subsequent) imagining of an ''Indonesian architecture.'' For van Romondt, it is important fcr Indonesia as a nation to recall its own tradition in order to overcome it – a position we might call an anti-traditional traditionalism.

Due to the political conflict over the island of West Guinea (today's Irian Jaya) in 1955 between the new Republic and its former colonizer, all Dutch lecturers were recalled to their homeland. All, that is, except for Vincent van Romondt who insisted on staying on and, keeping a low profile, led the only architectural school until 1962. Iwan Sudradjat (1991), an Indonesian architectural historian, reports that:

> under his direction the training programmes, which initially laid heavy stress on technical and engineering aspects, were gradually enriched. Aesthetic, cultural and historical considerations were gradually incorporated into the studio exercises, while lectures on Indonesian architectural heritage and excursions to different regions were introduced, to broaden students' minds and to intensify their appreciation of the architectural heritage in Indonesia. His teaching methods still exert a strong influence on the architectural education system in Indonesia today.
>
> (Sudradjat 1991: 187)

Van Romondt's proclamation to Indonesian architects to think and act beyond his or her technical expertise was to remain a continuous ''responsibility'' of generations to come. It is most strongly re-expressed by Professor Sidharta (1983), one of the first generation of Indonesian architects and former head of a major architectural school. Thirty years later, in the social field of the New Order, he wrote:

To Indonesian architects, I call: let us cultivate Indonesian architecture with full
consciousness and dedication. Do not think of architecture as merely a profession, but
above all as a national duty and obligation

(Sidharta 1983: 104).

TRADITION IN THE INTERNATIONAL FRAME

In an early issue of the first architectural journal published by the school of
architecture in Bandung,[6] the introduction is provided by a major article on the
architectural development of the (western) world:

> The following essay describes the development of architecture in the 'West,' which for
> us can be used as a reflection to explain our own architectural problem. Architecture, as
> an art devoted to people, cannot be separated from the society itself. The weakness of
> social developments in the 'West,' caused by the rapid growth of science and
> technology with all their impact, brings a social dimension to the attention of modern
> architecture. For us in Indonesia, who are living in a new social environment, undergoing
> a change and looking for an appropriate form, this [architectural development in the
> West] has been good for reflection. Though in many ways, the problems faced [in these
> two places] are not quite the same, a point can be made from the outset. The social
> dimension of Indonesian development, different though from that in the West, has to be
> placed as the basis for an Indonesian architecture.

(*Arsitektur* 1959: 10)

The article, written anonymously in collaboration with the editors, describes the
transformation in architectural ideas in Europe and the USA, starting from the
impact of the French Revolution to the genius of Frank Lloyd Wright. Euro-
American architectural dynamics are discussed in terms of stylistic changes within
the history of what has been taken as "modern architecture." Unlike what is
suggested in the introduction, there is no discussion of the socio-political forces
and cultural framework that gave rise to modern architecture: the history of
modern architecture is seen as purely a product of a philosophical attitude,
namely, the separation of humankind from nature. All the stylistic changes are
thus represented as the outcome of this paradigmatic perspective.

The article concludes with this emphasis: "they place humans at the center
of attention, however, not as man who carries the character of divinity, but as
the highest creature" (*Arsitektur* 1959: 13). The different social environment
(between Indonesian "cosmology" and the industrial West) is thus differentiated
in terms of belief systems.[7] As a result, the West is understood as no longer a
convenient source of inspiration. The article suggests that "architects have to ask
themselves what has been the aspiration of the innerself of the Indonesian
people" (*Arsitektur* 1959: 21). The answer seems to lie in what has been known
as indigenous or vernacular architecture referred to as "the raw material for
development" in which many of its representations are seen as comparable to
the achievement of Western modern architecture. Accordingly, the structural

principles of these ''vernacular'' buildings provide ''a basis of a hypermodern architecture'' (*Arsitektur* 1959: 21).

Following the article, we can see that the juxtaposition with the development of Western architecture is taken up in order to measure, as well as to bring into appearance, an Indonesian architectural tradition. The reference to the West was thus less a genuine reflection than an effort to foreground the existence of a genuinely ''Indonesian'' culture and architecture. The final paragraph concludes with a message not unlike that of van Romondt:

> It is not architecture that determines society, but society in its aspiration for housing and culture that provides architecture with its foundation. . . By meditating on the Indonesian attitude of life, its forms of interaction and social relations, architects could thus accelerate the birth of an Indonesian architecture.
>
> (*Arsitektur* 1959: 27)

The search for cultural norms and architectural forms for ''Indonesia'' registers the influence of Indonesian nationalism. At the core of the search has been the ''vernacular'' architectural representation, soon conceived of as a national cultural heritage full of potential for re-interpretation in the context of nation-building.[8] What is of particular importance here is not only that, in the early stages of nation-building, architecture and society are closely linked through national aspirations; but also a sense of authenticity and technological value are attributed to the cultural traditions. Though there is no trace of a nationally-prescribed style that affects the ''responsibility'' of Indonesian architects, the sense of crisis in architectural and cultural identity, prompted (though in no way caused) by van Romondt, has made many earlier attempts to foreground ''indigenous'' buildings as an important, if not authentic, component in the formation of an Indonesian architecture.

The structure of representation in the journal is also suggestive of the early nationalist imaginings of material progress. The journal can be seen as being composed of two parts, the first, largely a discussion of the urban and architectural development of the ''West'' as well as of Indonesian cities where the modernist architectural paradigm predominates. The second, only a few pages, is of the study excursions to places like Bali. The setting represents the complementarity of the two: the former is safe-guarded by the continuous presence of the latter, albeit in a ''marginal'' format; while the latter is implied by the remarkable presence of the former. Yet the attribution of Bali as a space of ''tradition,'' in the elite school of architecture, appears more as a sign of tradition faithfully guiding the increasing ''modernization'' of the urban center in Java. It assures us that no matter where we go, Bali is always with us ''there'' which, by definition, is ''here,'' in our own spiritual space of the nation. This homage to Bali has, in fact, been put into practice.

It was common practice for an architectural school, even in its infancy, to model itself on its European counterpart and arrange study excursions to places seen as having ''architectural quality.'' This pilgrimage supposedly enriches the students in experiencing the spaces and forms of architecture. For European architectural students, Rome was largely the place to meditate, but for the students of architecture in Indonesia, following the fashion of colonial orientalism, Bali was the favorite. Unlike the later stage of architectural discourses where living architectural traditions are rigorously subjected to architectural experimentation, the report on the early excursion by the school suggested the built environment of Bali as a place of spiritual learning and contemplation. The pilgrimage was more to create a spiritual balance, if not a confirmation, that the inner space of "Indonesia," which is not to literally suggest Bali, has always been "there," complementing (and also compensating for) postcolonial "modern" urban development.

However, it is also crucial to emphasize that the status of the "indigenous" cultural heritage in these early imaginings of Indonesian architecture is based on a largely technological assumption in which the timber frame is seen as parallel, if not superior, in terms of its design qualities, to the steel construction of the West. The distinction from the "western" tradition, for instance, is made by representing vernacular architecture as a "high" culture, parallel to, if not higher than, that of the "West." In this context, the fascination with vernacular architecture is less with its "authenticity" than with its promises of a future "high" technology. As we will see in the following section, the imagining of architecture in the New Order (after 1966), while still taking up this early "revolutionary" nationalist thought, has placed the importance of "authenticity" in the vernacular architecture as a means of distinguishing itself from that of the "west."[9] Moreover, the national framework has taken a form closer to the scopic regime of the apparatus of the state.

INDONESIAN ARCHITECTURE AND NATIONAL DEVELOPMENT

More than 20 years later, under the New Order, the theme of "Indonesian Architecture" re-appeared, not only in journals but at nationally organized congresses. Chosen as the theme for the 1982 national congress of architecture, this was followed by an increasing number of papers published sporadically in various media, from a highly (Western) theorized paper to a more spontaneous reaction regarding what should be done on the ground. Here, I will choose two inaugural lectures, one example from a professional journal, and two articles from a newspaper that illustrate the various cultural frameworks through which the New Order postcolonial architects imagine their conflictual identities.

In 1981, Professor Parmono Atmadi delivered in Gajah Mada University in Central Java perhaps the first inaugural lecture of architecture under the regime of the New Order. Entitled "Architecture and Its Development," the lecture is about architecture which, in its various definitions cited extensively from "western" literature, assumes a universal significance that, in all its Eurocentricity, seems to be relevant to measure the development of Indonesian architecture.

Deprived of the social, political and cultural circumstances within which these "western" architectural thoughts have arisen, their summary and translation are juxtaposed with the conditions governing the development of the architectural discipline in Indonesia. A striking imagery appeared in the lecture: the antiquity of the profession of architecture in Indonesia. Atmadi indicates that "Indonesia, since a long time ago, has given a special occupation to its architects. One of the examples is the Bugis or Makasar society who named their designer Panrita Bola. Here, the architect functions as a priest" (Atmadi 1984: 60). In a way, the appearance of the "architect" of the ancient regime in the margins of the discussion has the effect of overcoming, without excluding, the domination of exhaustive expositions of "western" theorists that occupy more than half the lecture.

After putting Indonesian architecture in the solid ground of "ancient" tradition, a point is finally made that the boundaries of architecture in Indonesia should be extended, not merely to accommodate "western" architectural discourses, but to facilitate the expanding vision of the nation–state itself. It is implicit, yet clear for Atmadi, that what are defined as national "problems" are also the concerns, and thus the scopic regime, of architecture in Indonesia. The will of the nation ('cita-cita bangsa') is also the will of Indonesian architect(ure). For example:

> The rapid growth of population and the large numbers of those who live below an acceptable standard has instructed architects to pay most of their attention to these problems, so that their works could be enjoyed by all members of the society. . . For that reason, particular attention should be paid to planning and design concepts so that their 'pembangunan' (development which is according to the government plan) could support the cultivation of the culture and civilization of the nation. . . Architects should not just focus on monumental buildings in the urban center, but also buildings that could be found in the rural area ('per-desa-an'). In this way the image of architects can be re-established *as a public servant.*
>
> (Atmadi 1984: 60, 61; emphasis added)

Here, there are at least two sets of contrasting imaginations in the construction of the "ideal" Indonesian architect. First is the elite space of the city in which architectural practice is concentrated. This is contrasted to the condition of the "desa" (rural). Second, the dominant role of architects as private practitioners serving the elite is contrasted with the role of the public servant working for the state. The overall message, nevertheless, is less one of suggesting a changing role for architects than to propose an expansive capability for Indonesian architects to function in all sectors of society. The "development" of Indonesia has effectively expanded the role of architects as public servants along with that of the government. The function of Indonesian architecture, as represented by Atmadi, is less autonomous, operating within the scopic regime of the nation–state in which a critical assessment of that state is unimaginable.

The second inaugural lecture delivered by Sidharta (1984) at the University of Diponegoro Semarang, three years after Atmadi,[10] provides a less significant link with the nation–state. Nevertheless, the discourse of "development," central to the nation–state's ideology, remains the essential theme of his lecture. Let us first look at what Sidharta thinks of the word "modern," a key term in his conceptualization of Indonesian architecture:

> I personally think that the word 'modern' could be used for the future of Indonesian Architecture, because 'modern' comes from the Latin word 'modo' which means 'just now.' I take 'modern' as a condition of not closing oneself off from new innovations that can be adapted into our condition. . .[The modern condition shows that] each nation–state has its national aspiration, norms, climates and local conditions that are the foundation of its architecture.
>
> (Sidharta 1984: 7)

Sidharta clearly understood that the time of the "modern" is not at all the time of "Europe"; it belongs perhaps to every single nation, it simply means "as of the present" to which Indonesia justifiably belongs. But spatially and notionally, "modern" is a "foreign" artefact which has to be "adapted into our condition." As such, the various categories of "modern" and the processes of "modernization" also simultaneously carry with them the forces of "localization." The double meaning of "modern" stems from the postcolonial hybrid subjectivity of Sidharta and has opened up a space for the national by way of "modernizing" its traditional order and simultaneously contextualising foreign cultural technologies.

Let us now see how the professional roles of the elite are asserted in this configuration. Sidharta suggests that:

> Indonesian architects should synthesize the innovation of advanced technology with architectural norms derived from the local condition and the cultural norms of the users. . . His responsibility is not only towards *his clients*, but to *the society* as a whole. This responsibility demands a way of life which is honest, truly open, ethical and not taking sides. He has to be very knowledgeable so that he can communicate successfully to everyone.
>
> (Sidharta 1984: 6 and 2; emphasis added)

Not unlike Atmadi's architect, here we can also see the role of architects as a Master, practising in between the clients (a metaphor for private, or indeed, the "foreign" component) and the society as a whole (representing the public interest of the Indonesian people). The knowledge the professional possesses enables him to take the measure of a contextualized "modernization" by holding, on one hand, the ("western") advanced technology, and on the other, the cultural norms of the local conditions. Not unlike Atmadi's architecture, the separation and convergence of the "traditional" and "modern" elements suggest that it is impossible to credit the one or the other exclusively.

As with Atmadi, a similar trope emerges in Sidharta's discussion of architectural theory. After surveying the state of architecture through the European canon, including the writings of Vitruvius, Ruskin, Durand, Corbusier, Mies van der Rohe, and Venturi, Sidharta concludes, with emphasis, that:

> Certainly, these Western theories should not be simply applied into the education and the profession of architecture in Indonesia. Our traditional architecture also has theories derived from the norms and standards related to the religious and belief systems or the way of life of the communities.
>
> (Sidharta 1984: 4)

Yet, unlike Atmadi, immediately after the juxtaposition with, and termination of, "Western" theories, the positive image of the "indigenous" element is also quickly passed over to give way to the "development" of "modern" Indonesia. For Sidharta:

> Traditional society is trapped under a static world view, saturated with magical power and thus does not have the courage to challenge the power on the top [of the magic world]. In these circumstances, architectural expression will be static and deprived of change.
>
> (Sidharta 1984: 4)

What we might pick up from these two inaugural lectures are the contradictions of architecture in Indonesia as an elite, if not "western," practice in a place composed of what has been characterized as "traditional." Yet, the *main task* of architecture, far from being ambiguous, has been to express a culture that has, from the outset, assumed the pre-existence of a "national" order for which architecture then provides a service.

THE QUEST FOR AUTONOMY

My final perspectives draw from the work of Josef Prijotomo and Rivai Gaos. Both are contemporary to, but younger than, Atmadi and Sidharta. Prijotomo, one of the most prolific contemporary Indonesian architectural critics, has published widely, especially in the local newspapers of Surabaya. Most of Prijotomo's writings are concerned with two closely-related (architectural) issues which, by now, form the standard themes in Indonesian architectural debate. One is how to remain "indigenous" in the midst of "foreign" influences; the other is how to remain "modern" within the traditional order of Indonesian society.

However, unlike most of his contemporaries and the previous generation, Prijotomo has a most "independent" perspective in regard to the position of architecture within the scopic regime of the nation–state. Generationally, he also represents the third phase of post-Independence Indonesian architectural thought. If van Romondt and others of his time conceived of architecture as working toward a (national) culture that needs to be defined less in relation to the "heart of Indonesia" (not to the state), and Atmadi and Sidharta placed architecture largely within the already defined framework of the nation–state, then Prijotomo understands architecture as generally an autonomous practice. Prijotomo conceives the dynamic of architectural change as parallel to the cultural formation of the nation–state, not simply as a response. Taking as his premise the post-modern architectural discourse that celebrates the liberal free interpretation of the "cultural heritage," Prijotomo's writings have the effect of distancing architecture from the domain of the political. He demonstrates the quasi-autonomy of architectural change as being beyond the political institutions; the two are related yet one cannot be subsumed under the other. Sharing the supposed universalism of aesthetic experiences, and liberating architecture from the control of the socio-political, Prijotomo is less interested in the possibility of identifying a national Indonesian architecture. Instead, he is more interested in interpreting Indonesia in terms of what it could provide for the advancement of architecture. The "national" element that most interests Prijotomo is the pluralism of the national ideology of "Bhinneka Tunggal Ika" (unity in diversity), that in the islands where virtual heterogeneity has been the norm, it would be a contradiction in terms to search for a single form of Indonesian architecture. As such, the single factor of an "Indonesian architecture" could, of course, be its immense diversity.

The quest for a "heterogenous" architecture of Indonesia is perhaps most elaborated in Prijotomo's discussion (1987) of modernist architecture. Here, like his fellows, Prijotomo shares the usefulness of maintaining the dichotomy of the "modern" and the "local" which he then brings together. Modernist architecture, for Prijotomo, is obsessed with rationality and science. Its universalism is destroying regional characteristics. It is insensitive and alien to the environmental context within which it stands. It is machine oriented and disregards the human emotional imperative. It disallows human symbolic expression. Lastly, it is a philosophical logic that demands a position of either/or, right/wrong instead of what Prijotomo found to be a more fruitful position of having both.

In my interpretation, this authoritative evaluation of (architectural) modernism, abstracted from the socio-political circumstances within which it developed in Europe, has prepared the grounds for Prijotomo to comment on the "nationalist" framework which could equally subsume local difference just as the Modernist had done. To maintain the heterogeneity of "Indonesia," Prijotomo suggested a "return" to the manifesto of the Indonesian 1945 Constitution that obliges an "openness towards foreign culture so long as it elevates the culture of our own" (Prijotomo 1987: 105). From a discussion centering on Western modernism, the arguments return to "we", who "have the obligation to refuse and accept foreign cultures, not vice versa" (Prijotomo 1987: 105). What is curious here is that the "we" does not represent the voice of the state. Instead it represents the irreducibility of Indonesian subjects that do not want to be subsumed under a modernist framework or the state's national mission. The consciousness of the "we" displaces, externally, the hegemonic position of architectural modernism, and internally, the nation–state by turning the "local" as the subject rather than the object of modernist/nationalist discourse. The rhetoric of "we" does not assume any singularity of the "nation." Instead, the appearance of "we" as subject was used in relation to the "diversity" of Indonesia. What is crucial here is the appropriation of the modernist architectural paradigm and the "diversity" framework of the state ideology to suggest a strategy for the creativity of architecture itself. This twist of architectural strategy made within the international framework of modernism and the national regime of power can be seen in the following statement:

> Architectural modernism has to be accepted cautiously and with alertness, while the treasury of Indonesian classical architecture has to be (re)activated. Thus, in essence, modernizing classical Indonesian architecture is expected much more than Indonesianizing modern architecture. . . The formal elements and components of regional architecture, including its non-physical symbols and meanings, are indeed richer than the sources of 'Western' architecture itself. 'Western' architecture only has Roman and Greek architecture as resources, while we, in Indonesia, owned not less than twenty seven primary sources for architecture (based on the number of provinces, not the number of regional architectures, of which there are more – author's comment).
>
> (Prijotomo 1987: 105, 107)

Prijotomo's theory is less the construction of an Indonesian architecture that would replace existing Modernist architecture, than the way architectural modernism is appropriated to make visible as well as to make modern the "heterogeneity" of Indonesia. Similarly, the ideology of the nation–state is appropriated to make space for autonomous, decentered and diverse ways of imagining architecture.

LOOKING FORWARD? THE TRADITIONAL COSMOPOLITANISM OF GAOS

In 1982, Prijotomo's contemporary, Rivai Gaos, wrote an article in an Indonesian architectural journal which the editor recalls as "stimulating," if not bewildering, in that he asked readers "to think, to search, and to find an architecture most suitable to us, the Indonesian people." [11] The 2000-word article entitled "Towards an Indonesian Architecture" (the same title as van Romondt's inaugural lecture), starts by quoting, approvingly, some words of Frank Lloyd Wright that "building upon the land is as natural to man as to other animals, birds and insects." Immediately after this, a "desa" (countryside) is romantically described suggesting that it, indeed, represents in a significant way the "organic architecture" of Wright concerning the integration between the natural landscape and the built environment:

> Let's imagine we go back to the countryside ('desa'). We will be welcomed not only by the small bridge made of coconut trees, but also by pieces of rock in the river which seem to enthusiastically appear on the surface to greet us. Every house we passed seems to invite us to sit or rest at their open verandah. No thorny gates and aggressive dogs could be found. Not only are we greeted by people, but also by the stone that supports the houses. They are all components of life that make us feel alive. We feel acknowledged as part of the big family.
>
> (Gaos 1982: 8)

Gaos, the author, is attempting to draw a parallel between the quality of his imagined "desa" and the principle of the "organic architecture" of Frank Lloyd Wright. For Gaos, however, the parallel that he imagined is actually an attempt to draw the attention of Indonesian architects to the *contrast* between the "desa" (country side) and the "kota" (city) in Indonesia; as, after co-ordinating the environment of "desa" *and* the architectural principle of Frank Lloyd Wright, Indonesia *and* the USA, within a shared temporality and platform, Gaos takes readers to Jakarta (the capital city of Indonesia).

According to Gaos, the capital city suffers from an excessive "modernization." Unlike his "desa," Jakarta is depicted as following the footsteps of what he imagines to be the "decaying" cities of Europe and the USA. Gaos describes the urban problems of Jakarta as simultaneous with urban problems in the West and thus both are co-ordinated within a single frame of time and space – both are seen as undergoing the age of urban decay. This co-ordination across time and space allows Gaos to predict that what had just happened to American cities would imminently happen to their counterparts in Indonesia. Gaos speaks to his Indonesian audience with the fullest confidence in the existence of urban problems in the West (on the other side of the world) through which his own Jakarta gains meaning. So, towards the end of the article, Gaos warns that the cities of Indonesia will be as decayed as the cities of Europe and the USA.

The architect then asks readers, where indeed shall we go, back to the "desa" or, following the path of what is thought to be, after all, the already "Euro-Americanized" Jakarta? The article concludes with what is perhaps a cosmopolitan hybrid solution to the city building:

> Yes, to follow the path [of Jakarta with all its Euro-Americanization] *and* also go back to the "desa." Taking the best [of theirs] of course. Change the bridge made of coconut trees to the concrete one if necessary. Use foundations instead of anchoring stones for the column of the house. Widen the windows, but don't isolate the house with a high and thorny fence. Use materials, measurement, system, and all that is new to advance architecture in Indonesia in order to strengthen our sense of humanity.
>
> (Gaos 1982:8)

Gaos' article is basically a critique of architecture and urbanism in Indonesia and is a suggestion of what is to be done in the future. But what is of interest to us is the appearance of "Frank Lloyd Wright" and "America" in what is, after all, an article directed at the condition of architecture and urbanism in Indonesia. We can observe, in his narrative, a striking parallel and also a contrast of imageries of both Jakarta and big cities in the USA and Europe, the Indonesian "desa" and the American architect. "Desa" is represented as a harmonious "indigenous" space, yet one to be overcome in the course of more "sensitive" development under the appropriate guidance of architectural principles. The desire to "model" the USA (through the figure of Frank Lloyd Wright) is combined with a dismissal of particular aspects of "Americanization." The "West" is thus both a subject of dismissal as well as the criterion for appraisal. The notion of "returning to desa" suggests that architects of Gaos' generation have been separated from, yet still quite easily identify with, the "desa" from which they perhaps came. Accordingly, part of the architect's spirit is with the "desa," while the other half, nevertheless, is with Frank Lloyd Wright. This split, and the simultaneous reconciliation, of identity allows Gaos to be proud of the tranquility of his "desa" while at the same time maintaining a professional, if not an imagined "contact" with Wright, the fellow professional half a world away. This long distance association with Wright allows the Indonesian architect, in indirect fashion, to imagine a cosmopolitan hybridity for a future kind of architecture in Indonesia.

In what perspective then does it make sense to reflect on this story? What sense, if not conclusion, can we make of these imaginings? To what conditions of the nation have Indonesian architects responded?

CONCLUSION

To arrive at a conclusion of these various imaginings, it may be helpful to refocus the specific thrust of the argument so far. First, the juxtapositions and separations between the "foreign" and "indigenous" elements are crucial to the formation of postcolonial Indonesian elite subjectivities. These contain a number of contradictions resulting from their multiple origins in practices such as those introduced by the Dutch, or better, the "West," then their own local-regional identity, and finally, their national subjectivity. Caught between their "traditional" milieu and the "modern" knowledge they have learned, the question for them is no longer which position to take but how to create a new cultural space, a third one inevitably, which will turn the contradictory relations into mutual interactions. This third space, as I have tried to show, takes the form of the *national* that, not unlike early nationalist thought, as Ruth McVey (1967: 129) aptly indicates, "was a coating that made palatable an otherwise bitter cultural pill."

I have also tried to show that, regardless of the stretch of the imagination, what matters for those involved in thinking of an Indonesian architecture is less how the nation has been constructed than the intellectual focus on how to promote, or even begin with, nationality. The undeniable presence of the "West" is not at all a threat in the making of Indonesian architectural culture since the notion of Indonesian architecture increasingly comes to represent not only what the foreign presence could not be, but what the Indonesian profession, in its particular postcolonial social and cultural order, could possibly be. As such, "western" or "modern" knowledge does not mean the legacy of (neo)colonialism. Instead it assumes a universal significance as an empty, though powerful, category that is subjected to a process of local translation which effaces its power. The "centrality" of the national "self" in the architectural culture of Indonesia is usefully problematic. It provides a crucial agency for the postcolonial subject to insert its integrity, yet this "authentic" self has never been thought out in terms of "what has made us what we are." Through the examples, we are, in effect, being shown the character of the nation towards which Indonesian architectural thought tends. The quest is less for a fulfillment of an architectural uniqueness that departs from the nation; instead, it is for a reunion and identification with the nation itself. This sense of nationality is profoundly expressed in a cartoon produced as a critical comment on the state of Indonesian architecture. In Figure 7.1, we see a man, supposedly an architect, searching in the dark with an electric torch to find an "Indonesian architecture." In Figure 7.2, an architect, in peasant outfit, is carrying on his back a rock on which sits a rich man in his armchair. The architect is climbing uphill following the sign that supposedly directs him to an "Indonesian architecture." In both, there are critical comments on the profession that frustratingly searches for its identity under the oppression of the rich. But what is important for us here is the sense of the ownership of an "Indonesian architecture." The cartoons tell us that no matter what an "Indonesian architecture" is and how to get there, the phenomenon is always there. It can, somehow, be *found* somewhere, in the dark or on the top of the hill, but always, within the nation.

If these overall points have any validity, a last, but most important, consideration has emerged: it involves the relationship between the *political* imagination of the profession and the *apolitical* demand of the nation–state. In what ways does the professional quest of cultural autonomy relate to the ideology of the nation–state, which demands the separation of architecture from political imagining? I began this chapter with the "gift" of political stability bestowed by the state to the profession in the latter's quest for professionalism.

Figure 7.1
MISSING: THE SEARCH
FOR "INDONESIAN
ARCHITECTURE"
Source: *Gallery-
Undip/Cakrawala
Arsitektur*, 1983

Figure 7.2
BURDEN OF
REPRESENTATION:
TOWARDS AN
"INDONESIAN"
ARCHITECTURE
Source: *Gallery-
Undip/Cakrawala
Arsitektur*, 1983

The change of political and economic structure, from colonial to postcolonial, from Sukarno's "revolution" to the New Order's "stability," demanded that architects combined their professionalism with the state's agenda of national development and national identity. However, this gift of the state given over to the profession does not necessarily mean that architecture in Indonesia is basically tailored by the cultural power of state. Throughout this chapter, I have tried to show the intellectual coherence of the architects on "nation" and identity, but this "national" lens is not in itself imagined through the optic of the state. Instead, the deep-seated traditional orientation of the state (see Chapter 3) may run in contradiction to the self-styled modernizers in the profession. The analysis of the political imagining of Indonesian architects is helpful in thinking about a peculiar form of resistance of the professional to the cultural ideology of the nation–state.

What has made the Indonesian professional community of architects represent an "Indonesian architecture" that appears to lie just beyond the limits of the "West" and, most importantly, the nation–state? The political imaginations of the architects I have described above, each in his own way, reveals a critical dialogue with the official imagining of the nation–state. The structure of their twisting arguments, and the syncretic references they provided, *could* all be read as an attempt to oppose the ideology of the nation–state which, by the 1980s, had been promoting the idea of "splendid ancestors" and the common inheritance of the past as the basis for "national culture."[12]

In Chapter 3, I suggested that a decade after Suharto established his government, the question of "what is Indonesia(n)?" began to trouble his regime. Twenty years after decolonization, the social imagination of Indonesia united against (Dutch) colonialism became obsolete. The rapid evaporation of Dutch power after decolonization brought the whole idea of "Indonesia(n)" into question. By the time of Suharto's regime, with the acceleration of globalization, it was determined that a new trope was needed to replace the old public memory of "Dutch colonialism." If the binding trope of (Dutch) colonialism and with it, Indonesian revolution (under Sukarno) are no longer a powerful memory for the present and the future, logically there are at least two imageries that present themselves as alternatives (Anderson 1965). One is to substantialize the pre-colonial past, and the other, to imagine the future in terms of a common project. And, as I have shown in Chapter 3, the imagery that the Indonesian state finally adopted, alas, was the first one, that is, to identify the nation with its common inheritance of the "splendid ancestors."

In the 1980s, the "Indonesia" of Indonesian architects was undergoing exactly this process of ancestral constitution through inward (or backward) looking political cultures. Their various imaginings of Indonesian architecture is, in a strange way, most usefully read as an implicit struggle between the professional and the whole emerging structure of hegemony of Suharto's "ancient regime." If we put their imaginings against the background of those of the state, what we find is a vision of an architect who is working *within*, as well as *against*, a particular socio-political environment. While pointing to the glory of the inherited past as the source of inspiration, these architects also show how much architecture in Indonesia is, or should be, tied to visions and hopes for the future. They suggest a way of imagining the future by collapsing global time and space, of bringing together Frank Lloyd Wright, "panrita bola", Jakarta, Bali, modernism and the "desa." Their imaginings say something about the common inheritance of the "splendid ancestors" but at the same time they place a lot of importance on comparing the national past with the architectural principles of the modern West. Even as the imaginings are constituted in ambiguous relations to the "West," these architects draw a feasible meeting line between the forward-looking vision of modern architecture and hopes for the future in the discourse of architecture in Indonesia.

In this sense, the political imaginings of these architects might be read, uneasily, as aiming to open up a space for an alternative vision. The site of the conflict is nothing other than the "nation." In this conflict over the cultural content of the nation, the "desa," the world cities, Western architects and theorists constitute a series of tropes by which a criticism can be launched and a new kind of "Indonesian architecture" can perhaps be invented. The forward-looking vision implied by "towards Indonesian architecture" promoted by Indonesian architects may thus be seen as a resistance of the professionals to the backward-looking cultural framework of the nation–state.

Yet, as I have also tried to argue, without a critical reflection on the ways in which the "nation" itself is constructed, not least through the prevailing political culture of the state, Indonesian architectural culture will remain passive in its relations to political power. And, to the extent that the profession subsequently became a large and complex institution, involved in the global transfer of technology and transnational capital, as well as in helping to construct the nationalist project (see Chapter 3), it has also been incorporated *within* these existing orders. It is also for this reason that it is necessary to examine the involvement of architecture in contemporary Indonesian political and cultural history.

Chapter 8: "Spectre of Comparisons"

Notes on Discourses of Architecture and Urban Design in Southeast Asia

> Isn't there in the East, notably in Oceania, a kind of rhizomatic model that contrasts in every respect with the Western model of the tree?
>
> (Guattari and Deleuze 1987: 18)

When I wrote "Professional and National Dreams" I felt confident that I had indicated certain paradigms used in some contemporary architectural discourses in Southeast Asia and had suggested a possible way of interpreting them. I have shown that the Indonesian architectural imagining of the "nation" is enabled precisely by the "western" paradigm it often rhetorically seeks to negate. "Modern architecture" has been driven by a metaphysical commitment to the universal character of its theory and practice across linguistic and cultural frontiers. This "universal" convention of representation is not only available for appropriation and replication *everywhere* but, most importantly, it also provides a series of local, if not national, variations in the forms of a "modern national architecture." It becomes possible for a series of nations: Indonesia, Malaysia, the Philippines, Singapore as much as for "the Thai team [to] adapt the basic design of a Thai-style house, but with a modernistic approach ... though the overwhelming impression is Thai."[1]

This possibility of replicating the modernist architectural paradigm, and of translating it into various national contexts, however, also suggests a way to imagine a *transnational regional* form of architecture and urban design. This chapter, however, is intended less to explain the socio-economic bases of existing "regional" alternative cultures and architectural strategies for postcolonial Southeast Asia, than to address why the "revision" is conceived in transnational "regional" forms – rather than in others, such as those of the "national."

Indeed, perhaps as a response in part to global cultural flows and contemporary processes of social and economic integration in the East and Southeast Asian region, there has been an increasing number of attempts to "unthink" the hegemonic architectural discourses of modernism and to "rethink" architecture through the histories and cultures of the Asian region.[2] These emergent discourses range from the (re)construction of the cultural traditions of the societies within the nation–states, to the (re)constitution of a transnational cultural heritage based on the common historical traits and topography of the region.[3]

This discourse, on "Asian identity and cultural heritage," began to emerge only in the 1980s. It was carried out regionally, for instance, in the first Asian Congress of Architects,[4] through a critique of foreign professional services whose architectural ideology was considered "insensitive" to local social and cultural values, and having a profoundly negative impact on the spatial development of the recipient countries. The infinite discourse of architectural modernism imported (largely, if not entirely) by foreign architects, was challenged by a new consensus which emphasized the importance of cultural identity; it drew on particular traditions that were seen as inherently embedded within the cultural space of the "Asian" region. The keynote speaker of the Congress, architect Leandro Locsin, from the Philippines, put the case in this manner:

> Western technology has introduced greater efficiency in production, but it has also led to the destruction of the environment, the pollution of air and water and the depletion of natural resources . . . The confrontation with Western culture has impelled us to delve into our Asian identity lest we lose that which is more precious. I venture to ask whether the present thrust towards modernization is complemented by a reaching back to the past, to rediscover one's history and to reaffirm the value of tradition.
>
> (As cited in Klassen 1984: 275)

And, referring to the housing trauma of urbanization shared by all countries in Asia, Locsin is convinced that "if we speak with one voice, there is much we can accomplish for we will be heard" (ibid.). "Cultural heritage" was thus staged as the strategic site within which alternative architectural ideas and practices in Asia were formulated. The congress emphasized the need for "Asian" architects to be involved "in the process of development, using the new technologies and guided by the diverse expression of architecture within the Asian region" (*Singapore Institute of Architects Journal* 1984). In addition to responding more effectively to the North–South political economic conflict and the consolidation of the professional class of architects in the Asian region, discourses on identity and heritage have broadened the cultural legitimacy of attempts by "Asian" architects to form and transform their own social environment. This venture requires both internal discourses within particular national cultural frameworks and across national dialogues with countries of the region. It is one that seeks to establish alternative forms of architecture and urban knowledge that are more proximate to the "regional" cultural setting than the mainstream regime of modernism.

In this course of re-writing histories and re-constructing architecture and urban planning in the Southeast Asian region, the idea that there was a pre-civilizational civilization comes to the fore. This not only become the starting point from which to imagine the specificity of the region; it is also the ideal means for recollecting origins, and for recovering the contradictions of the region's own creation.[5] In this effort to think of difference in the context of the continuing presence of the "West," "traditions" of Southeast Asia gradually appear to represent much that a "foreign" presence could not possibly be. Yet this potential "other" presence does not seem to assume a full ontological subject(ivity) of its own. Instead, in relation to its counterpart, it initially defines itself by re-fashioning the "foreign style" into what has been thought of as a style of its "own."[6]

The purpose of this chapter, therefore, is to consider some discourses of architecture in Southeast Asia that generate a collective subjectivity in and for the region, ones that negotiate with the basis of "western" architectural paradigms and that move beyond the framework of the nation. The chapter seeks to demonstrate the process of "intertwined histories, overlapping territories" (Said 1993), and of "global/localizing" processes (Wilson and Dirlik 1995). It seeks to demonstrate such a process of "cultural translation," of appropriating "western" knowledge for the development of Southeast Asian architecture, as part of the "re-writing" of architectural history. In so doing, it seeks to map a paradigm that is used to "localize" the transnational forces of architectural ideas by which the authority of the "West" is dislodged and the subject(ivity) of the "region" allowed to emerge.

Orientalism, I will argue, as a system of power and knowledge, has penetrated into many complex discourses that shape the construction of architectural culture in Southeast Asia. But in contrast to Said's earlier (1978) assumption that the objects of Orientalism cannot respond, this chapter argues that Southeast Asian architects have selectively *adopted* Orientalist categories as they negotiate their positions in the architectural world. Such "orientalism-in-reverse"[7] disturbs the idea of the simple dissemination of "western" knowledge as a system of total control.[8] "Western"-trained Asian architects have re-constructed material and symbolic resources to express their own agency in manipulating global schemes of cultural difference. This chapter will conclude with a reflection on the previous one, by looking at what theoretical, cultural and political shifts are implied by the architectural discourses of a region. To what conditions have these responded and how adequate have they been as a response?

COUNTERING LAND-BASED CIVILIZATION: SUMET JUMSAI AND THE WATER CULTURE OF SOUTHEAST ASIA

One of the most provocative architectural monographs published in the recent past from Southeast Asia is *Naga: Cultural Origins in Siam and West Pacific*.[9] The author, Sumet Jumsai (1988), a well-known Thai architect, characterized his own initial interest in the cultural origin of the region of Southeast Asia, understood as autonomous and culturally different (including the realm of architecture) from the Great Traditions of both the East and the West.[10] Taking the spatial imagination of the region as a whole, his intention, perhaps, is less to overcome the question of national identity than, more importantly, to counter the thesis that represents the cultures of the Southeast Asian region as the product of the historical processes of Indianization and Sinicization.[11] Against this, Sumet Jumsai proposes a series of unique cultures (and architectures) shared by the region of Southeast Asia, that are irreducible to the effects of "foreign" influences. The work is a clear example of a counter story of origins that negates the mainstream story of origin based on the nationally bounded imagination.

In *Naga*, by way of an exhaustive study of the origin of human migration, Jumsai arrives at the conclusion that Southeast Asia was once the center of the world. As the locus of human civilization, Southeast Asia was also the origin of civilization, and possibly, the hope of the future of human kind. Yet, as we will discover, the "original" culture of the region that Jumsai proposed cannot be the "origin," precisely because the realm of its enunciation is clearly enough defined by the dominant cultures it seeks to displace. Here is how Sumet Jumsai constructs his argument:

> Broadly speaking there are only two types of civilization on earth: one whose instinct is mainly based on tensile material and the other on compressive material. The former is the result of the aquatic skill and the survival instinct developed in the Quarternary period (or possibly before) and the subsequent migration to the 'Asian water front' when it was necessary to travel with the minimum of impedimenta. After the shift of world populations into the continental interior, generally in the northern latitudes, technology and the built environment had to rely substantially on stone quarried from mountains and other complementary compressive materials. The great monuments of Asia Minor, Egypt, Europe, the Indus Valley, and much of China belong to the civilization of compressive material. Ziggurats, pyramids, Stonehenge, and the Great Wall are pure compression structures, and so are houses, palaces, and temples which sit static on the ground. Even great Gothic cathedrals with their seemingly dynamic flying buttresses stand in place through a series of masonry point loads weighing down the outward thrust . . . The subsequent dominance of the land-based civilizations . . . meant that the concept and definition of humanity's progression (as represented in the notion of 'Stone Age') were squarely in (their) hands, particularly those in the Occident.
>
> (Sumet Jumsai 1988: 68–89)

The "beginning" of civilization is thus revised. Instead of the "land-based traditions," it is now the "water-based traditions" of Southeast Asia, or more broadly, the "West Pacific," with its aquatic cultures and tensile heritage that is the cradle of civilization. It is useful to see the diagram drawn by Jumsai (Figures 8.1 and 8.2) to revise the stages of what he calls the intercultural infusion.[12] The diagram showed the persisting centrality of the vertical flows of Southeast Asia, the longest of the others, despite the horizontal infusion of the "Great Traditions" of China, India and Europe. With Sumet Jumsai, the cultural flows of Hindu-Buddhism, Islam and Christianity are all necessarily incorporated to generate the traces of the existence, if not the superiority, of the Southeast Asian water-based traditions.

What is then the common denominator that forms the "water-based tradition" of the Southeast Asian architectural heritage as a whole? They are the cultures of rice agriculture, three-way basketry and, most important, the house on stilts.[13] This latter, according to Sumet Jumsai, is found historically everywhere in

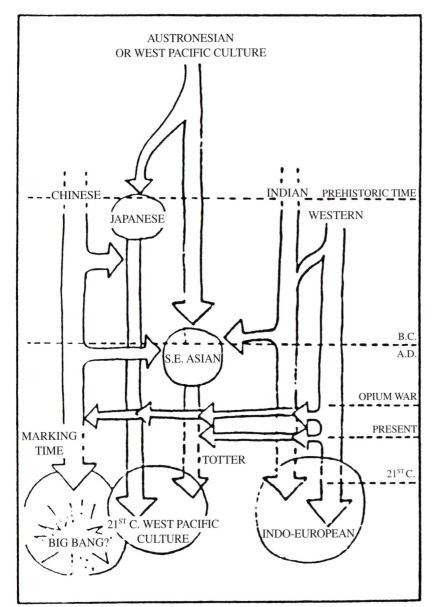

AUSTRONESIAN
OR WEST PACIFIC CULTURE

CHINESE

JAPANESE

INDIAN   PREHISTORIC TIME

WESTERN

S.E. ASIAN

B.C.

A.D.

OPIUM WAR

MARKING
TIME

PRESENT

TOTTER

21ST C.

BIG BANG?

21ST C. WEST PACIFIC
CULTURE

INDO-EUROPEAN

Figure 8.1
SOUTHEAST ASIAN-
CENTRIC WORLD
HISTORY
Source: Sumet Jumsai,
Mimar, 19, Jan–March
1986

the Western Pacific in an arc of more than 6,000 km across the equator from Melanesia and Indonesia to Japan. There, "on the 'Asia water front,' the same house type covers an area starting from Malaysia, Siam, and Indo-China to the foot of the Himalayas in Nepal and the Naga Hills in north-east India and South China" (Sumet Jumsai 1988: 80).

The water front architecture – the house on stilts – as against the land-based civilization of the "Great Traditions," has thus become the aquatic

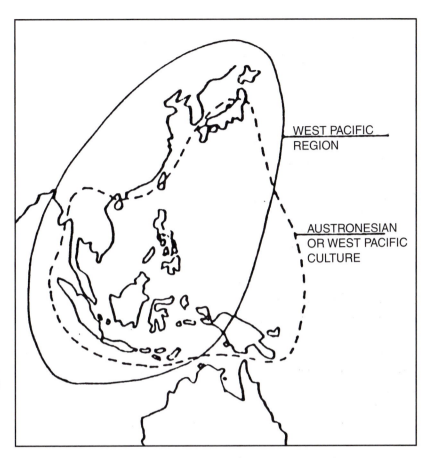

WEST PACIFIC
REGION

AUSTRONESIAN
OR WEST PACIFIC
CULTURE

Figure 8.2
SHARED TRADITION: THE
GEOGRAPHIC SPREAD OF
AUSTRONESIAN CULTURE
Source: Sumet Jumsai,
Mimar, 19, Jan–March
1986

tradition that exists from pre-historic time to the present state, though now near extinction as a result of the excessive forces of "modernization." What the emergence of this (floating) house on stilts does is to problematize and, ultimately, drive away any imagination of attachment to the ground – the sign of land-based civilization. The juxtaposition and separation of "foreign" land-based structures with the "indigenous" water-based built environment enables the latter to appear as self-sufficient and more authentic, more vulnerable as well as superior to its land-based counterpart.

Sumet Jumsai's reconstruction of the Southeast Asian architectural heritage, however, relies on the expressive correspondence of one set of houses on stilts with another and within the stretch of the "West Pacific" region. The effort is thus a kind of visual matching in which the systems of social and cultural specificity of each house seems to disappear. The "house on stilts," as an allegory of the regional culture, a collective possibility for the region to emerge as a distinctive and collective cultural discourse, only becomes visible as such by virtue of its isolation from the different, if not conflicting, socio-political grounds in which it is located.

For Sumet Jumsai, it is perhaps more important to represent the freshness of an "authentic" display of a unique "instinctive" cultural heritage that has made his effort reminiscent of the orientalist codification of the "East." Its representation is credited with the juxtaposing of the "Great land-based Traditions" with the "water-based" ones and separating them at the same time so that the latter now becomes a "civilization" that is equally "oriental", colossal, self-sufficient, and timeless.

The relevance of Sumet Jumsai's work for us is that it represents the will of a "water-based tradition" to become a center of civilization. At least it makes the world speak in and through the cultural conventions of the region that have so far been marginally represented by what Jumsai understands as the visual domination of the land-based civilization. For Sumet Jumsai, it would seem that the negation or inversion of "modernization" is crucial to the process of generating something altogether different. If this is allowed as the (hidden) agenda, then we might proceed by positing the fundamental features of Sumet Jumsai as a kind of impulse that postcolonial critics call "strategic essentialism." In this, there is a desire for a regional totality that is somehow, uneasily, conjoined with a desire for an alternative "development." Instead of just a monadic totality that celebrates the essentialism of cultural difference, what Sumet Jumsai shows us is a revision of orientalist codes in order to construct a cultural framework for an alternative "development" of the region of Southeast Asia. In this way Jumsai's architectural text can be seen as a re-statement of the region's expanding economy, or better, a cultural re-staging of the economic development of Thailand and its regional neighbors.

As the world economy is recentering to, as well as occasionally undermining, the Asia Pacific, it becomes possible to once again imagine the fluidity of the aquatic cultural representation. In the context of the global economy, Sumet Jumsai's discourse could be seen as constituting a future sense of regionality rather than attempting to excavate a past truth. The themes of "origins" and a "new era" are subtly linked precisely when world attention is placed on the (West) Pacific Rim as the center of capital accumulation. The conjuncture between Manuel Castells' (1989) technological "spaces of flow" fits nicely with Jumsai's insistence on the existence of the aquatic cultures of the West Pacific, which are now no longer peripheral.

The rise of Asian supercities might be generated by this residual aquatic instinct, something that is sure to happen to test Jumsai's predilection of a return to the instinct of the "sea creatures." Referring to Buckminster Fuller, an ecological futurist, Sumet Jumsai concludes:

> Future worlds will survive only if humans create more by using less – less material, less weight, less energy, etc . . . the trend for achieving more with less is now evident, as for example, the lunar landing module and other structures designed for space exploration, robotics, computer technology, and so on. In the next world upheaval . . . when the

planet once more enters the interglacial period, or as Vishnu puts on the garb of Indra and slays the serpent-cloud on top of Mount Meru, it is conceivable that the boatman's instinct, now dormant, will be replayed to ensure the survival of humanity.

(Sumet Jumsai 1988: 174)

Soon after *Naga* was published, Jumsai designed the Bank of Asia headquarters in the form of a robot (see Figure 8.3). Completed in 1986 for US$10 million, the "Robot Building" was labelled by Sumet Jumsai as "a statement in post high-tech architecture . . . that proclaims the demise of post-modernism as proliferated along the West Coast, as well as high-tech architecture as embodied in the Centre Pompidou and the Hongkong Bank building in Hongkong" (as cited in Boyd 1988: 48).

Sumet Jumsai's architectural philosophy is, according to a commentator, "high-tech in concept, but essentially human in form, flowing with energy and life-form, yet symbolic of the new technological age" (Boyd 1988: 48). This kind of architectural representation is perhaps what Jumsai imagined to be the more responsive architecture of the "mandala" and tensile technology in the transnational age of Asia. Nevertheless, the architectural imagining of Sumet Jumsai is best interpreted as aiming to open a space for other kinds of alternative historical narratives. In this imagining, the road would be cleared for future counter-hegemonic, popular and hopefully more critical appropriations of historical subjectivities.

THE BIOCLIMATIC CITY AND THE DISCOURSE OF TROPICAL ARCHITECTURE

As far as buildings can be seen as part of a rewriting of "history," it seems appropriate to interrogate the construction of "regionality" through the growth

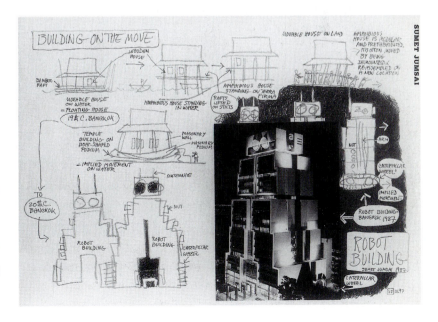

Figure 8.3
FROM HOUSE ON STILTS TO THE BANK OF BANGKOK
Source: Sumet Jumsai, *Cities on the Move*, Hou Hanru and Hans Ulrich Obrist (eds), Verlag Gerd Hatje, 1997

of high-rise buildings in Southeast Asia in the postcolonial era. Supposedly symbols of "modernity" and "progress," high-rise buildings are emblems of cities whose presence is assumed to convey, among other things, the internationality of the nation.[14] They are thus one of the most difficult building types to be localized, economically, technologically and symbolically. Perhaps that is the reason why high-rise buildings have been attributed with a significant degree of importance in representing the achievement of particular new "nation(s)." They provide an interesting case to see the ways in which contemporary Southeast Asian architects, as a result of changes in the political economy of their countries, have tried to make skyscrapers responsive to what are referred to as "local conditions." The site of this experiment is in the city which, as the keynote speaker of the first Congress of Asian Architects indicated, "is a place where one can be dehumanized and destroyed" (as cited in Klassen 1984: 275). Here, the geographical stretch of the "stilted houses," and the "water-based" philosophy of Sumet Jumsai seem to find a parallel in the discourse on the "bioclimatic city" and the "tropical towers" in the region.

Architects Ken Yeang (1987, 1987a, 1994) and Tay Kheng Soon (1989) of Malaysia and Singapore, most notably, have characterized their initial interest in a "tropical city" that presumably would not be realizable in areas that shared a different climatic environment. The relevance of their projects is that both, in their own ways, subscribe to a will that accepts the icon of "modernization," namely high-rise buildings, but "climatizes" them to suit the climatic environment of Southeast Asia. Without any awareness of, or interest in, the colonial origins of the concept of "tropical" from which the "temperateness" of European climates arises, Tay and Yeang have appropriated this classification to address the architectural desire of the economically "rising" Southeast Asia to seek its own identity (Figure 8.4). Here is the account of Ken Yeang, which starts:

> Economists have predicted for the 80s and early 90s that Asian economies would likely rank first in the world in terms of expansion. In an economic environment [this suggests] the need to develop an architectural urban aggregate form and fabric whose image and functions are related to the Asian life-style and independent identity of the local communities that it serves. Otherwise, the consequence would be a bland urban regional environment that is simply a repeat of the built mediocrities of international architecture found elsewhere. The need for a regionalist urban design is self-evident.
>
> (Yeang 1987a: 1)

The architectural programme is more explicitly described by Powell (1989) who, along with Tay and Yeang, has attempted to materialize the "tropical city":

> The concept of the Tropical City, might lead to the development of a distinctive local identity for the city. It might be held that for a city to have an identity, its place must have a clear conceptual framework that is recognisable, memorable, vivid, engaging of attention, and different from other locations . . . A distinctive city gives a sense of belonging to its inhabitants. The test of a place's identity is not the novelty of its

appearance, but the degree to which it is vividly remembered, used and identified by its people. This is the aesthetic justification for the 'tropical city.'

(Powell 1989: 105)

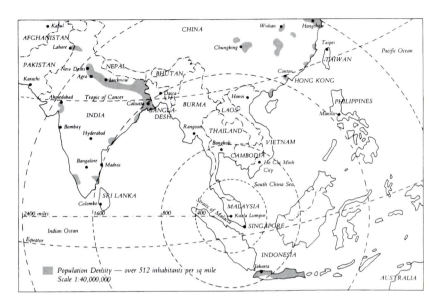

Figure 8.4
CENTERING THE REGION:
THE THEORETICAL AND
GEOGRAPHICAL BASES
FOR ASIAN REGIONALIST
ARCHITECTURE
Source: Ken Yeang,
Tropical Urban
Regionalism: Building in
a South-east Asian city,
Singapore: Concept
Media, 1987, p. 6

In these "manifestos," there is a crucial presupposition for a "tropical city." It is the notion of "identity" of the local communities. Instead of "Singaporean," "Chinese," or a "Malay," what is curiously proposed is an abstraction of "people," "Asian" and "independent identity" and a reference to a translocal pan-Asian *environment* that is deprived of any localized cultural categories. Tay (1989), perhaps the most conceptual of Southeast Asian architects today, has explained the reason and put the matter pointedly in his monograph:

> The aspect of tropicality arose regionally. It was spurred by the architectural identity quest stimulated by the government (in Kuala Lumpur), which desired a Malaysian identity in architecture. And various senior government members actually said that if architects didn't come up with a Malaysian identity in design, then the government would have to tell architects what to do. This alarmed the whole profession because everybody could see Minangkabau roofs coming up all over the place. The government was impatient with the slow pace of the development of visible symbols of Malaysian identity. This challenge took hold not only for that reason; it was also propelled by a disquiet amongst Malaysian architects at an implied ethnic sectarianism in the choice of ethnic symbols. That is one aspect of the problem. The other is that it took hold also because of tendencies among architects to follow the lead of architects in the developed world . . . In line with the eclectic phase of the so-called post-modernist architecture in the west, Asian architects are also beginning to incorporate their own ethnic and cultural symbols in their building

designs. This is historically absurd; it is also dangerous because it inadvertently
exacerbates ethnic cleavages that lie just below the surface of new-state cultures . . . Now,
it is in this context that there is a need for a more intrinsic design agenda for tropical
Asian countries. And that is to seek the design agenda from the *environment* itself, which
is specific to place and time. The new technological environment can also be brought in
as a generator of form and expression and to create a sense of cohesive identity which
transcends ethnicity and culture. This is the challenge to the creative design professions.

(Tay 1989: 8–11; emphasis added)

There is no doubt that Tay's formulation stemmed from a peculiar political
culture of Singapore which, from the beginning, believed that for the "plural
societies" of Southeast Asia to respond successfully to the first-ranking Asian
economy, local communities characterized by primordialism of identities are
officially rejected.[15] A distinctive city of the region, that follows the inhabitants'
senses of place and ways of life, is thus primarily based on its response to the
climatic environment which ultimately dismisses the discourses of "cultural
identity" based on visual iconic identification.

To achieve this translocal regionalist architecture, the preceding forms
of dominance represented by modernist architecture will thus have to be
rearticulated. Here, in a self-inscribed alterity to the modernist–international
architecture, the category of "tropical" climate becomes a symbol for a locally-
meaningful architecture. The series of high-rise buildings designed by Yeang and
partners, for example, put forward devices of climatic filtering, such as large-
scale wind shields, louvred screens, overhead pergolas, sunshading devices, wind
baffles and vegetation. These elements are hung and placed around or within
the modernist tower block (Figures 8.5, 8.6, and 8.7). The design diagram shows
them up as elements, each with its own integrity, floating in and on the imagined geometry as if, without these elements, there would be no "tropical skyscrapers." The insertion of these devices into an essentially high-rise modernist
structure presumably dispels the image of the modernist tower itself and thus
makes visible the specific climate of the region.

What is interesting here is the metamorphosis which these "tropical" projects inflect upon the modernist categories they seek to subordinate, namely, the
technique of incorporating climatic modifiers into what is essentially a modernist
structure. What the emergence of these climatic devices does is to problematize,
and ultimately dispel, the image of the "modernist box" itself. Yet, on the other
hand, the interpenetration of the devices, touching each other without sacrific-
ing their own "identity," are curiously mediated by the "modernist" structure
which presupposes an ultimate rejoining of the "tropical" with the "modern"
and the re-identification of the latter with the former.

This represents a process of architectural "localization," a cultural negotiation of the authority of the "international style" that the ultimate alignment is
established only when the latter is deprived of exercising an absolute dominance.
Only by positing the "modernist box" as its counterposition and representing it

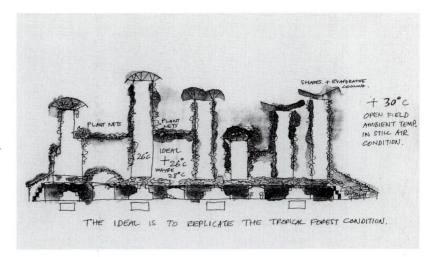

Figure 8.5
"THE IDEAL IS TO
REPLICATE THE TROPICAL
FOREST CONDITION"
Source: Tay Kheng Soon,
Megacities in the Tropics,
Singapore: Southeast
Asian Studies Program,
1989

in terms of crisis does "tropical architecture" gain its distinctive identity with a will to assert its own authority.

In this sense, in masking the "modernist box," there is no immediate rejection of the modernist paradigm itself nor the determinants out of which it comes. Indeed, the climatic devices are all "dependent" upon the structure of the building which, typologically, is not unlike those constructed all over the world. Perhaps the obligation to come to terms with the city fabric has informed a change in the architectural sign system so that the whole cultural patterning of the city is reduced to the problem of an apolitical "climate." This climatic essentialism might as well be read, economically, as a cultural restructuring of late capitalist development whose expansion is no longer mediated by the dissemination of the old standardized "modernist box." However, this regionalist approach adopted by Tay and Yeang should also be read *politically* as representing the contention with primordialism in the construction of a "modern" post-colonial nation. The modernist box lying behind the climatic device is articulated to speak a language beyond that of universal modernism. Instead, it now goes through the condition that allows the non-political climatic expression of identity – an issue that has become an important attribute for the postcolonial countries in the Malay Peninsula.

By defining the "tropical skyscrapers" as a distinctive structure of the region, Tay and Yeang enable the realities and possibilities of postcolonial nation–states to speak of their own "regional" authority. Within the narrative of "nation-building," with its prime interest of national integration and regional network, all other levels of difference have to be suppressed to give way to the distinctiveness of climate as "culture." Yet, with this technical optimism, they also take for granted that sustainable development will be increasingly dependent on modern scientific and technological expertise, which is supposed to be objective and non-political. The emergence of Southeast Asia as one of the important loci of the world-economy has assumed a trust in science and technology as a

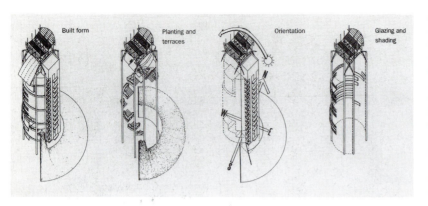

Figure 8.6
REFASHIONING,
RESISTING OR
ACCOMMODATING
MODERNIST
SKYSCRAPERS? THE
CLIMATIC DEVICES OF
THE MENARA
MESINIAGA (1989–92),
SUBANG JAYA,
SELANGOR, MALAYSIA
Source: Ken Yeang,
Bioclimatic Skyscrapers,
1994, p. 12

fundamental force of the future. Once again "modern science and technology have been regarded as an unambiguously progressive, necessary and neutral means for realizing undisputed political objectives such as growth, progress and development" (Moser 1995: 3). The architectural discourse of Tay and Yeang contests both Western hegemony and nationalist primordialism through the supposedly "non-political" language of nature, science and technology, a position we might call the politics of non-political architecture.

CONCLUSION

The tropical skyscrapers of Tay and Yeang and the "water-civilization" of Jumsai, while different in their philosophical thinking and tactics towards modernist architecture, are all attempts to think through the impasse of mainstream architectural discourses. Yet their self-representation is derived from a "western" discourse that is used and appropriated as a strategy to inform their own position and subjectivity. Jumsai, Tay and Yeang, each in their own way, do not resist the idiom of "Western" discourses; instead they appropriate them by finding local parallels. The identification with the modernist paradigm through a moment of self-inscribed alterity, turn upside down the subject/object of history, enabling the region to emerge as a subject of history. Whereas before, the "water-based traditions" and the idea of the "tropical" suffer from the domination of their counterpart, today it becomes the challenging subject that moves the history of architecture in the region, and in the case of Sumet Jumsai, even the prime mover of world history itself. What has been reproduced then is the "authenticity" and "sovereignty" of "water-based traditions" in the case of Jumsai, and the regionality of the "tropical" in the example of Tay and Yeang. Southeast Asian architectural identity is thus achieved by virtue of its continuous involvement with the modernist chain that preceded its appearance as a subject of histories. The construction of "cultural difference" is thus enabled by the imagined structure of "foreign" materials, a condition enabled to a fundamental degree by a re-articulation of modernist codes. The postcolonial architectural discourses have

Figure 8.7
TROPICAL MODERNITY:
THE CLIMATIC
SOUTHEAST ASIAN
TOWER
Source: Ken Yeang,
Bioclimatic Skyscrapers,
1994, p. 61

to be understood by aligning them within the larger eurocentric structure of knowledge that preceded them, and against which they have come into being.

But in what *political* perspective does it make sense to reflect on these various architectural imaginings of Southeast Asia architects? This, and the previous chapter revaled to us, I believe, at least two misconceptions in our common understanding of the architecture, or architectural thinking, of postcolonial nations. The first misconception is that what is going on is "Westernization," with all the connotations this word might imply including the idea of "Western" knowledge as a system of total control. For this notion makes us forget, or ignore, the profound processes of cultural translation, of appropriating "Western" knowledge for the unthinking and rethinking of the local political and architectural cultures of the recipient countries.

"Westernization," as a system of power and knowledge, has indeed penetrated into many complex discourses that shape the construction of architectural culture in postcolonial Southeast Asia. But, contrary to the assumption that the objects of "Westernization" cannot respond, the Western-trained architect, as I have shown, has selectively adopted Western categories and techniques as he or she has negotiated their positions in the architectural world. Perhaps even more important, "Western" discourses of architecture provide cultural resources by which an *implicit* critical commentary on the nation's political cultures can be launched. We may, therefore, want to remove the idea of "Westernization" as a global process by which the "West" controls knowledge production in the postcolonial or dependent world, and replace it with a term which more adequately describes this process of cultural translation. We need a term that will allow us to understand the significant global spread of the standardized conceptions of modern architecture, but *along with* their reworking by postcolonial architects who cross over them, or use them for different ends, and often with remarkable political and cultural implications.

"Westernization" or "Americanization" may seem to be uncomplicated ideas but, as in the cases I have discussed, these terms may suggest a different meaning. Seen from one side, "Westernization" appears to suggest a destination, a process of arrival, by replication, at some imagined place called the "West." But seen from the other side of the globe, "Westernization" could mean something quite the opposite. It could point to a departure, an exit from something one wants to leave behind, which does not necessarily imply that one would then arrive at, or replicate, a particular place called the "West." With this inverted lens, therefore, we can look at the adventure of "modern architecture" in various parts of the world, grasping its standardized grammar more in terms of the diversity it has created and, more importantly, the localized, decentered, and hopefully *critical*, forward-looking visions it has generated.

The second misconception, related to, and growing partly out of, the first is that architecture and epoch are in some ways fundamentally related. This misconception makes it hard to refuse the belief that an "Indonesian architecture" (for instance) should both possess and express its own distinctive character. This drive for one's own culture was quite often accompanied by the search for a glorious past and "splendid ancestors" (Anderson 1999). This narrative of looking backward puts an immense importance on what has been known as a trace of spatial and temporal "origins". It gains meaning by reference to the possession of a particular past and within a certain bounded territory. This narrative makes us forget that "modern architecture" was, in fact, initiated as a common project, an enterprise that directs people's imagination (of all places) towards the future. It also makes us forget the remarkable spread of a forward-looking vision in much of the postcolonial world that seeks to leave behind the past and the imagery of the "nation" in order to negotiate a new identity.

What we have in these two misconceptions is the sharing of the intellectual paradigm of "telos" in history, one which generates two interrelated but profoundly contrasting trajectories of loyalty. The first is the narrative of progress towards the "West" as the future, in which case the architecture of the postcolonial world evolved through the practices of "Westernization," "modernization" and "Americanization." The second is the story of a return to the common inheritance of "splendid ancestors" and a past with which the nation identifies itself in its quest for "development." These two loyalties typically give rise to a vision that is not only utopic but also quite often dangerous.

The tropical skyscrapers of Tay and Yeang, the water civilization of Jumsai, and the "political" imaginings of Indonesian architects, while different in their philosophical thinking and tactics about architectural cultures in Southeast Asia, are all attempts to think through the impasse of "national" imagining and the universalizing claims of international modernism. The identification with the modernist paradigm enables a form of unbounded regional architectural imagination that re-examined, interrogated and, where possible, problematized both the ideologies of universal modernism and the bounded history of the nation–state. These architects jointly define architecture in its capacity to address the social and political conditions of the spaces within which their works are embedded.

However, the question really is whether their anxieties about nationalism and modernization, and the stretch of their critical imagination of architecture, can also include a critique of late capitalist expansion in their search for a localized, popular and typically unbounded regional experience. As for global capitalism it is easier to align its demand with supra-national regional spaces than with some unaccommodating nation–states. To this extent, the architecture of these Southeast Asian architects has tended to be incorporated into, and adapted for, the order of the world-economy, rather than to provide a site to interrogate it.

Conclusion: Beyond the Postcolonial?

Nationalism was recognized both to have constituted the single most important site of resistance to colonialism, at the same time that it provides the most salient demonstration of the power of colonialism to reproduce itself.

(Dirks 1992: 15)

What I have aimed to demonstrate in the previous pages is that the realm of architecture and urban design is not only essential for understanding the political and cultural development of contemporary Indonesia, but that architecture and urban design have also played a central and, indeed, critical role in shaping the norms and forms of the country's society, culture and politics.

Though each of the previous (interrelated) chapters has had its own locus and focus, the study as a whole has had four main objectives. The first, and most important, has been to demonstrate the cultural formation of collective "national" subjectivities in the postcolonial Indonesian world and the contribution of architecture and urban design discourses to this process. The second has been to write a political history of postcolonial architecture and urban design which recognizes its colonial "origins," not only for the sake of its past, but, more particularly, for the questioning of the present as well as the future. The third objective has been to transcend the criticism of the modernist paradigm in architecture and urban design as merely "colonial" and see how this can be appropriated in the interests of, as well as against, a country-specific, national culture. Finally, my aim has been to get away from an analysis of postcolonial history, simply in terms of "East/West" encounters and consider other nexus of power – not least, those of the supra-national region – that generate different types of "modernity."

All these purposes have been anchored, however, by one overall aim: to enable the present subjects of Indonesia to live with, rather than to suppress by means of "nationalism," the differences, gaps and contradictions of their condition, and thereby learn to live together, rigorously, but also with self reflection and understanding. A fund of illustrative materials, narratives and arguments –

including colonial derivation, western ideas, Sukarno's syncretic modernism, Suharto's repressive traditionalism, the New Order's bestiality, the kampung's "origins," the architect's political imaginations, and Indonesian Chinese amnesiac Utopianism – have all been drawn upon to remind ourselves and the citizens of *present* day Indonesia of its hybrid modernity. It remains to be seen if, with the end of Suharto's regime, the new generation it helped to construct will want to articulate this hybrid modernity rather than (as under the New Order) suppress it.

The themes of these chapters – the colonial "origins" of contemporary Indonesian culture, the violent genealogy of the New Order, the hybrid modernities of the protesting New Order's generation – are all conditions best conveyed through the notion of "postcoloniality." Whatever the controversy surrounding recent theories of "postcolonialism," their value can only be evaluated in terms of how one can adequately address the complex conditions that attend the aftermath of "formal" colonial occupation. In the following pages, I first address these questions of postcoloniality and the relevance, if any, of contemporary postcolonial theories and criticism to the case of Indonesia. In the final section, I return to the topic of architecture and spatial politics and the formation of collective subjectivity.

NATIONALISM AND THE MUTED LEGACY OF COLONIALISM

In his study of Third World nationalism, Partha Chatterjee (1993; 1996) argues that the cultural forms of imagining the nation by nationalist elites are conducted through a separation of culture into material and spiritual domains. This very separation offers nationalism an inner space, uncontaminated by "foreign" elements, over which it declares its sovereignty long before any political confrontation with colonial rule. It is this inner space where nationalism launches its project of combining a multiplicity of social groups under a single overarching community and, on this basis, initiates material progress along the lines of its "foreign" counterparts. In other words, the supposed spirituality of the nation's identity in turn affects the materiality (and the physicality) of a whole set of institutions where it seeks to enforce this identity. In this sense, the material and physical development pursued by decolonized nation–states is subjected to the control, or indeed, the absorption, of the supposedly eternal and unified inner spiritual space of the nation. Therefore, as this book has shown, the pursuit of "development" in Indonesia, as well, perhaps, as in other Third World countries, is far from eroding "traditional" cultures. Instead, the former has been undertaken entirely within the continuous creation of the latter.

One illustration of the way modern "development" is embarked on through the production of "traditional" culture can be seen in the construction of political legitimacy, under the notion of "development" in Indonesia. In his analysis of the concept of "development" in New Order Indonesia, Ariel Heryanto (1988) indicates that Indonesian's idea of "development," known as "pembangunan," while sharing something with broad theories of modernization, is constituted through a traditional concept of authority. The leader of the New Order is bestowed with a title, "Father of Development," which indicates that he is performing a familial role not of his will but the will of destiny. As "development" is thought to be a "natural" process, it could therefore only be conceived by an equally "natural" authority within a family of traditional structure.[1] A Minister points out:

> The title Father of Indonesian Development ('Bapak Pembangunan Indonesia') will be the property of only one person and is not to be given to any other person. This means that the Father of Indonesian Development is one ('manunggal') with our present national leader, Pak Harto.
>
> (Minister Abdul Gafur, as cited in Heryanto 1988: 21)[2]

In engaging with the international ideology of progress, the New Order thus operates the "stages of development" through a local concept of authority that will ultimately lead the nation to "lepas-landas" (take-off) to the dreamworld promised by "development."

This aspect of postcoloniality, at least in the case of Indonesia as I have shown throughout the study, is not merely an outcome of globalization; instead it is inextricably merged with the colonial legacy which, paradoxically, made it possible for Indonesian nationalists to imagine a specifically "Indonesian" (precolonial) culture. The cultivation and promotion of the "authentic" and "ancient" in Indonesian civilization under the Dutch also provided the basis for a postcolonial narrative of "progress" and the construction of different "stages of development." This had the effect of placing "Indonesia" within its "own" genealogy and apparently outside colonial legacies.

As this perspective gradually took on a discourse of anti-colonial nationalism, a dichotomy was established between, on one side, colonized "Indonesia" and, on the other, the Dutch colonizer. Indonesia was thus formally remembered, by its own politicians and intellectuals, in terms of its "own" development, a process which was assumed to have evolved out of its own genealogy. A generalized understanding of "tradition," imagined as long existing within a cultural terrain of the "nation," was recognized as a "local" heritage. Through this somewhat (un)intended cultural inheritance we can begin to understand the way in which the representation of the "Indies" under Dutch colonialism, as a political representation of Indonesian heritage with its application in the sphere of architecture and urban design, anticipated, in our case, the search for an "Indonesian architecture" by the architects of the New Order.

In this way, colonial representations provided a cultural framework in which postcolonial "official nationalism" could imagine not merely its "imperial" identity, but could also reproduce "tradition" as a kind of protective armour with which to shield the state from the contradictions of capitalist "development." Caught up in this environment, the architects of the New Order, through their works, represent a form of cultural inheritance that is central to the New Order's ideology of "development" and "stability" and one that is also grounded upon "traditional rituals" (Pemberton 1994).

How far postcolonial architects respond to the official nationalism of the New Order and the demands of capitalist market relations are open questions. Their roles as "specific intellectuals," to use Foucault's term (Rabinow 1989), working in the postcolonial social and technocratic environment, might have situated them as professionals, demonstrating artistic and scientific integrity, outside the socio-political realm. Yet as both they, as well as their projects, are necessarily constituted under specific constraints of power, they also participate in the construction of a rationality that ultimately produces Indonesian "traditions." As producers of "culture" they find themselves serving the interests of political reaction and caught up in the dream-state of "development."

In this respect, the practice of Indonesian architects resembles the dominant writers of the New Order in the realm of literature, as I have intimated in Chapters 3 and 7. Keith Foulcher (1995: 149, 161), a critic of Indonesian literature, suggests that:

> The construction of a postcolonialist identity upon and through the dislocations wrought by colonialism has never been a central motive in Indonesian creative expression, nor has it been a major concern of literary critical debate . . . Indonesian literature, in both its radical and conservative traditions, became linked to the aspirations of the state, on the side of building the future, incorporating the marginal, and subduing the breakaway.[3]

For postcolonial Indonesian creative writers, the issues at stake are "how can the national and nationalist project be furthered?" and "what is to be incorporated into it?" They are not concerned with critical questions, as often asked by postcolonial critics in the First World, such as "what has made us what we are?" (Foulcher 1995: 161).

Foulcher provides an answer to the question as to why this is the case. Indonesians never thought of themselves as being part of a colonial legacy because they were encouraged, by Dutch orientalist discourse, to remain "Indonesian." One important factor here was the language:

> Dutch orientalist views on the education of the native population had won the day, not only in terms of colonial debates, but also in determining that the colonial language could not be the language of the postcolonial state.
>
> (Foulcher 1995: 162)

Part of the colonial project was to promote an officially sanctioned indigenous "lingua franca" with the ultimate aim that it should become a "national" language. In these symbolic terms, then, the "Indonesian" language becomes a language of both the colonizer and the colonized. What we have is a situation where colonial power, rather than denying the images and languages of the colonized, in fact contributed to the formation of what, in postcolonial times, was to be institutionalized as the official representation of Indonesia.[4] This phenomenon, therefore, poses a serious question for standard postcolonial criticism that takes the colonial "language" as its prime target of displacement (Ashcroft et al. 1989).

If we take "bahasa Indonesia" – the official language of Indonesia – as "a powerful tool for the state's project of incorporation, subduing the fragmenting tendencies of regional loyalties," (Foulcher 1995: 161) in the same way as the colonial language had previously done in many parts of Africa, India, the Americas and parts of Southeast Asia, then what we have in postcolonial Indonesia is a replaying of the "political rationalities" of colonial power.[5] The territorial expansion of "bahasa Indonesia" becomes a smaller-scale version of the spread of English within the British Empire. In this way, the "postcolonial" of Indonesia has to be understood not merely in the "typical" postcolonial genre of criticizing "Europe," but also as a strand in the critique of an authoritarian, centralizing, neo-colonial, or better, neo-feudal "official nationalism" of the New Order regime.[6]

One crucial dimension of postcolonial studies is the interrogation of the colonial past in order to remind the present of its origin in colonial oppression. For the Suharto regime of Indonesia, there is neither a painful memory of colonial subordination, nor a burden to disown its colonial past. Colonial history is not a significant part of Suharto's modern history of Indonesia. Therefore, it has merely been suppressed, or appropriated to support the pride and heroism of the proto-Indonesian state. Suharto's Indonesia was not compelled to share the anxieties of postcoloniality with other places elsewhere, which is:

> to negotiate the contradictions arising from its indisputable historical belatedness . . . its postcoloniality, or political and chronological derivation from colonialism, on the one hand, and its cultural obligation to be meaningfully inaugural and inventive on the other.
>
> (Gandhi 1998: 6)

Indonesia's New Order lacked this anxiety. Colonial history, seen from the optic of the ruling regime, represents only a fragmented rupture of the longer and continuing history of the "Javanese" empire (Pemberton 1994). The mobilization of the resources of the New Order's culture to cope with the seemingly dreadful transformation of society that accompanied colonialism is outside the imagination of the country. Such a construction is too passive to accommodate the mode of aggressive resignation characteristic of the New Order. Colonial techniques of representation are a lure rather than a threat; and the regime, as I have shown in many cultural and geographical sites above, rose to appropriate these techniques in its own fashion. Colonialism did not subordinate the self-invention of the postcolonial subject. Instead, it provided a framework for the New Order to generate a political culture which had the effect of strengthening, rather than weakening, "traditional" symbolism.

What postcolonial critics have observed in independent nation–states after colonialism, namely, a will to forget the colonial past, cannot be found among the desire of the postcolonial elite of Indonesia. There is, therefore, no "new" world that is expected to emerge from the "physical" ruins of colonialism. Instead, the main concern has always been how to restore "power" to the present as expressed in the state's question, "how can a national project be promoted"? Perhaps the only "real" anxiety harboured by the governing elite of the New Order concerns the political illegitimacy which accompanied the violence of its rise to power. The emergence of the New Order was fraught with anxiety and fears of failure of its own regime in relation to the previous regime it overthrew, and *not* in relation to the outside world. Postcolonial amnesia in Indonesian experience is therefore not an urge for a historical self-invention after colonialism, as suggested by postcolonial studies, but an erasure of the memories of its immediate illegitimate past. As such, the Indonesian experience reveals the limit of "postcolonial studies" as they have so far been represented in the literature. Today, the postcolonial nation is struggling not only with a singular past, namely, the colonial history of "East"/"West", but also with its own immediate, and often more intimate but no less violent, set of histories after decolonization.

ARCHITECTURE, SPATIAL POLITICS AND SUBJECT FORMATION

How might this "postcoloniality" of Indonesia affect discourses of architecture and urban planning? The pursuit of modern architecture and urban design under the continuous grounding of "culture" has been a paradigm shared by sensitive architects working for, as well as in, the postcolonial world. On this score, "culture" has been understood as lying within the space of the nation. Architects and planners, as both custodians and developers of that "culture," produced architecture and space that represents the cultural and technological development of that nation. The starting point remains of taking architecture as an object of national discourse, rather than as its subject. What remains unexplored in this search for a "postcolonial national architecture" is the repertoire of "culture" itself: "what has made it what it is"? And what are the various roles of architecture and urban design in registering colonial and postcolonial histories?

Examining this aspect of architecture and urban planning, this study has been concerned with the postcolonial question of "what has made us what we are?" In responding to this inquiry, I have represented architecture and urban design as a technology that is involved in techniques of regulation and strategies of identity formation that are both disciplining and empowering. My study has sought to show the importance of architecture and space in the formation of collective subjectivities, a connection that is conspicuously missing in the postcolonial (literary) attempts to account for subject formation. Scholars of colonial discourse, from the social sciences to the humanities, frequently discuss "space," but generally their works hardly touch on the real, physical and spatial representation of colonial encounters. While spatial metaphors are used (such as "third space," spaces of ambivalence, and "in-between space"), the making of postcolonial subjects phrased as hybrid, contradictory, and ambivalent are all noticeably unmediated by the material properties of space (Jacobs 1996; King

1999; Myers 1999). It seems that these subjects are constructed out of thin air and outside the realm of a material environment.

Unlike many recent colonial discourse analyses that discuss "space" but barely touch on the real, physical outcomes of colonialism's spatial (inter)ventions, this study has represented urban spaces as capable of deploying techniques that appeals to the viewer's identification with a subject position. By showing the practices of spatial and architectural representation involved in the making and unmaking of political cultures, I have aimed to show the constitutive role of space in the formation and transformation of subjectivity. Here the city is less the object of national discourses, but is, instead, its subject which is actively involved in the making and unmaking of cultures and identities, in producing national subjects that are both obedient and "modern." The method is no longer simply to represent in the city what the nation, following the end of colonial rule, has produced, but to use the city for the process of production.

Apart from seeing architecture as a "form of dominance" of colonial and postcolonial enterprise, I have endeavored to show how architecture and urban design, as a "noun" instead of as a "verb" (Mitchell 1994: 1), simultaneously represents both a colonization *and* a decolonization of cultures. I have treated architecture and urban planning as social and political means of representation in which a postcolonial nation, and its subjects, altered city space for themselves. "For the ex-colony," as Appadurai (1995: 23) points out, "decolonization is a dialogue with the colonial past, and not a simple dismantling of colonial habits and modes of life." I argue, in the case of Indonesia, that the dialogue with the colonial past has resulted, among other things, in the reproduction of a form of colonialism itself.

Notes

INTRODUCTION

1. O'Neill (1993) and Macdonald (1995) indicate that there are no signs of continuity with traditional Indonesian architecture in the Friday Mosque (today it is called "Masjid Istiqal"). Instead, architectural traditions of the Ottoman Empire were more significantly expressed.

2. Between 1982 and 1988, 394 standard-design mosques were constructed in 26 provinces (Sumintardja 1988).

3. The Demak Mosque was reputedly built in 1498 to be a kind of "relic" or "trace," a monument that would stand perpetually as a concrete, material site both for pilgrimage and as an embodiment of supernatural power. It was to be the sacred site of power of the realm of Java and at the same time, a talisman ("pusaka") for the rulers of that realm. Almost 500 years after its erection by the Islamic saints ("wali"), the Grand Mosque of Demak still remains a force in Indonesian governance. President Suharto assured the assemblage that the restoration of the Demak Mosque was neither a waste of money nor a luxury, but integral to the nation's development – in the largest sense of the word. The president saw the restoration as part of an effort to build up the nation's spiritual capital ("modal rohani") into a source of working capital that would powerfully propel all aspects of national development (Florida 1995: 321, 324).

4. See Young (1991); Chakrabarty (1992); Dirks (1992); Stoler and Cooper (1997).

5. Of course, such geopolitical essentialism would both deny the existence of a diversity of so-called "European" perspectives as well as essentialize "non-European" viewpoints.

6. See also Cooper (1987); Celik (1997); Myers (1997); Perera (1998).

7. For a discussion of this in the realm of Indonesian literature, see Foulcher (1995). Foulcher also indicates the absence of the sense of cultural "inauthenticity" in the literatures of postcolonial Indonesia. This sense of "inauthenticity" is considered to be a founding moment of postcolonial consciousness.

8 "Official nationalism" refers to a form of nationalism represented and promoted by the nation–state (Anderson 1991: Chapter 6).

9 For a critique of Mbembe's methodology, see Coronil (1992).

10 As Michel Foucault (1982: 30–1) indicated, "I would like to write the history of this prison, with all the political investments of the body that it gathers together in its closed architecture. Why? Simply because I am interested in the past? No, if one means by that writing a history of the past in terms of the present. Yes, if one means writing the history of the present."

11 Historian M.C. Ricklefs (1993: 151–62) characterizes this time as "a new colonial age," and discusses it in terms of "the emergence of the idea of Indonesia."

12 The effect of print capitalism and technological change on the political consciousness of both the colonizer and colonized are noted in Adam (1995), Anderson (1996), and Shiraishi (1990).

13 For example, Noyes (1992); Pratt (1992); Said (1993); Bhabha (1994); McClintock (1994); Young (1995). "Space," as it is used in these analyses of colonial power, is metaphorical, or imagined rather than concrete and material. The exception is Jacobs (1996); Lee (1999) and Abbas (1997). See also the critique of Myers (1999).

Chapter 1: "ORIGINS" REVISITED

1 See King (1976, 1990); Rabinow (1989); AlSayyad (1992); Wright (1992); Crinson (1996); Yeoh (1996); Home (1997); Nalbantoglu and Wong (1997).

2 For an account of the effect of mechanical reproduction on the imagining of (post)colonial property with political implications, see Anderson (1991: Chapter 10).

3 For a discussion on this technique of the colonial exhibition, see Mitchell (1991: 15–21).

4 For a discussion of ideologies behind colonial efforts to appear as the guardian of local tradition, see Anderson (1991: 180–1).

5 This was perhaps the time when the term "Indonesia" entered the imagination of both the colonizer and the colonized. The term "Indonesia" was first conceived in 1850 by the English ethnologist, G.W. Earl, to designate the inhabitants of the archipelago called "Indunesians" or "Melayunesians." It was then a working concept for scholars in geography and ethnography to imagine the whole islands of the Malay archipelago. However, the term was then suppressed by the colonizer because it was suddenly invested with a connotation of what the colonized could not possibly be: anti-colonialism and political independence of the territory from the Dutch. See Kroef (1951); Ave (1989).

6 The notion of "specific intellectual" is from Foucault. In his study, Paul Rabinow (1989: 16) used the term to describe the "technocratic" actors, not by virtue of their genius or superior cultural background, but because each "embodied and articulated, in diverse and often contradictory ways, an essential dimension of the [French] practice and ethos of social modernity. They were neither heroes nor villains nor anonymous citizens. They were pragmatic technicians seeking to find scientific and practical solutions to public problems in times of crises: hence they qualify as intellectuals."

7 In the eyes of Europeans interested in European architecture in the colonies, the Dutch were considered to have failed. As an observer indicated in 1940, "In all the

Indies there is not a single architectural work, not a sign of a real monument worthy of the Dutch, though the latter have lived in Batavia for more than three centuries." The observer cited the great historian of Southeast Asia, Furnivall, who "tells us that he mistook the office of a regent for a bicycle-shed; too many administrative buildings are no more impressive than automobile garages. As for the two 'palaces' of the governor-general, they are old, commonplace, ridiculous structures utterly without character" (Bousquet 1940: 91–2).

8 It is important to note that this switching of standards in evaluating the built environment of the Dutch East Indies was an aspect of the changing criteria in the Netherlands. Architecture in Europe was itself undergoing crises of identity following the institutionalization of its experts, and the demand for professional autonomy. Within the Netherlands, architecture was torn between engineering and art, the two domains that claim hegemony over housing and urban planning (Stieber 1998). While architects reacted against the tendency of many of their profession to focus on technical issues at the expense of aesthetic ones, they also held different ideologies. For instance, the architectural movement of De Stijl in Holland believed in the universality of "abstract geometric" form, and thus more easily accepted the machine as a means of universal production. In contrast, the Amsterdam School aspired to the artistic conception of originality and craft expressionism. De Klerk, leader of the Amsterdam school, was himself attracted to the "Nieuwe Kunst (1892–1904)" (a Dutch version of Art Nouveau, formed in opposition to rationalism and functionalism) when his group worked in the Cuypers atelier which, to a certain degree, was influenced by Indonesian art. The Amsterdam School found its momentum in the Dutch government because it sought to restore the original character of the city and represent the dignity of the working class. Looking at the intertwined architectural histories of metropole and colony, we may start to link the attention given to the "working class" in the metropole with an interest in vernacular architecture in the colony. An informed analysis of this theme is essential and much needed.

9 For a discussion on this theme, see Coedes (1968). For a polemic against this thesis and more in favor of that based on a "genius loci" of the indigenous culture, see van Leur (1955); see also Kroef (1951a). For a lucid exploration of the theme see Wolters (1982).

10 Wolff Schoemaker, however, in his architectural practice, tried to combine a modernist architectural paradigm with the art deco of his mentor Frank Lloyd Wright. See Wiryomartono (1995: 137–40).

11 A Dutch architect, Cuypers, established a successful office in Batavia in 1909, and from 1910 till 1929, 14 buildings for the Bank of Java were built in self-styled colonial–neoclassical–art deco style. See C. Passchier AvB (1988).

12 For a brief discussion on architectural modernism and art deco movements in the city of Bandung, see Wiryomartono (1995: 132–5).

13 For Berlage's 1924 lecture after a brief visit to the Indies, see H.P. Berlage, *Mijn Indische Reis: Gedachten over Cultuur en Kunst*, Rotterdam: Brusse's Uitgeversmaatschappij N.V. 1931.

14 How Maclaine Pont and Thomas Karsten arrived *politically* at the position of formulat-
    ing the idea of "Indies architecture" is beyond the scope of this study. Their student
    life at the Technische Hoogeschool at Delft might have contributed to their intellec-
    tual development, since there was a climate of Social radicalism on the campus at
    that time. For a biographical sketch of Henri Maclaine Pont, see Jessup (1989);
    Leerdam (1995); and for a brief bibliography of Thomas Karsten, see Cobban (1992:
    335–6); Bogaers and Ruijter (1986).

15 Van Doorn (1982: 26) points out that the University of Delft became the engineers'
    network for the colony in 1920s.

16 This view was also behind the idea of offering a university with a faculty in the
    humanities in Batavia in the 1930s that would focus primarily on "indigenous culture
    and its evolutionary history." Debate formed around the issues of whether Dutch civil-
    ization should provide the intellectual foundations of the curriculum or whether the
    Indonesians should be given their own space in analysing their own society and
    history. The short-lived institutions of higher learning in the humanities established
    under Dutch colonialism (1940–1) was set to motivate Indonesians to study the devel-
    opment of their own cultures, rather than to "absorb Western civilization." See
    Gouda (1995: 218–19).

17 Owing to my lack of familiarity with the Dutch language, my discussion on Karsten's
    architectural work (including those of Pont) is based on my interpretation of his
    drawing and statements as they appear in citations in the works of Jessup (1982a,
    1982b). The works of Jessup, perhaps the only authoritative work on "Indies architec-
    ture" written in English, remains essential to my basic understanding of this architec-
    tural movement.

18 Henri Maclaine Pont, "Javaansche Architectuur," *Djawa*, 3e Jrg, 1923, 112–27,
    159–70; 4e Jrg, 1924, 44–73.

19 In 1924, Maclaine Pont was also involved in undertaking an archeological project for the
    reconstruction of the ruins of the fourteenth-century Majapahit kingdom (Leerdam
    1995). The nobility of the indigenous civilization was seen as an important factor to
    provide a consciousness of self-sufficiency indispensible for the emergence of a modern
    society. The colonial excavation of "indigenous" civilization, however, also contributed
    to the rise of nationalism. For this latter aspect, see Oetomo (1961); Reid (1979).

20 Anthony King (1976: 58–66) has written about the unplanned emergence of British
    colonial third culture in India. Since the late nineteenth century, colonial Indonesia
    was subjected by a policy that regulated cultural differences based on racial cat-
    egories. This had put an end to a period of an emerging unplanned "Indische
    culture" in the early colonial society of Indonesia (Milone 1966–7). Indeed, we could
    conceive the Ethical Policy as an institutionalized "third culture." For a discussion of
    Indonesian "third culture" as it is formed through colonial policy, see Doorn (1983);
    Stoler (1989, 1992).

21 The notion of "logos" is from Alberto Perez-Gomez (1983: 311) who argues that it
    emerged in the "West" from the "undifferentiated product of a technological world-
    view." This, according to him, has led to the geometry of the Bauhaus, the inter-
    national style, and the modern movement in architecture.

22   Jessup (1982: 36) suggests that the Bandoeng Technische Hoogeschool was "remarkable in being the first of its kind in the Indies."

23   For the young Sukarno, Bandung Technical College was a "white" world where, in
1921, there were only eleven Indonesians among the largely Dutch student body. In
the midst of studying the same engineering subjects as the Dutch, Sukarno (1966: 53)
recalled, "I don't know what magic I possessed. I only know that my presence alone
was sufficient to shut up the belittlers and command respect."

Chapter 2: MODERN ARCHITECTURE AND TRADITIONAL POLITY

1   In this essay, the terms "modernity" and "modern" are used interchangeably as social
and cultural concepts, while "modernist" and "modernism" are used to represent an
architectural and urban design movement, developed in Europe in the 1920s. For a
history of modernist "international style" architecture, see Frampton (1980).

2   See King (1976, 1990, 1995); Rabinow (1989); AlSayyad (1992); Wright (1992);
Crinson (1996); Yeoh (1996); Home (1997); Nalbantoglu and Wong (1997).

3   In Boddy's account, Sukarno was assumed to be a dictator who cherished "modernist
architecture" and disregarded traditional Indonesian spatial and architectural concepts.

4   Kampung refers to the unplanned poor settlements that grow in the urban area,
usually built without any support of utilities from the municipality. For a nuanced discussion on various types of kampung, see Ford (1993) and Part II of this book.

5   Addressing the Parliament in 1966, Sukarno reminded them: "As you know, I am an
architect. Besides, I have been roaming far and wide abroad . . . and everywhere, in
every country, I've seen that the Parliament Building is always the most prestigious . . .
Oh yes, I am indeed a megalomaniac. . ." (as cited in Leclerc 1993: 54). Sukarno had
been dissatisfied with the Parliament – both the building and the people in it.

6   Official figures in this period show the doubling of the population from 1948
(823,000) to 1952 (1,782,000), and again, to 1965 (3,813,000). These numbers do
not take into account the large number of temporary migrants (Abeyasekere 1987:
171).

7   For Takdir Alisjahbana, the incorporation of the neighborhood regions only served a
limited class of the Jakarta population. ". . . due largely to [the] increased affluence,
Djakarta has grown so as to encompass not only the glittering new satellite town of
Kebajoran, but also the area between Bogor and Tjiandjur, where the Djakarta rich
spend their leisure time" (as quoted in Feith and Castles 1970: 322).

8   In this plan, the "kampung's problems" were solved by proposing a simplified "slum
clearance programme." During the period of the Outline Plan, the mayor stated that
under rapid urban transformation, it was difficult to know the aspirations and needs
of Jakarta's citizens, especially those newly arrived from the countryside or other
regions in Indonesia. The Outline Plan proposed only 11 per cent of the budget for
housing which would provide only 1,000 houses each year, when about 14,000 were
required. And the provision of this "modern" housing required "a slum clearance
programme" by which kampung dwellers would be displaced without accommodation (Abeyasekere 1987: 201).

9   "The 350 years of colonialism" was a catchphrase of Sukarno who knew perfectly well, as Anderson (1990: 200) indicates, that "many parts of Indonesia only experienced colonial rule in the twentieth century and many parts of Java only seriously encountered colonialism in the eighteenth century." The claim of the long-term suffering makes sense when we see Sukarno as the latest Javanese ruler who had experienced a series of defeats and catastrophes under Dutch rule (ibid).

10   Sukarno's involvement in the city's display was substantial. Henk Ngantung, an artist of no previous experience in administration, was appointed to be Deputy, and later, Governor of Jakarta from 1960–5. He wrote later that his position as Governor was due to the president and "throughout my term of office there was practically no development or important event . . . that was not blessed or tackled directly or indirectly by Bung Karno (Sukarno)." Ngantung's official memoirs, like those of other Jakarta Mayors and Governors before 1966, are found in *Karya Jaya* (1977). The above citation is from Abeyasekere (1987: 169–70).

11   The Games for the "New Emerging Forces" were only held in 1963, after the Asian Games. Held in Jakarta under the name of GANEFO I (the First Games of the New Emerging Forces), 51 countries from the "non First World" were represented. The Games were established to rival the "Western"-sponsored Olympic Games at the time (Pauker 1965).

12   The notion of "the beacon of the New Emerging Forces" is from Sukarno's speech in 1962. The New Emerging Forces were the new nation–states of Asia and Africa which held their first "Non-alliance" conference in 1955 in Bandung, 100 miles southwest of Jakarta. See Daerah Khusus Ibukota (1962: 30).

13   The 1962 Asian Games generated the largest issue of stamps in the 1950s and 1960s in which public works projects were represented. Leclerc indicates that along with GANEFO (Games of the New Emerging Forces), the "cloverleaf, stadium, conference hall, press center, hotel, all organized a passage way, a space for receiving, gathering, informing, marked out by statues, obelisks, spouting fountains. The outline of the center" (Leclerc 1994: 40).

14   For a parallel discourse of nation-building in the "Third World" using modernist architecture and urban design to represent and transform societies, see Holston (1989); Needell (1995); Bozdogan (1997). For a different strategy, see Vale (1992).

15   Edward Said (1978) has written about Orientalism as a western discourse that created an eternal unchanging platonic vision of the Orient. Anderson's assessment of Javanese culture, while sharing this orientalist paradigm, should be understood as a political interpretation which served to criticize the ways cultures and symbols of the past are institutionalized to justify the power of the ruling regime. Anderson makes a distinction between the capitalized Power and the non-capitalized power. The former represents an ancient Javanese cultural order; the latter is "modern", carrying with it a sense of cultural organization capable of conducting planned change. Here I only use power in a capitalized sense.

16   Thus the fourteenth-century king of Majapahit, as Geertz (1983: 130) indicates, proposed his kingdom in the following diagram. At the center and apex, stood the king; around him and at his feet, the palace; around the palace is the capital composed of

a "reliable, submissive" number of relatively self-contained royal compounds; around the capital, is the realm of the bondsmen's dwellings of impermanent building materials "getting ready to show obedience" at the periphery. See also Tambiah (1985).

17 One striking illustration of this spatial concept, as Anderson (1990: 45) indicates, can be found in the titles of the three of the four rulers in contemporary Java – "Pakubuwana" (Nail of the Universe), "Hamengku Buwana" (Sustainer of the Universe), and "Paku Alam" (Nail of the World) (Anderson 1990).

18 In the Javanese language, there is no etymological distinction between the idea of capital city and that of kingdom; instead, the word *negari* was used to include both. See Anderson (1990: 41); see also Kulke (1991).

19 In his published critique of Sukarno's "Guided Democracy," banned soon afterward, Vice-President Hatta pointed out, ". . . his aim is to realize a true democracy, a 'gotong royong' democracy like that of Indonesian society as it originally existed. He condemns Western-style democracy . . . [that] has broken up national unity and led to the work of development being neglected . . . The guided democracy he has in mind was a means of implementing a planned development by vigorous action under a single leadership . . . Soekarno's guided democracy has become a dictatorship supported by certain groups . . ." Mohammad Hatta in 1960 as cited in Feith and Castles (1970: 139–40).

20 Muhammad Yamin was absorbed into the imagined territory of the Majapahit's mandala. In his address given to a plenary session of the Investigating Committee for the Preparation of Indonesian Independence, a committee which had been proclaimed by the Japanese Military Government in March 1945, Yamin proposed an expanding territory of Indonesia similar to the mandala space of Majapahit kingdom. He stated "As history shows, Papua and the islands adjacent to it have been inhabited by the Indonesian people since time immemorial . . . Papua is within the sphere of Austronesia which is centered on Indonesia . . . What I mean by Papua in this context is that part which used to be ruled by the Dutch . . . Portuguese Timor and North Borneo, being outside the territory of former Dutch rule, constitute enclaves . . . so these areas should come within the control and complete the unity of the State of Indonesia . . . [T]he Malay Peninsula, including the four states (Perlis, Kedah, Kelantan, and Trengganu, the unfederated states of Malaya) . . . was part of Indonesia proper, and its original inhabitants were the same stock as ours (Islamic Indonesia) . . . Uniting Malaya to Indonesia would mean strengthening our position and perfecting our unity in a way which accords with our national aspirations and is consistent with our geopolitical interests as regards air, land and sea. It has been the express and sincere wish of the people there to join us . . . (as quoted in Feith and Castles 1970: 438).

21 At the beginning, the design of the monument was the subject of a nationwide competition held in 1956 in which 222 architects, artists and engineers received a briefing from the President who wanted the Monument ("tugu") to be "a symbol of virile grandeur and bravery . . . an emblem of the people's will to soar on high . . . of rising up to the firmament." However, this aspiration was realized only after the president himself took over the design in 1961 with the help of the "palace architect," Soedarsono. The building site was soon opened, while the 1951 Proclamation

Monument, erected at the very place independence was proclaimed (Sukarno's office at the time) was torn down. See Leclerc (1993: 40–1).

22 As phrased in a report on the National Monument, *Tugu Nasional: Laporan Pemban-gunan*, Jakarta 1978, quoted in Leclerc (1993: 46).

23 At home, artists and architects were gathered by Sukarno to discuss the progress of projects for buildings, statues, streets and gardens. To inspire and educate, architects were taken by Sukarno on his overseas tour (Abeyasekere 1987: 168).

24 Malaysia was identified by the Guided Democracy of Indonesia as a nation of neo-colonial power, since British bases would remain after the independence of the country (1957). For a brief but fuller picture, see Ricklefs (1993: 272–4).

25 In addition to these, the national economy was also facing severe problems, with the Indonesian currency devalued by 75 per cent. A monetary purge was ordered with the effect of reducing the money supply from 34 billion rupiah to 21 billion rupiah at one stroke (Ricklefs 1993: 262–7).

26 It is interesting to see the display models of the city's master plan as they appear in the figures of this chapter: the central boulevard and the Asian Games complex among others. The effect of the representation, the origin of which was reasonably architectural in tradition, is undoubtedly political. It appears here as a fragment of "modern" imagery, wholly detached from its geographical context. In its miniature form, prepared for a bird's-eye-view, the existing and neighboring kampung was summarily removed. The modern architectural space is instantly recognizable as a powerful emblem of what, in the imagination, an exemplary center is *supposed to be*, in contrast to the reality which existed outside the exhibition hall.

27 For an important investigation on this eventful night, see the report of Cornell schol-ars in 1966 (Anderson, McVey and Bunnell, 1971).

28 The institutional and architectural transformation as intended by modernists is too complex to be elaborated on here. It is sufficient to suggest that "the modernist strat-egy of defamiliarization intends to make the city strange. It consists in the attempt to impose a new urban order through a set of transformations that negate previous expectations about urban life" (Holston 1989: 55).

29 For a discussion on tradition as "ideology," instead of as a subject formation of the ruling class, see Hobsbawm (1983).

Chapter 3: RECREATING ORIGINS

1 However, the "cultural roots" of Professor Budihardjo may be broad and heteroge-nous, not in any essential sense reflecting the New Order's conservatism.

2 In essence, the economy of the New Order's Indonesia had relied upon the value of oil, foreign "aid" and multinational corporate investment. Domestic capital, apart from that of the ethnic Chinese, is rather weak. The oil boom of the 1970s and early 1980s had somewhat changed the attitude of the state towards the regulation of foreign investments which, for a short period, enjoyed the privilege of capital accu-mulation (Winters 1996: Chapter 3).

3 The January 1974 "Malari" event was a social protest along a wide spectrum of issues, one of them involving class and ethnic conflict. It also marked, after almost a

decade, the end of a positive relationship between students, especially at the University of Indonesia, and the New Order regime.

4   This section draws for its insights on two important discussions on this project: Anderson (1990) and Pemberton (1994a). Anderson provides a socio-political background behind the emergence of the project and argues that "Beautiful Indonesia" represents the New Order's search for "new" continuity to the past. Similarly Pemberton also discusses the project as an erasure of the past. However, he further argues that this "invented tradition" has a strange effect, offering "authenticity" to the minds of Indonesians. I would extend their argument by focusing on the creation of the other side of "tradition," namely, "development" that completes the "power" of Javanese culture.

5   Mini is a popular name for the Beautiful Indonesia in Miniature Park. The park seems to provide for the Indonesians, in Berlant's (1993: 407) words, "a consciousness of the nation with no imagination of agency . . . in other words, national knowledge has itself become a modality of national amnesia, [an] incitement to forgetting that leaves simply the patriotic trace for real and metaphorically infantilized citizens, that confirms that the nation exists and that we are in it."

6   Booklet prepared for Mrs Suharto as cited in Sumintardja (1972). Sumintardja, one of the co-ordinators of the Regional Housing Center, indicates that the typical traditional domestic building in Indonesia was never constructed to endure for "hundreds of years."

7   For a discussion of replica and monument in the age of official nationalism, see Anderson (1998: 46–57).

8   Sudradjat (1991: 101) reported that the State Department of Inventory Project and Documentation of Regional Cultures published monographs on a series of regional houses between 1981–7: Bali (1981/2); East of Nusa Tenggara (1981/2); Irian Jaya (1981/2); West of Nusa Tenggara (1981/2); Central Java (1982); Jogyakarta (1982); West Java (1982); Riau (1983/4); Aceh (1984); Central Kalimantan (1985); South Kalimantan (1985); South Sumatra (1985) Central Sulawesi (1986); Jambi (1986); Lampung (1986); North Sulawesi (1986); North Sumatra (1986); Southeast Sulawesi (1986); West Kalimantan (1986).

9   The experiment brought together some 60 students. The methodology was said to be derived from Demetri Porphyrios' "Building and Rational Architecture," *Architectural Design*, 54, June 16, 1984. Prijotomo's experiment has been further theorized in "Bentuk Dalam Arsitektur Klasik Indonesia" (Form in Indonesian Classical Architecture) in his imaginative *Dinamika Arstektur Indonesia*.

10 *Tempo*, "Joglo = Jogya – Solo," June 1, 1984: 58; and "Membongkar Pilar Yunani" (Dismantling Greece's Pillar), September 1, 1984: 18. This event initiated discussion among a group of architects, mainly academics, who strongly disagreed with the governor's idea.

11 I would like to thank Iwan Sudradjat for providing me with materials on the recent extension of the Institute of Technology at Bandung.

12 Iwan Sudradjat, correspondence, July 8, 1996.

13 Constructed with loans provided by Japanese capital, the buildings in the "modern"

zone characterize the shift of global economic power from one established upon the colonial connection to another based on the regional capitalist network.

14 Here we might speculate that the word "modern" is used to signify the transnationality of this final zone of the campus, instead of Indonesian "moderen" which would have been parallel to the other phonologically-adapted coinages "konservasi/historis" and "transisi."

15 As quoted in *Mimar*, 12, 42, March 1992: 65–9. Like the extension of the Institute of Technology at Bandung, the new campus of the University of Indonesia was designed by a consortium of Indonesian architects. It was inaugurated by President Suharto in 1985. For an opinion on the success of the new campus to represent "Indonesian Architecture," see Wiwiek Usmi ("Bentuk Tradisional, Wajah Sebuah Kampus Baru" (Traditional in Form, The Face of A New Campus), *Asri*, 53, 1987: 21–6); Zein Wiryoprawiro, ("Citra Arsitektur Indonesia Untuk Kampus Baru U.I." (An Image of An Indonesian Architecture For the New Campus of the University of Indonesia), *Konstruksi*, 12, 117, 1988).

16 The very strategy of reviewing typological characteristics of significant buildings and then abstracting their archetypes into a generic principle from which a design process starts is far from "traditional." It is inherited from the functionalist science of architecture first introduced by French architectural theorist, Jacques-Nicolas-Louis Durand (1760–1834). See Perez-Gomez (1983: Chapter 9).

17 For a critique of campus normalization of Indonesian Universities, see Akhmadi (1981).

18 Buildings identified as "lokal," "tradisional," "daerah" have often been understood as possessing the principles (characterized by use of the English letter C) of Continuity and Connectivity of Culture, Climate and Craft which, in the time of economic development, would supposedly prevent an architectural, if not national, crisis of identity. See Budihardjo (1991: 55).

19 This "tradition" seems to pervade other cultural productions. In the realm of literature, as Foulcher (1995: 149) points out, "the construction of a postcolonialist identity upon and through the dislocations wrought by colonialism has never been a central motif in Indonesian creative expression, nor has it been a major concern of literary critical debate."

20 On the American involvement of architects and urban planners in the Third World's development, see "U.S. Building Abroad," *Architectural Forum*, 102, January 1955: 98–119.

21 Interest in the built environment of the "non-western" world proliferated after the influential work of Amos Rapoport (1969) and others, paradigmatic of architectural anthropology that studied "non-western" architecture. For a discussion on early pioneers in this area, see Oliver's introduction to Paul Oliver (ed.) (1996). For a discussion on architectural regionalism within the academic tradition, see Colquhoun (1997).

22 *Indonesia Property Report*, 1, 2, 1995: 90.

Chapter 4: THE VIOLENCE OF CATEGORIES

1 Though the city, in most historical cases, is defined as both the target and theme of national representation, there have been cases, at particular historical moments, where the nation takes its identity in the space of the rural.

2 Benedict Anderson (1991: Chapter 10) indicates that this possibility of imagining "others" as part of "the same" is made possible by a range of representations associated with the state apparatus, such as newspapers, maps, and museums. By analogy, architecture and the city is one of these representations. We could say that communities are produced through the material and spatial environment. They are not constructed out of thin air. In this sense, the city, while embodying the state, is forming and transforming national subjectivity. For a discussion on space (including its formal and material properties) as both the product of and the condition of possibility of social relations, see Lefebvre (1991).

3 For a study of the political cultures of the postcolonial nation–state through the ways in which monumental buildings such as the capitol are represented, see Vale (1992).

4 As cited in *Kompas* May 22, 1998, "perusuh menjarah" means "rioters loot."

5 Political theorist Claude Lefort (1986: 306) indicates that the embodiment of the people by the figure of the supreme leader is a solution adopted by a society whose united imaginary is threatened. Lefort writes, "The Egocrat coincides with himself, as society is supposed to coincide with itself. An impossible swallowing up of the body in the head begins to take place, as does an impossible swallowing up of the head in the body. The attraction of the whole is no longer dissociated from the attraction of the parts." This process of embodiment, as I will show, needs a spatial and architectural representation.

6 The accelerating economic crises, the increasing internal political conflicts, social unrest and rebellions in the Outer Islands marked the period of the end of the 1950s. All these events undermined the authority of the center. This perhaps explains why "populist politics" was not initiated before the late 1950s. For a fuller account on the relationship between city building and the decline of Sukarno's rule, See Chapter 2.

7 John Pemberton suggested that the term "rakyat," which I would take as the revolutionary subject of Sukarno's populist politics, today appears as an absent body. In Siegel's (1998) account, this body appears as an imagined figure invested with the meaning of criminality, death and menace. Reference to Pemberton's account is in Siegel (1998: 141).

8 The number killed has never been exactly calculated. It was estimated at some 4,000. Outside estimates have doubled this figure (Pemberton 1994: 317).

9 For a fuller analysis of this theme, see Foucault's discussion of the torture and execution of the failed regicide Damiens in 1757.

10 The events took place during the visit of Japanese Prime Minister, Kakuei Tanaka. The reasons for the upheaval ranged from economic disparities among social groups, corruption in the state's development policies – which served the interests of "foreigners" and the rich – to internal conflicts within the Indonesian military. Student protests expanded into large-scale riots when unemployed youths joined in and began burning and looting shops and cars. In the course of two days before the army intervened, at least 11 people died and 137 were injured, while 552 cars and 117 buildings were damaged (Abeyasekere 1987: 240). The Malari incident, as the riot came to be known, shocked the government to its very roots particularly by "its

inability to maintain law and order during the visit of an extremely important guest" (as cited in Schwarz 1994: 34).

11 "Tut Wuri Handayani" of the New Order is a corrupted version of the theory of Ki Hadjar Dewantara, the founder of the pre-war, and pre-Independent Indonesian education system.

12 For an extended discussion of the notion of "development" ("pembangunan") see Heryanto (1988). Heryanto indicates that the ideological keyword of the New Order, "pembangunan," is essentially based on modernization theory, but is conducted under a tradition-like polity. See the conclusion of this book.

13 For a discussion on the relations between the Indonesian family and the state, see Shiraishi (1997).

14 "Kampung" is generally understood as the "residential area for lower classes in town or city" (Echols and Shadily 1992: 258). It is characterized as an unregistered, unregulated residential area whose buildings are not in conformity with building regulations. It is important to notice that "kampung" is a generalized term that could hardly capture the varieties of built environment contained by it. There are kampungs with largely permanent structures, and there are also kampungs with temporary dwellings. A kampung could also be composed of two storey stone houses with garages and temporary quarters made of bamboo and leaves. For a typological analysis of kampungs, see Ford (1993). It is often reported that two thirds of the Jakartan population live in a kampung (Darrundono 1991).

15 Ralph Gakenheimer, professor of urban planning at the MIT and consultant on transportation issues for the Indonesian government, cited in Michael Specter, "Letter from Jakarta," *Far Eastern Economic Review*, March 8, 1984.

16 For a parallel urban experience in Southeast Asia, see Tadiar (1993).

17 *Kompas*, April 13, 1996.

18 As cited in Margot Cohen, *Far Eastern Economic Review*, March 13, 1997: 46.

19 The real estate housing exhibition has become an important arena for agencies involved in marketing, consulting, information services and the production of architectural knowledge. In 1994, for instance, there were no less than 88 housing exhibitions in major cities of Indonesia, varying in scale, but with similar subject matter. See *Katalog Pameran ke-9 Rumah dan Interior 1995*, Jakarta Convention Center, 13–21 January 1995.

20 Beyond this phenomenal observation by sociologists, there was little agreement concerning "the definition of the middle class and the identification of its value." H.W. Dick (1990: 63). Richard Robison (1996), who has been dealing with this phenomenon, used the term "middle class" to cover a large range of subjects, institutionalized under Suharto's regime, from the upper middle class businessmen, military groups and politicians to the populist lower middle class students, minor officials and religious workers. These accounts, valuable as they are, take "middle class" as a sociological category based on occupation without showing how it is constructed through material and spatial representation such as the form of the city itself. In what ways do those with "middle class" status, made possible by the policy and social

environment of the New Order, represent themselves either stylistically, socially, spatially, architecturally, in relation to their kampung and/or countryside counterparts?

21 "Presiden Suharto canangkan gerakan disiplin nasional," *Kompas*, May 21, 1995: 1. I am indebted to Larry Chavis Jr (1997) for the references in this paragraph.

22 "Military launches disciplinary programme," *Jakarta Post*, May 24, 1995: 3.

23 Budi Winarno et al., "Disiplin nasional: tertib bersama kader berompi," *Sinar*, December 9, 1995: 83.

Chapter 5: COLONIAL REPLICA

1 I use the term "middle class" (Robison 1996) to cover a large range of social subjects conceivable under Suharto's regime, from businessmen, military groups and politicians to the populist students, minor officials and religious workers who represent themselves either stylistically, socially or economically, as "above" their kampung and/or countryside counterparts (see Chapter 4).

2 I suspect this perception of the kampung derives from the kampung's relation to the city. Wiryomartono (1995: 171–82) uses the term "kampung-kota" to depict the inseparable and dependent relations of the kampung and the city. For a study on the history of and change in a kampung in Jakarta over time, see Jellinek (1991).

3 For a study of the micropolitics of a kampung in Jakarta under the New Order, see Jellinek (1991).

4 Rabinow (1989) has elaborated on these men who were "neither heroes nor villains nor anonymous citizens. But they were pragmatic technicians seeking to find solutions to public problems in time of crises" (Rabinow 1989: 16).

5 The notion of "social modernity" is used by Rabinow (1989: 15) to represent the beginnings of a modern understanding of society as a historical and natural whole, as well as the beginnings of society as a target of state intervention. Here, it was on the level of knowledge about social and biological milieu that "opened the way for new scientific discourses, new administrative practices, and new conceptions of social order, and hence ushered in a long period of experimentation with spatial/scientific/social technologies."

6 It was in this era too, as Shiraishi (1990: 27) indicates, that a daughter of the regent of Jepara, R.A. Kartini, began her first letter to her Dutch pen pal with the sentence "I have so desired to make an acquaintance with a 'modern' girl."

7 The Kampung Question (Kampongvraagstuk) consisted of a collective concern of colonial social reformers towards the physical and "inhuman" condition of the kampung. See Heiden (1990) and Cobban (1993).

8 The first "kampung improvement" scheme took place in 1925, after elaborate studies by Dutch urban planners and social reformers. They made visible the insanitary condition of the kampung which threatened public health in the city (Milone 1966: 30).

9 For an overview of Karsten's work, see Bogaers and Ruijter (1986) and Cobban (1992).

10 The most well-known report of the urban condition of the Indies by Thomas Karsten is compiled under "Town Development in the Indies," in W.F. Wertheim et al. (1954). I suspect this collection is the only English translation of the Dutch documents on urban planning.

11   For Nas (1986), Karsten's approach is an "Applied Urban Development Sociology," which conceived that "the aspects of the problems that arise are planological, sociological, administrative, juridical and historical" (Nas 1986: 95–6).

12   For a panoramic description of Batavia in terms of conflicting ideals as well as mutual relations between communities of Arabs, Chinese, Eurasians, and Europeans, see Abeyasekere (1987: Chapter 3).

13   For the best depiction of this issue, see Toer (1982, 1990a).

14   For a discussion on Karsten's town planning concept in the context of European planning, see Cobban (1992).

15   Rabinow (1989: 132) used the example of a colonial experiment conducted by biologist de Lanessan to describe the transformation of two Indochinese men who eat the same food and live in the same climate though coming from different villages. One is to be made a sailor, another a rifleman. After a few years, differences appear. The sailor becomes muscular and his character European; the rifleman grows thin and peaceful. The explanation was believed to lie in the food (the sailor ate French food) and the milieu (the villager imitates, and is influenced by, his French mate).

16   For a discussion on how to develop Javanese cultures from a perspective of the Javanese elites, see Shiraishi (1981).

17   Along with concern about the political and cultural relevance of Javanese tradition to "progress," the Volksraad (People's Council), founded in 1918, and the earlier indigenous elite's grouping of Budi Utomo, began to discuss the condition of the kampung. The civilization of Java was thus linked to the understanding of the kampung in Java.

18   At the turn of the century, the Dutch colony in the Indies had expanded to make up the whole territory of present day Indonesia, except for East Timor.

19   The economic pressure that pushed the Dutch to pursue "agricultural products" saleable on world markets resulted in an indigenous (Javanese) economy that was kept fundamentally unchanged. As a result, as Clifford Geertz points out, "[t]hey brought Indonesia's crops into the 'modern world' but not the people." (as cited in Otten 1986: 119).

20   The concern about Javanese civilization was related to the Dutch Ethical Policy, which understood it to be a potential cultural model for the Outer Islands of the Netherlands Indies as a whole. Governor-General van Limburg, in his opening speech to the Volksraad's Congress for Javanese cultural development, remarked: "[the Volksraad] will be able to attain perfection as the organ to express the will of the population of the whole Netherlands Indies only after civilization has come to maturity in all parts of the archipelago" (cited in Shiraishi 1981: 93). Here, the Governor-General was referring to Javanese civilization as a potential agent for the perfection of the whole Netherlands Indies.

21   The "ten commandments of colonization" were drawn up by C.C.J. Maassen, an official of the Department of the Interior in charge of agricultural colonization in the later 1930s (cited from Pelzer 1948: 210).

22   Since the ideal Indonesian family was formed under the patriarchal state, the gender dimension was already marked from the beginning. Women, while they could find themselves classified as "undesirable people," could not, however, be classified as

"transmigrants." They therefore have no claims at all to the "benefits" provided by the programme.

23 Neo-colonialism is a less straightforward form of domination (economic, cultural and ideological) and one that can be seen as a continuation of formal colonialism, which has been overthrown. (Said 1993: 5–12).

Chapter 6: CUSTODIANS OF (TRANS)NATIONALITY

1 Mohammad Hatta, Vice-presidential address to an All-Indonesian Cultural Congress held at Bandung in 1952. First published in Indonesia, *Madjalah Kebudayaan*, III, Jan–Mar, 1952: 20–30.

2 "Exile is the nursery of nationality," claimed the English politician–historian, Lord Acton. Anderson points out that the first explicitly Indonesian–nationalist organization, the Perhimpoenan Indonesia, was established (in 1922) half a globe away from the Netherlands Indies. See Anderson 1998: Chapter 3.

3 Ariel Heryanto, "A Class Act," *Far Eastern Economic Review*, June 16, 1994: 30.

4 *Media Indonesia*, June 7, 1998.

5 On the relation between Indonesian nationalism and anti-Sinicism at the turn of the century, see Takashi Shiraishi (1997).

6 This chapter uses the notion "Indonesian" to represent "indigenous" people, though "indigenous people" here is ambivalent as many "Chinese Indonesians" could also be considered "indigenous" (socially, historically, culturally, and linguistically). What those considering Indonesian Chinese as "different national subjects," as an "exclusive community" and so on, often neglect to mention is the lack of acceptance by "Indonesians" of the "Indonesian Chinese."

7 For a discussion on how Suharto's Indonesia could largely be seen as a regime produced and sustained by foreign and domestic capital, see Winters 1996. Under this regime, the Indonesian Chinese was produced as a subject who is economically "powerful," but politically a pariah. See also note 11.

8 Emily Thorton, "Name Dropping," *Far Eastern Economic Review*, 158, 29, July 20, 1995: 74.

9 Purwanto Setiawan SH, "Selamat Tinggal Istilah Asing," *Gatra*, June 17, 1995: 8.

10 James Riady, "Lippo Group Hails Nationalism," *Indonesia Business Weekly*, 3, 26, June 12, 1995: 35.

11 The misleading idea that all Indonesian Chinese are rich and that they all become rich through a collusion with government officials at the expense of the "indigenous people" has caused endless tension among many people. This knowledge has also been used by the leaders of the state to control the Chinese by routinely unleashing society's deep resentment against them as a way to remind them of their precarious position. Heryanto (1998) notes the conspicuous invisibility of reports on the existence of the Chinese poor.

12 The country's ten giant developers control up to 70 per cent of land for housing projects in the Jakarta, Bogor, Tangerang and Bekasi (Jabotabek) area. See "The New Suburbia: Chasing the Indonesian Dream," *Economic and Business Review Indonesia*, 156, April 8, 1995: 8. See also "Gonjang-Ganjing Bisnis Property" (Ups and downs of

the property business), *Info Business*, 32nd edition, Year II, 16 July 1996. This issue of *Info Business* has a listing of 20 of the largest property and real estates companies, of which at least 18 can be recognized as owned by ethnic Chinese (60–1).

13   "Will the Bubble Burst?" *Economic and Business Review Indonesia*, 141, December 24, 1994: 6–15.

14   Akbar Tandjung, "New Towns and Satellite Cities: Problems and Prospects," *Indonesia Property Report*, 1, 2, 1995.

15   "The New Suburbia," op. cit: 6.

16   The identity formation of the Chinese in diaspora, according to Aihwa Ong (1993, and Ong and Nonini 1997), should be understood in intersecting national and trans-national political arenas. For a recent collection on the historical background of the Chinese in Southeast Asia, see Reid (ed.) (1996).

17   "Chinese New Year is a family affair," *Jakarta Post*, February 18, 1996: 1.

18   In her observation of the cultural orientation of the Indonesian businessmen of Chinese descent, Mely G. Tan indicated that Ciputra, among others, pays serious attention to Feng Shui (the Chinese art of geomancy). The norms of Feng Shui may have gained considerable influence in the Indonesian real estate business, but the forms in which it is publicly represented are "western," instead of explicity "Chinese." For a discussion on the influence of Feng Shui on the business of the ethnic Chinese, see Mely G. Tan (1996).

19   The convergence of "English" and "Chinese" was most clearly represented in the recently completed elite school of Pelita Harapan, built as part of the Lippo Village. It provoked debate as it became the "favorite" school of many of the rich Indonesian Chinese families, among others, since the youngest students will spend up to 80 per cent of their time speaking English. See Margot Cohen, "Eton of the East: Elite School Raises the Hackles of Nationalists," *Far Eastern Economic Review*, July 22, 1993: 20, 22.

20   Some scholars have argued that there has been a softening of racial and cultural tension at the popular level between indigenous Indonesians and their ethnic Chinese counterparts during the Suharto regime. It was the state that generated – from behind – "anti-Chinese" sentiments at particular strategic moments to legitimize its rule (Heryanto 1998). While this observation is correct, it undermines the complexity of the kind of political culture in Indonesia that demands an understanding beyond a mere state/civil society division.

21   Susumu Awanohara, "The Perennial Problem," *Far Eastern Economic Review*, September 6, 1984: 26–7.

22   *Media Indonesia*, August 5, 1998.

23   In Heryanto's words, "the Chinese have been branded asocial and unpatriotic, and blamed for supposedly pursuing selfish interests and for remaining aloof from much of national life" (1998: 103).

24   This has been the reason why Lieutenant General Prabowo resented the Chinese. See Margaret Scott's interview, "Indonesia Reborn?" *The New York Review of Books*, August 13, 1998.

25   At its aftermath, the May riot has been considered, above all, as a "moral" move-

ment. See "Bukan untuk tandingi pemerintah Majelis Amanat rakyat adalah gerakan moral," *Media Indonesia*, May 16, 1998; see also "Wiranto: Reformasi berarti peringatan bagi bangsa," *Antara*, September 19, 1998.

Chapter 7: Professional and National Dreams

1   See, for instance, Vale (1992); Perera (1998).

2   "Stability" in this context could be understood as an institutionalization of cultures and traditions to suit a regime based on military authoritarianism and a capitalist economy (see Chapter 3).

3   Homi Bhabha (1984) indicates that the construction of the colonial Other will be recognizably the same as the colonizer but still different: "not quite/not white." He gives the example of an Indian, educated in English, who works in the Indian civil service and mediates between the colonial power and the colonized people. This Indian becomes, in certain respects, "English." The production of this mimic English-man produces a disturbing effect for the colonizer. While Bhabha's inquiry is focussed on the psychological effect on the colonizer, here I examine the "colonized" who negotiates his or her "whiteness" within the social field of the decolonized nation.

4   A series of inaugural lectures on architecture by Dutch professors had been given in the Dutch East Indies "technical school" since the 1920s. All remained in Dutch, but only that by van Romondt was published in Indonesian in the same year (1954), as *Menuju Ke Suatu Arsitektur Indonesia* (Towards an Indonesian Architecture). The reason for this might be that this was the only postcolonial inaugural lecture by a Dutch professor. V.R. van Romondt (1903-74) taught architecture at Bandung Institute of Technology in which he was also the first chair of the department until his retirement in 1962. A total of 110 Indonesian architects graduated under his tenure. See Wastu Pragantha (1983).

5   The idea of "transition" was not clearly explained; for van Romondt, it could supposedly describe a stage of development that would transform Indonesia from an agriculturally-based society into an industrial one or it could also meant a transition from Dutch colonialism into an Indonesian national state.

6   Considered to be the first architectural journal published after the transfer of sovereignty, *Arsitektur* was established in 1958 by "Ikatan Mahasiswa Arsitektur – Gunadharma" (Architectural Students Union called Gunadharma – a name given to the creator of the ancient monument of Borobudur) edited by Hario Sabrang and Kwee Hin Goan.

7   The belief in God under the Indonesian national philosophy of "Pancasila" is represented as incompatible with the "modernity" of the West.

8   This view has been paradigmatic. Most prominently found in the works of Josef Prijotomo and Eko Budihardjo, architectural theorists and critics who became prominent in the 1980s after their return from further study in the United States and England. Budihardjo (1991: 55) identifies the uniqueness of Indonesian "vernacular" architecture in terms of the five principles of the English letter "C": Continuity and Connectivity of Culture, Climate, and Craft. Cultivation of these attributes in the time of national development would supposedly prevent an architectural crisis of identity.

9   In this respect, despite his anti-traditionalist stance, van Romondt's awareness of the importance of an Indonesian architectural tradition in constituting an "Indonesian architecture," soon conferred on him the title of "father of Indonesian traditional architecture" by his former students.

10   The article entitled "Menuju Arsitektur Indonesia" (Towards Indonesian Architecture) was reprinted as the lead article in Kadardono's edition (1984) of *Arsitektur Indonesia 2: Masalah dan Potensi*, a collection of essays used for teaching history and theory of architecture in the schools of architecture in Surabaya.

11   Sidharta, "Peran Arsitek, Pendidikan dan Masa Depan Arsitektur Indonesia," (The Role of Architects, Education and the Future of Indonesian Architecture), *Media IAI*, October, 1984; reprinted in Kadardono (ed.) (1984). Professor Sidharta was one of the first generation of architects graduating from Bandung Institute of Technology in 1958. He continued his studies in the Department of Architecture, University of Washington, Seattle, USA in the mid-1960s and has been a professor in Diponegoro University, Semarang, Central Java since 1984. A reference to Ki Hajar Dewantara, the founder of the Indonesian Indigenous "national" school at the turn of the century, was indeed given in the 1982 congress "Towards Indonesian Architecture." It says, "Kihajar Dewantara indicates that a national cultural identity is produced and developed through a continuous attempt to meld the existing cultural values with foreign ones" (Pragantha 1981: 29).

12   Anderson (1999) characterizes Indonesian "official" nationalism as being based on seeking "absolutely splendid ancestors" betraying therefore the "forward-looking" character of nationalism initiated by the earlier nationalists.

Chapter 8: "SPECTRE OF COMPARISONS"

1   Cited from *Asian Architect and Contractor*, June 1989: 44.

2   For a discussion of the effect of the collapse of Southeast Asian economies, and its impact on the architectural and urban transformation of major cities in China, see King and Kusno (2000).

3   See the reports of the Asian Congress of Architects, first held in October 25–28, 1984, Manila, Philippines (see *Singapore Institute of Architects Journal*, no. 127, December 1984); The meeting of the Architects Regional Council of Asia (ARCASIA) which now includes 15 nations in Asia (See *ARCHASIA*, 1994: content); see also collections of papers and debates in the Aga Khan Award for Architecture (1983).

4   See the series of reports in the *Singapore Institute of Architects Journal*, particularly no. 127, Dec. 1984, that covers the first congress on Asian architecture. See also the detailed review of the congress by Winand Klassen (1984).

5   For a discussion on the contradictory creation of a region in Asia by Euro-American forces, see Arif Dirlik (1992).

6   Southeast Asian historian, Oliver W. Wolters, calls this processes a "localization" of foreign materials in various Southeast Asian contexts. See Wolters (1982) especially pages 52–94. What is important here is not the existence or the truth of local statements that are presumably other than the "foreign" materials but rather, how the local subjects "discovered" their cultural ancestry in and through this interaction with the "foreign."

7   The notion of "orientalism in reverse" is used by Sadik Jalal al-'Azm (1981) to describe a phenomenon in which the victim of Orientalism applies the readily available structures, styles and ontological biases of Orientalism upon themselves.

8   This maneuver can be seen as a kind of "subversive strategy" used in postcolonial criticism to represent the subaltern agency in order to negotiate its own authority through a process of displacing colonial strategies. See Spivak (1988).

9   The notion of "naga" in sanskrit means serpent, a creature equated with water which, for Jumsai, is the original space of human civilization. But the application of the term "naga" has also been understood as "based on the factor of aboriginality, that is to say the fact of their being aboriginal or native to the regions inhabited by them and their ancestors from time immemorial" (Singaravelu 1970). Thailand is the only area of the territory that was not formally colonized by European imperial powers, but it was certainly affected by imperialism as well as by Orientalist scholarship. This historical specificity of Thailand, though not explored here or in Jumsai's own text, should circumscribe any reading of modern Thai's cultural discourses. For a discussion on the modern politics of Thailand, see Anderson (1998) and Thongchai Winichakul (1994).

10 Jumsai was referring to the "land-based" civilization that "marginalized" his "water-based" civilization. Indeed the term "Southeast Asia" reflects the Orientalist's structure of knowledge that represents Southeast Asia as a periphery of the two Great Traditions: the South of China and East of India. In this perspective, Southeast Asia represents "familiar shapes of India to the West and China to the North." For a discussion of the polemic surrounding the term "Southeast Asia," see Emmerson (1984).

11 For a discussion on the long-standing thesis of the "Indianization of Southeast Asia," see Wolters (1982).

12 One might compare this diagram with the "tree of architecture" drawn by Banister Fletcher for the canonical "eurocentric" account of modern architecture.

13 For a concise, but more focused discussion of the house on stilts (with a steep thatched roof) as the common heritage of Southeast Asian countries, see also Sumet Jumsai (1983, 1986).

14 The erection of high-rise monuments is perhaps what Deyan Sudjic suggests is an effort to "make nowhere suddenly into somewhere." The effort, however, works not merely in terms of physical height, but also in relation to the forms (and not less the norms) that the tower assumes (as cited in King 1996).

15 For Singapore's politics of development, see Wee (1993). Notice here the paradox of Singapore's leader, Lee Kuan Yew who, in the last quarter of his rule, propagated the "Confucian" ethic as the basis of "modern" Singapore.

Conclusion: BEYOND THE POSTCOLONIAL?

1   As Heryanto (1988: 21) indicates "In the Indonesian family . . . there is a prohibition against children 'mendurhaka' (sinning) against their Father, no matter how culpable the Father in the eyes of his children. A Father is a father to his children not only during his life time, but even after his death. Likewise, children have only one natal father, not only in their lifetimes but even after their deaths."

2   From the original text proposed for the bestowal of the title "Father of Development" on President Suharto, written by Minister Abdul Gafur and his team, as cited in Heryanto (ibid.).

3   With the exception of the works of Pramodya Ananta Toer, Foulcher also indicates the *absence* of the sense of cultural inauthenticity, a founding moment of postcolonialism in other cases, in the literatures of postcolonial Indonesia.

4   For an interesting account of the role of "lingua franca" in the formation of political identities in the Indies of 1920s, see James Siegel (1997).

5   "Political rationalities" are "a form of power not merely coincident with colonialism," but are concerned above all, "with disabling old forms of life by systematically breaking down their conditions, and with constructing in their place new conditions so as to enable – indeed, so as to oblige – new forms of life to come into being." See Scott (1995: 193).

6   For an account of the ways "Bahasa Indonesia" is used *against* the authoritarian, neo-feudal "official" nationalism of the Suharto regime, see Anderson (1996a).

References

Abbas, M.A. (1997) *Hong Kong: Culture and the Politics of Disappearance*, Minneapolis: University of Minnesota Press.

Abeyasekere, S. (1987) *Jakarta: A History*, Singapore: Oxford University Press.

Adam, A. (1995) *The Vernacular Press: The Emergence of Modern Indonesian Consciousness*, Ithaca: Cornell University, Southeast Asia Program, 1995.

Aga Khan Award for Architecture (1983) *Architecture and Identity: Proceedings of the Regional Seminar,* Kuala Lumpur, Malaysia, July 25–27.

—— (1983a) *Architecture and Community: Building in the Islamic World Today*, Islamic Publications Ltd.

Akhmadi, H. (1981) *Breaking the Chains of Oppression of the Indonesian People: Defence Statement at His Trial on Charges of Insulting the Head of the State*, Ithaca: Cornell University, Modern Indonesian Project.

AlSayyad, N. (ed.) (1992) *Forms of Dominance: On the Architecture and Urbanism of the Colonial Entreprise,* Aldershot: Avebury.

Anderson, B. (1965) 'Indonesia: Unity vs. Progress,' *Current History*, February: 75–81.

Anderson, B., McVey, R. and Bunnell, F. (1971). *A Preliminary Analysis of the October 1, 1965, Coup in Indonesia*, Ithaca, N.Y. Cornell Modern Indonesia Project, Interim Report Series.

Anderson, B. (1990) *Language and Power: Exploring Political Cultures in Indonesia*, Ithaca: Cornell University Press.

—— (1991) *Imagined Communities: Reflections on the Origin and Spread of Nationalism*, London: Verso (revised edition).

—— (1992) 'The Influence of the East Timor Issue on Indonesian Politics,' lecture at the Catholic University of Braga, Portugal, May 27, 1992.

—— (1996) 'Language, Fantasy, Revolution: Java 1900–1950,' in Lev, D. and McVey, R. (eds) *Making Indonesia: Essays on Modern Indonesia in Honor of George McT. Kahin*, Ithaca: Cornell University, Southeast Asia Program.

Anderson, B. (1996a) 'Colonial Language Policies in Indonesia and the Philippines: A Contrast in Intended Aims and Unintended Outcomes,' in Gracia-Moreno, L. and Pfeiffer, P. (eds) *Text and Nation: Cross Disciplinary Essays on Cultural and National Identities*, Columbia: Camden House.

—— (1998) *The Spectre of Comparisons: Nationalism, Southeast Asia, and the World*, London: Verso.

—— (1999) ''Indonesian Nationalism Today and in the Future,'' *New Left Review*, 235, May/June: 3–17.

Appadurai, A. (1995) 'Playing with Modernity: The Decolonization of Indian Cricket,' in Breckenridge, C. (ed.) *Consuming Modernity: Public Culture in a South Asian World*, Minneapolis: University of Minnesota Press.

Appadurai, A. and Breckenridge, C. (1995) 'Public Modernity in India,' in Breckenridge, C. (ed.) *Consuming Modernity: Public Culture in a South Asian World*, Minneapolis: University of Minnesota Press.

Arsitek Indonesia (1985) 'Ikatan Arsitek Indonesia: proses pembentukan dan kegiatannya hingga saat ini,' *Arsitek Indonesia*, February: 9–10.

Arsitektur (1959) 'Perkembangan Pendapat Arsitektonis Dalam Abad 20,' *Arsitektur* 2, 2: 10–13, 21, 27.

Ashcroft, B., Griffiths, G. and Tiffin, H. (1989) *The Empire Writes Back: Theory and Practice in Post-colonial Literatures,* New York: Routledge.

Atmadi, P. (1984) 'Arsitektur dan Perkembangannya di Indonesia,' *Cipta*, 64: 55–63.

Ave, Jan B. (1989) '' 'Indonesia,' 'Insulinde,' and 'Nusantara': Dotting the I's and Crossing the T,'' *BKI*, Deel 145, Afl. 2 and 3: 220–34.

Berlant, L. (1993) 'Theory of Infantile Citizenship,' *Public Culture*, 5: 1–16.

Bhabha, H. (1983) 'Difference, Discrimination, and the Discourse of Colonialism,' in Barker, F. et al. (eds) *The Politics of Theory,* Colchester, England: University of Essex.

—— (1991) 'The Postcolonial Critic – Homi Bhabha interviewed by David Bennett and Terry Collits,' *Arena*, 96: 47–63.

—— (1994) *The Location of Culture,* New York: Routledge.

Boddy, T. (1983) 'The Political Uses of Urban Design: The Jakarta Example,' in Webster, D. (ed.) *The Southeast Asian Environment*, Ottawa: University of Ottawa Press.

Bogaers, E. and Ruijter, P. (1986) 'Ir. Thomas Karsten and Indonesian Town Planning, 1915–1940,' in Nas, P. (ed.) *The Indonesian City: Studies in Urban Development and Planning*, Dordrecht: Foris Publication.

Bousquet, G.H. (1940) *A French View of the Netherlands Indies*, London: Oxford University Press.

Boyd, A. (1988) ''New wave design for 'fun,' '' *Asian Architect and Contractor,* Dec: 46–9.

Bozdogan, S. (1997) 'The Predicament of Modernism in Turkish Architectural Culture,' in Bozdogan, S. and Kasaba, R. (eds) *Rethinking Modernity and National Identity in Turkey*, Seattle: University of Washington Press.

Braudel, F. (1988) *The Identity of France*, Reynolds, S. (trans.), New York: Harper and Row.

Buck-Morss, S. (1995) 'The City as Dreamworld and Catastrophe,' *October*, 73, Summer: 3–26.

Budihardjo, E. (ed.) (1983) *Menuju Arsitektur Indonesia,* Bandung: Alumni.

—— (1991) 'Menuju arsitektur yang beridentitas,' *Sketsa*, 06/09: 52–7.

—— (1998) 'Lebih jauh dengan Prof. Ir. H. Eko Budihardjo Msc,' *Kompas*, May 10.

Cairns, S. (1997) "Re-Surfacing: Architecture, 'Wayang,' and the 'Javanese House,'" in Nalbantoglu, G.B. and Wong C.T. (eds) *Postcolonial Space(s),* New York: Princeton Architectural Press.

Castells, M. (1989) *The Informational City: Information Technology, Economic Restructuring and the Urban–Regional Process,* New York: Basil Blackwell.

Celik, Z. (1997) *Urban Forms and Colonial Confrontations: Algiers under French Rule*, Berkeley: University of California Press.

Chakrabarty, D. (1992) 'Postcoloniality and the Artifice of History: Who Speaks of "Indian" Pasts?' *Representations*, 37, Winter: 1–26.

—— (1998) 'Revisiting the Tradition/Modernity Binary,' in Vlastos, S. (ed.) *Mirror of Modernity: Invented Traditions of Modern Japan*, Berkeley: University of California.

Chatterjee, P. (1993) *Nationalist Thought and the Colonial World: A Derivative Discourse*, Minneapolis: University of Minnesota Press.

—— (1996) 'Whose Imagined Community?' in Balakrishnan, G. (ed.) *Mapping the Nation,* London: Verso.

Chavis Jr, L. (1997) 'Hiding English, the Money, and the Chinese: Building Unity through Languages and Discipline,' MA Thesis, Asian Studies: Southeast Asia, Ithaca: Cornell University, August 1997.

Clifford, J. (1988) *The Predicament of Culture: Twentieth Century Ethnography, Literature, and Art*, Cambridge: Harvard University Press.

Cobban, J. (1988) 'Kampungs and Conflict in Colonial Semarang,' *Journal of Southeast Asian Studies*, 19, 2: 266–91.

—— (1992) 'Exporting Planning: the Work of Thomas Karsten in Colonial Indonesia,' *Planning Perspectives*, 7: 329–44.

—— (1993) 'Public Housing in Colonial Indonesia, 1900–1940,' *Modern Asian Studies*, 27, 4: 871–96.

Coedes, G. (1968) *The Indianized States of Southeast Asia*, Vella, W. (ed.), Cowing, S. (trans.), Honolulu: East-West Center Press.

Colquhoun, A. (1997) 'The Concept of Regionalism,' in Nalbantoglu G.B. and Wong, C.T. (eds) *Postcolonial Space(s),* New York: Princeton Architectural Press.

Constant (1993) 'The Great Game to Come,' in Ockman, J. (ed.) *Architecture Culture 1943–1968*, New York: Rizzoli.

Cooper, F. (1987) *On the African Waterfront: Urban Disorder and the Transformation of Work in Colonial Mombasa*, New Haven: Yale University Press.

Coronil, F. (1992) 'Can Postcoloniality be Decolonized? Imperial Banality and Postcolonial Power,' *Public Culture*, 5, 1, Fall: 89–108.

Crinson, M. (1996) *Empire Building: Orientalism and Victorian Architecture*, London: Routledge.

Daerah Khusus Ibukota (1962) *Peringatan Ulang Tahun ke 435 Kota Djakarta*, Jakarta, Pemerintah DKI.

Damais, S. (1979) *Bung Karno dan Seni*, Jakarta: Yayasan Bung Karno.

Darrundono (1991) 'Penanganan Kampung Pengharapan,' *Sketsa*, 06/09: 76–81.

Dick, H.W. (1990) 'Further Reflections on the Middle Class,' in Tanter, R. and Young K. (eds) *The Politics of Middle Class Indonesia*, Monash Papers on Southeast Asia, no. 19, Clayton: Monash University.

Dirks, N. (ed.) (1992) *Colonialism and Culture*, Ann Arbor: University of Michigan Press.

Dirlik, A. (1992) 'The Asia Pacific Idea: Reality and Representation in the Invention of a Regional Structure,' *Journal of World History*, 3, 1: 55–79.

Doorn, J. van (1982) *The Engineers and the Colonial System: Technocratic Tendencies in the Dutch East Indies*, Rotterdam: Comparative Asian Studies Programme 6.

—— (1983) *A Divided Society: Segmentation and Mediation in Late-Colonial Indonesia*, Rotterdam: Comparative Asian Studies Programme 7.

Dumarcay, J. (1987) *The House in Southeast Asia*, Singapore: Oxford University Press.

Echols, J. and Shadily, H. (1990) *Kamus Indonesia – Inggris*, Jakarta: Gramedia.

—— (1992) *Kamus Indonesia – Inggris*, Jakarta: Gramedia (revised edition).

Emmerson, D. (1984) " 'Southeast Asia': What's in a Name?" *Journal of Southeast Asian Studies*, 15, 1: 1–21.

Feith, H. (1962) *The Decline of Constitutional Democracy in Indonesia*, Ithaca: Cornell University Press.

Feith, H. and Castles, L. (eds) (1970) *Indonesian Political Thinking: 1945–1965*, Ithaca: Cornell University Press.

Florida, N. (1995) *Writing the Past, Inscribing the Future: History as Prophecy in Colonial Java*, Durham: Duke University Press.

Ford, L. (1993) 'A Model of Indonesian City Structure,' *Geographical Review*, 83, 4: 374–96.

Foucault, M. (1977) *Discipline and Punish: The Birth of the Prison*, Sheridan, A. (trans.), New York: Penguin Books.

—— (1982) 'The Subject and Power,' in Dreyfus, H. and Rabinow P., *Michel Foucault: Beyond Structuralism and Hermeneutics*, Chicago: University of Chicago Press.

Foulcher, K. (1995) 'In Search of the Postcolonial in Indonesian Literature,' *Sojourn*, 10, 2: 147–71.

Frampton, K. (1980) *Modern Architecture: A Critical History*, London: Thames and Hudson.

Frederick, W. (1983) 'Hidden Change in Late Colonial Urban Society in Indonesia,' *Journal of Southeast Asian Studies*, 14, 2: 345–71.

Frederick, W. (1989) *Visions and Heat: The Making of the Indonesian Revolution*, Athens: Ohio University Press.

Fuller, M. (1996) 'Wherever You Go, There You Are: Fascist Plans for the Colonial City of Addis Abbaba and the Colonizing Suburb of EUR'42,' *Journal of Contemporary History*, 31: 397–418.

Gandhi, L. (1998) *Postcolonial Theory: A Critical Introduction*, New York: Columbia University Press.

Gaos, R. (1982) 'Menuju Arsitektur Indonesia,' *IAI Media*, February.

Geertz, C. (1980) *Negara: The Theater State in Nineteenth Century Bali*, New Jersey: Princeton University Press.

—— (1983) *Local Knowledge: Further Essays in Interpretive Anthropology*, New York: Basic Books.

Giedion, S. (1954) 'Forget the International Style: the State of Contemporary Architecture, I: the Regional Approach,' in *Architectural Record*, 115: 132–7.

Goodfellow, R. (1995) 'Api dalam Sekam: The New Order and the Ideology of Anti-Communism,' Working Paper 95, Monash University, Clayton.

Gouda, F. (1995) *Dutch Culture Overseas: Colonial Practice in the Netherland Indies 1900–1942*, Amsterdam: Amsterdam University Press.

Guattari, F. and Deleuze, G. (1987) *A Thousand Plateaus: Capitalism and Schizophrenia*, Minneapolis: University of Minnesota Press.

Hanna, W. (1961) *Bung Karno's Indonesia*, New York: American Universities Field Staff Inc., WAH-13–'59.

Hardjono, J.M. (1977) *Transmigration in Indonesia*, Kuala Lumpur: Oxford University Press.

Heiden, C.N. van der (1990) 'Town Planning in the Dutch Indies,' *Planning Perspectives*, 5: 63–84.

Heryanto, A. (1988) "The Development of 'Development'," Lutz, N. (trans.), *Indonesia*, 46: 1–24.

—— (1998) 'Ethnic Identities and Erasure: Chinese Indonesians in Public Culture,' in Khan, J. (ed.) *Southeast Asian Identities: Culture and Politics of Representation in Indonesia, Malaysia, Singapore and Thailand,* Singapore: Institute of Southeast Asian Studies.

Hinds, G.A. (1965) 'Regional Architecture for a Developing Country,' *AIA Journal*, February: 31–6.

Hobsbawm, E. (1983) 'Introduction: Inventing Traditions,' in *The Invention of Tradition*, Hobsbawm, E. and Ranger, T. (eds). Cambridge: Cambridge University Press.

Holston, J. (1989) *The Modernist City: An Anthropological Critique of Brasilia*, Chicago: Chicago University Press.

Home, R. (1997) *Of Planting and Planning: The Making of British Colonial Cities*, London: E. and F.N. Spon.

Hooker, V. (ed.) (1993) *Culture and Society in New Order Indonesia*, Kuala Lumpur: Oxford University Press.

Ingleson, J. (1981) "Bound Hand and Foot": Railway workers and the 1923 strike in Java, *Indonesia*, 31: 53–87.

Ikatan Arsitek Indonesia (1985) *Kongres 35 Tahun Pendidikan Sarjana Arsitektur di Indonesia*, Jakarta: Ikatan Arsitek Indonesia.

Jacobs, J.M. (1996) *Edge of Empire: Postcolonialism and the City*. London: Routledge.

Jalal al-'Azm, S. (1981) 'Orientalism and Orientalism in Reverse,' *Khamsin*, 8: 5–26.

Jameson, F. (1991) *Postmodernism or the Cultural Logic of Late Capitalism*, Durham: Duke University Press.

Jellinek, L. (1991) *The Wheel of Fortune: The History of a Poor Community in Jakarta*, Honolulu: University of Hawaii Press.

Jessup, H. (1980) 'The Architecture of Henri Maclaine Pont: Colonial Style and Native Tradition in Indonesia,' *Lotus International*, 26: 108–13.

—— (1982) 'Four Dutch Buildings in Indonesia I: Henri Maclaine Pont's Institute of Technology, Bandung,' *Orientations*, 13, 9: 32–9.

—— (1982a) 'Four Dutch Buildings in Indonesia II: Thomas Karsten's Folk Theater, Semarang,' *Orientations*, 13, 10: 24–32.

—— (1982b) 'Four Dutch Buildings in Indonesia III: Thomas Karsten's Sonobudoyo Museum, Yogyakarta,' *Orientations*, 13, 11: 24–31.

—— (1985) 'Dutch Architectural Visions of the Indonesian Tradition,' *Muqarnas*, 3: 138–61.

—— (1989) 'Netherlands Architecture in Indonesia, 1900–1942," PhD Dissertation, Courtauld Institute of Art, University of London.

Jumsai, S. (1983) 'House on Stilts, Pointer to Southeast Asian Cultural Origins,' in Aga Khan Award for Architecture, *Architecture and Identity: Proceedings of the Regional Seminar*, Kuala Lumpur, Malaysia, July 25–27.

—— (1986) 'The West Pacific Region vs. Punk Architecture,' *Mimar*, 19, 1986, p. 22–23.

—— (1988) *Naga: Cultural Origins in Siam and the West Pacific*, Singapore: Oxford University Press.

Kadardono (compiler) (1984) *Arsitektur Indonesia 1–3: Masalah dan Potensi*, Surabaya, Institute of Technology.

Karsten, T. (1958) 'Town development in the Indies,' in Wertheim, W.F. et al. (eds) *The Indonesian Town*, Hague: W. van Hoeve Ltds.

Karya Jaya (1977) *Karya Jaya: Kenang-Kenangan Lima Kepala Daerah Jakarta, 1945–1966*, Jakarta: Pemerintah Daerah Khusus Ibukota.

King, A.D. (1976) *Colonial Urban Development: Culture, Social Power and Environment*, London: Routledge and Kegan Paul.

—— (1990) *Urbanism, Colonialism and the World-Economy: Cultural and Spatial Foundations of the World Urban System,* London: Routledge.

—— (1995) *The Bungalow: The Production of a Global Culture*, New York: Oxford University Press.

—— (1996) 'Worlds in the City: Manhattan Transfer and the Ascendence of Spectacular Space,' *Planning Perspectives*, 11: 97–114.

—— (1999) '(Post)colonial Geographies: Material and Symbolic,' *Historical Geography*, 27: 99–118.

King, A.D. and Kusno, A. (2000) 'On Be(ij)ing in the World: "Postmodernism," "Globalization," and the Making of Transnational Space in China,' in Dirlik A. and Zhang, X. (eds) *Postmodernism and China*, Durham: Duke University Press (forthcoming).

Klassen, W. (1984) 'First Asian Congress of Architects and Asian Identity: A Search for a Meaningful Role,' *Philippine Quarterly of Culture and Society*, 12: 271–305.

Kompas (1995) 'Stigma Itu . . .' and 'Yang Amat Dibutuhkan, Konsultan Pembangunan,' *Kompas*, April 17,1995.

Kostof, S. (1995) *A History of Architecture: Settings and Rituals*, New York: Oxford University Press.

Krausse, G. (1988) 'From Sunda Kelapa to Jabotabek: A Socio-Cultural Profile of Indonesia's Capital City,' in Gerald Krausse (ed.) *Urban Society in Southeast Asia: Political and Cultural Issues*, Hongkong: Asian Research Service.

Kroef, J.M. van der (1951) 'The Term Indonesia: Its Origin and Usage,' *Journal of the American Oriental Society*, 71: 166–71.

—— (1951a) 'The Hinduization of Indonesia Reconsidered,' *The Far Eastern Quarterly*, 11, 1: 17–30.

—— (1954) *Indonesia in the Modern World: Vol.I*, Bandung: Masa Baru.

—— (1985) " 'Petrus': Patterns of Prophylactic Murder in Java," *Asian Survey*, 25, 7: 745–59.

Kulke, H. (1991) 'Epigraphical References to the "City" and the "State" in Early Indonesia,' *Indonesia*, 52: 3–22.

Leaf, M. (1991) 'Land Regulation and Housing Development in Jakarta, Indonesia: From the Big Village to the "Modern City",' PhD Dissertation, University of California at Berkeley.

—— (1994) 'The Suburbanisation of Jakarta: a Concurrence of Economics and Ideology,' *Third World Planning Review*, 16, 4: 343–56.

Leaf, M. and Dowell, D. (1991) 'The Price of Land in Jakarta,' *Urban Studies*, 28, 5: 707–22.

Leclerc, J. (1993) 'Mirrors and the Lighthouse: A Search for Meaning in the Monuments and Great Works of Sukarno's Jakarta, 1960–1966,' in Nas, P. (ed.) *Urban Symbolism*, Leiden: E.J. Brill.

—— (1994) 'The Political Iconology of the Indonesian Postage Stamp (1950–1970),' *Indonesia*, 57: 15–48.

Lee, L.O. (1999) *Shanghai Modem: The Flowering of a New Urban Culture in China, 1930–1945*, Cambrdige, Mass: Harvard University Press.

Leerdam, B.F. van (1995) *Architect Henri Maclaine Pont: Een Speurtocht naar het wezenlijke van de Javaanse architectuur*, CIP – Gegevens Koninklijke Bibliotheek, Den Haag.

Lefebvre, H. (1991) *The Production of Space,* Nicholson-Smith, D. (trans.), Oxford: Basil Blackwell.

Lefort, C. (1986) 'The Image of the Body and Totalitarianism,' in *Political Forms of Modern Society*, Cambridge, MA: MIT Press.

Leigh, B. (1991) 'Making the Indonesian State: The Role of School Texts,' *Review of Indonesian and Malaysian Affairs*, 25, 1: 17–43.

Leur, J.C. van (1955) *Indonesian Trade and Society: Essays in Asian Social and Economic History*, The Hague: W. van Hoeve, Ltd.

Macdonald, G. (1995) 'Indonesia's Medan Merdeka: National Identity and the Built Environment,' *Antipode*, 27, 3: 270–93.

McClintock, A. (1994) *Imperial Leather: Race, Gender and Sexuality in the Colonial Conquest*, London: Routledge.

McGee, T. (1994) 'The Future of Urbanisation in Developing Countries: The Case of Indonesia,' *Third World Planning Review*, 16, 1: iii–xii.

McVey, R. (1967) 'Taman Siswa and the Indonesian National Awakening,' *Indonesia*, 4, October: 128–49.

Mahasin, A. (1990) 'The Santri Middle Class: An Insider's View,' in Tanter, R. and Young, K. (eds) *The Politics of Middle Class Indonesia*, Monash papers on Southeast Asia, no. 19, Clayton: Monash Univeristy.

Markus, T. (1993) *Buildings and Power: Freedom and Control in the Origin of Modern Building Types*, London: Routledge.

Mbembe, A. (1992) 'The Banality of Power and the Aesthetics of Vulgarity in the Postcolony,' Roitman, J. (trans.), *Public Culture*, 4, 2: 1–30.

Milone, P. (1966–7) 'Indische Culture, and Its Relationship to Urban Life', *Comparative Studies in Society and History*, vol. 9, July–October: 407–26.

—— (1966) *Urban Areas in Indonesia: Administrative and Census Concepts*, Berkeley: University of California, Institute of International Studies Research Series, no. 10.

Mitchell, T. (1991) *Colonizing Egypt*, Berkeley: University of California Press.

—— (1997) 'Society, Economy, and the State Effect,' in *State/Culture: State Formation After the Cultural Turn*. Steinmetz, G. (ed.) Ithaca: Cornell University Press.

Mitchell, W.J.T. (ed.) (1994) *Landscape and Power*. Chicago: University of Chicago Press.

Moerkerken, P.H. van Jr and Noordhoff, R. (1922) *Atlas Gambar-gambar akan dipakai untuk pengadjaran Ilmoe Boemi*, Amsterdam: S.L. van Looy.

Mohamad, G. (1994) 'City,' in *Sidelines*, Linsay, J. (trans.), South Melbourne, Victoria: Hyland House.

Moser, I. (1995) 'Introduction: Mobilizing Critical Communities and Discourses on Modern Biotechnology,' in Shiva, V. and Moser, I. (eds) *Biopolitics: A Feminist and Ecological Reader on Biotechnology,* London: Zed Books.

Myers, G. (1997) 'Sticks and Stones: Colonialism and Zanzibar Housing,' *Africa*, 67: 253–71.

—— (1999) 'Colonial Discourse and Africa's Colonized Middle: Ajit Singh's Architecture,' *Historical Geography*, 27: 27–55.

Nalbantoglu, G.B. and Wong C.T. (eds) (1997) *Postcolonial Space(s),* New York: Princeton Architectural Press.

Nas, P.J. (ed.) (1986) 'From Problem to Planning: An Example of Applied Urban Development Sociology from 1938,' in Nas, P. (ed.) *The Indonesian City: Studies in Urban Development and Planning*, Dordrecht: Foris Publication.

Nas, P.J. (ed.) (1995) *Issues in Urban Development: Case Studies from Indonesia*, Leiden: Research School CNWS.

Needell, J. (1995) 'Rio de Janeiro and Buenos Aires: Public Space and Public Consciousness in 'Fin-de-Siècle' Latin America,' *Comparative Studies in Society and History*, 37, 3: 519–40.

Nora, P. (1989) 'Between Memory and History: Les Lieux de Memoire,' Roudebush, M. (trans.), *Representations*, 26, Spring: 7–25.

Noyes, J. (1992) *Colonial Space: Spatiality in the Discourse of German South West Africa*, Reading: Harwood Academic Publishers.

O'Connor, R. (1995) 'Indigenous Urbanism: Class, City and Society in Southeast Asia,' *Journal of Southeast Asian Studies*, 26, 1, March: 30–45.

Oetomo, B. (1961) 'Some Remarks on Modern Indonesian Historiography,' in Hall, D.G.E. (ed.) *Historians of South East Asia,* London: Oxford University Press.

Oliver, P. (ed.) (1996) *Encyclopedia of Vernacular Architecture of the World*, 2 vols, Cambridge University Press.

O'Neill, H. (1993) 'Islamic Architecture under the New Order,' in Hooker, V. (ed.) *Culture and Society in New Order Indonesia*, Kuala Lumpur: Oxford University Press.

Ong, A. (1993) 'On the Edge of Empires: Flexible Citizenship Among Chinese in Diaspora,' *Positions*, 1, 3, Winter: 749–78.

Ong, A. and Nonini, D. (eds) (1997) *Ungrounded Empires: The Cultural Politics of Modern Chinese Transnationalism,* London: Routledge.

Otten, M. (1986) *Transmigrasi: Indonesian Resettlement Policy, 1965–1985*, International Work Group for Indigenous Affairs Document 57, Copenhagen: IWGIA Publication.

Passchier AvB, C. (1988) 'The Modern Movement of Architecture in Indonesia,' Paper presented to a seminar on 'Change and Heritage in Indonesian Cities,' Jakarta, September 28–29.

Pauker, E. (1965) 'Ganefo I: Sports and Politics in Djakarta,' *Asian Survey*, 5: 171–85.

Pelzer, K. (1948) *Pioneer Settlement in the Asiatic Tropics*, New York: American Geographical Society.

Pemberton, J. (1994) *On the Subject of "Java,"* Ithaca: Cornell University Press.

—— (1994a) 'Recollections from "Beautiful Indonesia" (Somewhere Beyond the Postmodern),' *Public Culture*, 6: 241–62.

Perera, N. (1998) *Society and Space: Colonialism, Nationalism, and Postcolonial Identity in Sri Lanka*, Boulder: Westview Press.

Perez-Gomez, A. (1983) *Architecture and the Crises of Modern Science*, Cambridge, MA: MIT Press.

Podo, H. and Sullivan, J. (1986) *Kamus Ungkapan Indonesia-Inggris*, Jakarta: Gramedia.

Polle, V. and Hofstee, P. (1986) 'Urban Kampung Improvement and the Use of Aerial Photography for Data Collection,' in Nas, P. (ed.) *The Indonesian City*, Dordrecht, Holland: Foris Publications.

Powell, R. (1989) *Ken Yeang: Rethinking the Environmental Filter*, Singapore: Landmark Books.

Pragantha, W. (1983) 'Dua Tokoh Pembentuk Arsitektur Indonesia,' in Eko Budi-hardjo (ed.) *Menuju Arsitektur Indonesia*, Bandung: Alumni.

—— (1984) 'Menuju Arsitektur Indonesia,' in Kadardono (ed.) *Arsitektur Indonesia: Masalah dan Potensi 2*, Surabaya: Surabaya Institute of Technology.

Pratt, M.L. (1992) *Imperial Eyes: Travel Writing and Tranculturalation*, New York: Routledge.

Prawirohardjo, D. and Sularto, R. (1984), 'Menuju Arsitektur Indonesia,' in Kadardono (ed.) *Arsitektur Indonesia: Masalah dan Potensi 2*, Surabaya: Surabaya Institute of Technology.

Prijotomo, J. (1984) *Ideas and Forms of Javanese Architecture*, Yogyakarta: Gajah Mada University Press.

—— (1984a) 'The Face of Kampung and Street Architecture,' lecture given at Perhimpunan Persahabatan Indonesia Amerika, Surabaya, May 25.

—— (1987) *Dinamika Arsitektur Indonesia*, Surabaya: Surabaya Institute of Technology.

—— (1988) 'The Indonesian Elements in the Architecture of 1900–1930,' Paper presented in the seminar on 'Change and Heritage in Indonesian Cities,' Jakarta, September 28–29.

Rabinow, P. (1989) *French Modern: Norms and Forms of the Social Environment*, Cambridge: MIT Press.

—— (1982) 'Ordonnance, Discipline, Regulation, Some Reflections on Urbanism,' in *Humanities in Society*, 5, 3–4: 267–78.

Rapoport, A. (1969) *House Form and Culture*, New Jersey: Prentice Hall.

Reid, A. (ed.) (1979) 'The Nationalist Quest for an Indonesian Past,' in Reid, A. and Marr, D. (eds) *Perceptions of the Past in Southeast Asia*, Singapore: Heinemann.

—— (1996) *Sojourners and Settlers: Histories of Southeast Asia and the Chinese,* New South Wales: Allen and Unwin.

Ricklefs, M.C. (1993) *A History of Modern Indonesia since c.1300*, Stanford, California: Stanford University Press.

Robison, R. (1996) 'The Middle Class and the Bourgeosie in Indonesia,' in Robison, R. and Goodman, D. (eds) *The New Rich in Asia: Mobile Phones, McDonalds and Middle Class Revolution,* London: Routledge.

Romondt, V. van (1954) *Menuju Ke Suatu Arsitektur Indonesia*, Djakarta: Noordhoff-Kolff N.V.

Rukmana, S.H. (1990) 'Teknologi Penghemat Biaya,' *45 Years Public Works Department*, Jakarta: Public Works Department.

Sadikin, A. (1992) *Bang Ali: Demi Jakarta (1966–1977)*, Jakarta: Pustaka Sinar Harapan.

Said, E. (1978) *Orientalism*, New York: Random House.

—— (1989) 'Representing the Colonized: Anthropology's Interlocutors,' *Critical Inquiry*, 15, Winter: 205–25.

—— (1993) *Culture and Imperialism,* New York: Alfred Knopf.

Schmutzer, E.J.M. (1977) *Dutch Colonial Policy and the Search for Identity in Indonesia, 1920–1931*, Leiden: E.J. Brill.

Schwarz, A. (1994) *A Nation in Waiting: Indonesia in the 1990s*, Boulder: Westview Press.

Scott, D. (1995) 'Colonial Governmentality,' *Social Text*, 43, Fall: 191–220.

Shiraishi, S. (1986) 'Silakan Masuk, Silakan Duduk: Reflections in a Sitting Room in Java,' *Indonesia*, 41: 89–130.

—— (1997) *Young Heroes: The Indonesian Family in Politics*, Ithaca: Cornell University, Southeast Asia Program.

Shiraishi, T. (1981) 'The Dispute Between Tjipto Mangoenkoesoemo and Soetatmo Soeriokoesoemo: Pandita vs, Satria,' *Indonesia*, 32, October: 93–108.

—— (1990) *An Age in Motion: Popular Radicalism in Java 1912–1926*, Ithaca: Cornell University Press.

—— (1996) 'Rewriting the Indonesian State,' in Lev, D. and McVey, R. (eds) *Making Indonesia,* Ithaca: Cornell University, Southeast Asia Program.

—— (1997) 'Anti-Sinicism in Java's New Order,' in Chirot, D. and Reid, A. (eds) *Essential Outsiders: Chinese and Jews in the Modern Transformation of Southeast Asia and Central Europe*, Seattle: University of Washington Press.

Sidharta (1983) 'Arsitektur Indonesia modern yang kita dambakan,' in Budihardjo, E. (ed.) *Menuju Arsitektur Indonesia*, Bandung: Bandung Alumni.

—— (1984) 'Peran Arsitek, Pendidikan dan Masa Depan Arsitektur Indonesia,' *Media IAI*, October.

Siegel, J. (1986) *Solo in the New Order: Language and Hierarchy in an Indonesian City*, Princeton: Princeton University Press.

—— (1997) *Fetish, Recognition, Revolution*, Princeton: Princeton University Press.

—— (1998) *A New Criminal Type in Jakarta: Counter-Revolution Today*, Durham: Duke University Press.

—— (1999) 'Early Thoughts on the Violence of May 13 and 14, 1998, in Jakarta,' *Indonesia*, 66, October: 75–108.

Singapore Institute of Architects Journal (1984), no. 127, December.

Singaravelu, S. (1970) 'The Legends of the Naga-Princess in South India and Southeast Asia,' in Bunnag, T. and Smithies, M. (eds) *In Memoriam Phya Anuman Rajadhon*, Bangkok: The Siam Society.

Smith, M.P. (2001) *Transnationalism and Urban Theory*, Basil Blackwell (forthcoming).

Snuijff, S. (1914) *Architecture in Netherlands East India*, Netherlands East Indian San Francisco Committee, Department of Agriculture, Industry and Commerce, No. 11, Semarang-Soerabaja-Den Haag: Van Dorp and Co.

Spivak, G. (1987) *In Other Worlds: Essays in Cultural Politics*, London: Methuen.

—— (1988) 'Subaltern Studies: Deconstructing Historiography,' in Guha, R. and Spivak, G. (eds) *Selected Subaltern Studies*, New York: Oxford University Press.

Stieber, N. (1998) *Housing Design and Society in Amsterdam: Reconfiguring Urban Order and Identity, 1900–1920*, Chicago: Chicago University Press.

Stoler, A. (1989) 'Rethinking Colonial Categories: European Communities and the Boundaries of Rule,' *Comparative Studies in Society and History*, 31, 1: 134–61.

—— (1992) 'Sexual Affronts and Racial Frontiers: European Identities and the Cultural Politics of Exclusion in Colonial Southeast Asia,' *Comparative Studies in Society and History*, 34, 1: 514–52.

Stoler, A. and Cooper, F. (eds) (1997) *Tensions of Empire: Colonial Cultures in a Bourgeois World*, Berkeley: University of California Press.

Sudradjat, I. (1991) 'A Study of Indonesian Architectural History,' PhD Dissertation, Department of Architecture, University of Sydney.

Suharto (1991) *Soeharto: My Thoughts, Words and Deeds*, Jakarta: PT. Citra Lamtoro Gung Persada.

Sukarno (1962) 'Transformation of Djakarta Raya,' in *Indonesia 1962*, Department of Foreign Affairs, Republic of Indonesia.

—— (1962) 'Amanat Presiden Sukarno pada peringatan Ulang Tahun ke 435 kota Djakarta di Gedung Olah Raga Djakarta pada tanggal 22 Djuni 1962,' Jakarta: Ministry of Information edition no. 218.

—— (1966) *Sukarno: An Autobiography as Told to Cindy Adams*, Hongkong: Gunung Agung.

Sumintardja, D. (1972) "Indonesia in Miniature?" *Masalah Bangunan*, 17, 3–4: 8–11.

—— (1988) 'Buildings for Worship in Indonesia During the Dutch Period,' Unpublished paper presented at 'Change and Heritage in Indonesian Cities,' September 28–29, Jakarta.

Supomo, S. (1979) 'The Image of Majapahit in Later Javanese and Indonesian Writing,' in Reid, A. and Marr, D. (eds) *Perceptions of the Past in Southeast Asia*, Singapore: Heinemann.

Tadiar, N. (1993) 'Manila's New Metropolitan Form,' *Differences*, Fall, 5, 3: 154–78.

Taman Mini Indonesia Indah (1975) *Kenang-kenangan Peresmian Pembukaan Taman Mini Indonesia Indah*, Jakarta: Taman Mini Indonesia Indah.

Tambiah, S. (1985) 'The Galactic Polity in Southeast Asia,' in *Culture, Thought and Social Action*, Cambridge: Harvard University Press.

Tan, M.G. (1996) 'Fengshui and the Road to Success: the Persistence of a Traditional Belief System in the Face of Market Expansion,' Paper presented at the third seminar on 'Socio and Cultural Dimensions of Market Expansion,' Goethe Institute, University of Bielefeld and Gajah Mada University, Yogyakarta, Indonesia, August 26–27.

Tanter, R. and Young, K. (eds) (1990) *The Politics of Middle Class Indonesia*, Monash Papers on Southeast Asia, no. 19, Clayton: Monash University.

Tay Kheng Soon (1989) *Megacities in the Tropics: Towards an Architectural Agenda for the Future*, Singapore: Institute of Southeast Asian Studies.

Taylor, P. (1996) 'Embedded Statism and the Social Sciences: Opening Up to New Spaces,' *Environment and Planning A*, 28: 1917–28.

Teeuw, A. (1967) *Modern Indonesian Literature*, The Hague: Nijhoff.

Tickell, P. (1981) 'Introduction: Mas Marco Kantodikromo and Early Indonesian Literature,' in *Three Short Stories by Mas Marco Kartodikromo (c 1890–1932)*, translated and introduced by Paul Tickell, Centre of Southeast Asian Studies, Monash University, Melbourne.

Tiwon, S. (1996) 'Models and Maniacs: Articulating the Female in Indonesia,' in Sears, L. (ed.) *Fantasizing the Feminine in Indonesia*, Durham: Duke University Press.

Tjahjono, G. (1989) 'Center and Duality in the Javanese Dwelling,' in Bourdier, J.P. and AlSayyad, N. (eds) *Dwelling, Settlements and Tradition: Cross Cultural Perspectives*, Lanham: University Press of America.

Toer, P.A. (1955) 'Letter to a Friend from the Country,' in Aveling, H. (ed. and trans.), *From Surabaya to Armageddon*, Singapore: Heinemann Books.

—— (1982) *Child of All Nations*, New York: Penguin Books.

—— (1990) 'My Kampung,' Sumit Mandal (trans.), *Indonesia*, 61, April: 25–31.

—— (1990a) *Footsteps*, New York: W. Morrow.

Tongchai Winichakul (1994) *Siam Mapped: A History of the Geo-Body of a Nation*, Honolulu: University of Hawaii Press.

Vale, L. (1992) *Architecture, Power and National Identity*, New Haven: Yale University Press.

Vittachi, T. (1967) *The Fall of Sukarno*, London: Andre Deutsche.

Wee, C.J.W.-L. (1993) 'Contending with Primordialism: The "Modern" Construction of Postcolonial Singapore,' *Positions*, 1, 3: 715–44.

Wertheim, W.F. (1987) 'Colonial and Postcolonial Cities as Arenas of Conflict,' *Bijdragen Tot de Tall Land-en Volkenkunde*, deel 143, 4e Aflevering: 539–44.

Wertheim, W.F. et al. (eds) (1954) *The Indonesian Town*, The Hague: W. van Hoeve Ltd.

Wertheim, W.F. and Giap T.S. (1962) 'Social Change in Java, 1900–1930,' *Pacific Affairs*, 35: 223–31 and 240–7.

Wilson, R. and Dirlik, A. (eds) (1995) *Asia/Pacific as Space of Cultural Production*, Durham: Duke University Press.

Winters, J. (1996) *Power in Motion: Capital Mobility and the Indonesian State*, Ithaca: Cornell University Press.

Wiryomartono, B. (1995) *Seni Bangunan dan Seni Binakota di Indonesia*, Jakarta: Gramedia.

Wolters, O. (1982) *History, Culture, and the Region in Southeast Asian Perspectives*, Singapore: Institute of Southeast Asian Studies.

Wright, G. (1991) *The Politics of Urban Design in French Colonial Urbanism*, Chicago: Chicago University Press.

Yeang, K. (1987) *Tropical Urban Regionalism: Building in a Southeast Asian City*, Singapore: Concept Media.

Yeang, K. (1987a) *The Tropical Verandah City: Some Urban Design Ideas for Kuala Lumpur*, Petaling Jaya: Longman Malaysia.

—— (1992) "Designing the Tropical Skyscraper," *Mimar* 42, March.

—— (1994) *Bioclimatic Skyscrapers*, London: Artemis.

Yeoh, B. (1996) *Contesting Space: Power Relations and the Urban Built Environment in Colonial Singapore*, Kuala Lumpur: Oxford University Press.

Young, R. (1991) *White Mythologies: Writing History and the West*, New York: Routledge.

—— (1995) *Colonial Desire: Hybridity in Theory, Culture and Race*, New York: Routledge.

Index

Abeyasekere, Susan 54, 60, 71
Anderson, Benedict 16, 50, 60, 64;
      comparisons 8; New Order
      73, 76; professionalism 174;
      tradition 89; urban space 98
Appadurai, Arjun 69, 212
Arsitek Indonesia 10–11
Art Deco 31
Arts and Crafts movement 44–5
Asian Congress of Architects 191, 198
Asian Games 56–7, 60, 65, 102
Association of Indonesian Architects (IAI)
      94, 170
Ataturk, Kemal 128
Atmadi, Parmono 178–81
Authority 60–2, 65–6

Bahasa Indonesia 156–7, 210
Bali 26, 86, 177–8
Bandarhardjo housing complex 123–5
Bandung Institute of Technology (ITB –
      formerly Bandoeng
      Technische Hoogeschool) 30,
      43–6, 60, 81–5, 87–90, 170
Bank of Asia 197
Bauhaus 62
Beautiful Indonesia in Miniature Park 72,
      74–9, 94
Berlage, H.P. 32
Bhabha, Homi 47, 69, 91
Bioclimatic cities 197–201
Breckenridge, Carol 69
Buddhism 193
Building Research Institute 78–9

Cairns, Stephen 38–9
Castell, Manuel 196
Catholicism 104
Centralism 60–2

Centre Pompidou 197
Chakrabarty, Dipesh 6
Chatterjee, Partha 26, 47–8, 207
Chavis, Larry Jr 156
Chinese 144, 152–63, 165–6; citizenship
      207; Revolution 131
Ciputra 158–9
Cityscapes 156–61
Class system 99, 132–3, 152–9; identity
      148–9; riots 164; urban
      design 145
Classical architecture 79–81, 86
Clifford, James 27
Colonial Third Culture 8–10
Co-prosperity 29
Communism 103, 158
Comparisons 8–10, 190–204
Compression structure 193
Conrad, Joseph 13
Constitution 182
Containment policy 160
Crinson, Mark 37
Culture-building 149–50, 158, 162–6;
      architecture 169; political
      14–16; water-based 193–6

Democracy 51, 72, 91
Department of Agriculture, Industry and
      Commerce 29
Department of Culture and Education 75, 78
Department of Social Affairs 139
Dependency thesis 120
Design 120–43
Developers 145
Development policy 71–3, 89, 93, 106; fear
      165; nationalism 155, 207–8;
      political culture 120;
      transmigration 141; urban
      space 109, 117, 119

Dick, H.W. 116
Dutch Pavilion 26, 27

East Timor 75, 104
Education 43–6
Egypt 37, 193
Elites 111–15
Empire 62–6
Ethical Policy 16, 26–31, 43–5, 47; People's
    Theatre 38; political culture
    125, 127, 129, 142;
    resettlement 135, 138
Eurasians 152
Europe 6, 9, 176, 178; influence 180–2,
    184, 193, 210

Facades 125, 128–30
Fear 165–6
Feudal values 42
Foucault, Michel 12, 105, 111, 209
Foulcher, Keith 209
France 12
Frederick, William 127
Friday Mosque 1–3
Fuller, Buckminster 196
Fuller, Mia 59
Functionalism 125
Furnivall, John 127
Futurism 62

Gajah Mada University 178
Gali 104–5, 117, 164
Games of the New Emerging Forces
    (GANEFO) 56
Gandhi, Mahatma 128
GANEFO see Games of the New Emerging
    Forces
Gaos, Rivai 181, 183–5
Garden cities 124–5
Geertz, Clifford 56
Gender issues 113, 137, 139, 148–9
Giedion, Sigfried 92
Global Governance 122
Gouda, Frances 26, 40–2
Greater Netherlands 29–31
Guided Democracy project 51–2, 54, 56,
    60–2, 65–6, 68

Habibie, B.J. 84
Hatta, Mohammad 149–50
Heryanto, A. 207
Hinds, George A. 92
Hinduism 26, 86, 193
Holston, James 67
Hongkong Bank 197
Housing 112, 124, 153–4, 157–8, 162,
    194–6
Housing and Interior Exhibition 112

Idenburg, A.W.F. 28
Identity cards 160

Identity formation 26, 47, 50–2, 57–9;
    Chinese 160–6; housing 113;
    kampung 124–5, 128, 134;
    middle class 116; monuments
    65; nationalism 209; political
    culture 14–16; professionalism
    170–2, 186–8; revision
    148–52; Sukarno 100–3;
    tradition 72–3, 75;
    transformation 156; urban
    space 97–8, 105, 110
Identity-formation, tropical architecture
    198–201
Imagination 97–8, 169–89
Independence 50
India 8–9, 30
Indies architecture 30–3, 37–8, 43–4, 47
Indigenous architecture see Vernacular
    architecture
International Colonial Exhibition 26–9
International Style 68, 92, 200
Irian Jaya 64, 102, 139, 175
Islam 131, 193
Ismail, Taufiq 66
Italy 59

Jakarta 17, 49, 67–70, 98–103, 116–17;
    control 104; culture-building
    150–1; fear 165; housing
    112, 157–8; migrants 153;
    professionalism 184, 188;
    riots 106, 154–6, 160,
    162–4; Suharto 121–2; traffic
    jams 146–7; transmigration
    140; urban space 109–10
Jakarta Post 93–4
Java 26, 30, 32–3, 35–9; centralism 60–2,
    70; culture-building 3, 81,
    151; nationalism 210; pre-
    colonial 51–2; resettlement
    programmes 135–40;
    vernacular architecture 177
Jockeys 147
Joglo style 81
Jumsai, Sumet 192–8, 202, 203–5

Kampung 52–3, 60, 66–7, 99; Chinese
    161; culture-building 151–4;
    fear 165; modernism 207;
    political culture 120–30, 142;
    space 108–18, 145–8;
    transmigration 140; urban
    planning 134–7
Karsten, Thomas 8, 13, 25, 32–8, 47–8;
    Koningsplein 55; nationalism
    152, 154; urban planning
    129–35, 136; zoning 145
King, Anthony 8–9
Kompas 122–3
Kostof, Spiro 4
Kota 173–4, 184

Krausse, Gerald 153
Kroef, Justuf M. van der 53

Language 156–7, 209–10
Le Corbusier 62
Lefebvre, Henri 5
Locsin, Leandro 191
Logos 43
Long-houses 141
Looting 164
Lyautey, Hubert 12–13

McGee, Terry 153–4
Machiavelli, Niccolò 117
Maclaine Pont, Henri 13, 25, 32–3, 37;
        Bandung Institute of
        Technology 81, 89; milieu
        39–45, 47–8
McVey, Ruth 185
Mada, Gadjah 63
Mahasin, Aswab 116
Majapahit 62–3, 68
Malari incident 106
Malaysia 64, 102, 194, 198–9
Mangkunegoro, King 74
Maoism 62
Marginalization 146
Marriages 139
Mbembe, Achille 15
Media 100, 116, 127
Middle class 109–11, 115–19, 122; housing
        157–9; Jakarta 162;
        nationalism 155; prestige
        144–66; professionalism
        171; riots 164–5; zoning
        132–3
Migrants 108, 140, 151–2, 153
Milieu 25–48, 133–9, 148, 152, 169
Military 104, 117, 146
Minangkabau 44–5, 199
Ministry of Education and Cultural Affairs
        78, 156
Modernism 1, 29–33, 49–50, 52, 54–60,
        68–9; International Style 92;
        professionalism 182–3;
        Southeast Asia 190;
        translation 60–2; tropical
        architecture 200–1
Modernity 9, 49–53, 70, 90, 125, 127,
        132–33; fear 165–6; future
        trends 206; identity formation
        149; kampung 135; political
        culture 121; riots 162–4;
        social 125; Suharto 156;
        syncretic 67–70, 207; zoning
        systems 133
Mohamad, Goenawan 162
Mohammad Ali Mosque 4
Mojopahit 62
Monuments 62–6, 71, 74, 102
Mythos 92

Naming 156–61
National Awakening Day 117
National Discipline Campaign 117
National Monument 63–4, 71
National subjects 97, 105–15, 117
Nationalism 17, 29, 43, 50, 55; Chinese
        158, 160; class 152–6;
        colonial legacy 207–11;
        culture-building 149–50;
        dreams 169–89; future
        trends 206; language 156–7;
        space 144–5; tradition
        89–91; urban space 97–8
Neoclassicism 30, 68, 133
New Order 2–4, 67, 71–94, 98–9, 105–6;
        Chinese 157–8; comparisons
        8, 13; culture-building
        170–1, 175; family life 113,
        115; fear 165; modernism
        207; nationalism 153–5, 208,
        210–11; political culture
        120–2, 125; professionalism
        178, 187; repression 146;
        transmigration 141; urban
        space 103–5, 109, 111,
        117–19
Nora, Pierre 15–16
Notosusanto, Nugroho 71

O'Connor, Richard 148

Pancasila Democracy 72, 91
Parliament House 99, 103
Pemberton, John 75, 78, 89
Pendapa 34–6, 38–9
People's Theatre, Semarang 33–8
Police 146, 160, 165
Political cultures 14–15, 120–43
Political imagination 169–89
Politicization 29
Populist politics 102–3, 109, 117–18
Porphyrios, Demetri 80
Postcolonial studies 5–8, 206, 212;
        Postcolonial condition: 8–10,
        15–16
Postmodernism 15, 93–4
Powell, Robert 198
Power relations 105, 122, 145, 147
Prijotomo, Josef 79, 181–3
Privatization 162
Professionalism 12–14, 169–89
Public Works Department 29–30, 123

Quarternary period 193

Rabinow, Paul 12–13, 31, 133
Race 148–9, 152–6
Rationalization 37, 39–40, 45–6
Real estate 111–13, 146, 148, 156, 158
Regional Housing Center 76
Regionalism 92–3

Resettlement programmes 135–9
Riots 99–100, 106, 142, 154–5; modernity 162–4; race 158–9, 160
Rosidi, Ayip 53, 150
Rukmana, Mrs 109–10

Sadikin, Ali 107–9, 116–17, 139, 151–2
Said, Edward 12–13, 142, 192
St Mark's, Alexandria 37
Schoemaker, Wolff 30
Security guards 146
Selection rules 136–7
Sex see Gender issues
Shiraishi, Saya 113
Shiraishi, Takashi 16
Shock therapy 104
Shopping malls 111, 118, 155–6
Sidharta 175–6, 180–1
Siegel, James 103–5, 117, 155–6, 162, 164
Singapore 7, 198–9
Snuijff, S. 29 33
Sociaal-Technische Vereeniging van Democratische Ingenieurs en Architecten (STV) 32
Social categories 97–119
Social control 104, 106, 117
Sonobudoyo Museum 33
Southeast Asia 190–204, 210
Space 5–9, 54–60, 62–6, 97–119; Chinese 160; nationalism 144–52; organization 122; planning 135–6; politics 211–12; transmigration 139; zoning system 132–3
Specific intellectuals 29, 125–7
Status 130–3
Streets 103–9, 117–18, 133
Students 99–100, 106, 118, 154
STV see Sociaal-Technische Vereeniging van Democratische Ingenieurs en Architecten
Subject formation 4–5, 15, 97–99, 118–19, 211–12
Subjectivity 12–14, 40–43, 169–172, 185–89
Sudradjat, Iwan 40, 78–9, 91, 175
Suharto, Mrs 74, 76–7
Suharto, President 2–4, 8, 71–4, 115–19; fear 165–6; Jakarta 121–2; modernism 156, 207; nationalism 154–5, 210; political culture 125; professionalism 188; transmigration 141; urban violence 98–109
Sukarno, President 1, 3–4, 46–7, 49–70, 66–70; egalitarianism 106–7; modernism 207; National Monument 71; nationalism 78, 152; political culture 120–2, 128; professionalism 171, 187–8; tradition 92; urban space 98, 117–19

Sulawesi 65
Sumatra 26, 30, 45, 65
Surveillance 105
Symbolism 51, 53–61, 63, 66, 71; Chinese 158, 164; long-houses 141; riots 155; tradition 74, 77, 80; urban space 103, 106
Syncretic modernity 31–3, 67–70, 207

Tay Kheng Soon 198–9, 201–2, 205
Technische Hoogeschool, Delft 32, 172
Techno-cosmopolitanism 31
Tensile structure 193
Third World 7, 92–3
Three-in-one zones 146–7
Toer, Pramoedya Ananta 66–7, 97–8, 119
Traditional architecture 71–94; see also Vernacular architecture
Traffic jams 146–7
Transmigration 135–41
Transnationality 144–66, 190
Trisakti University 99
Tropical architecture 197–201

Underclass 99–100, 105, 118, 155, 159, 164
Underdevelopment 145
United Nations (UN) 52–4, 64
United States (US) 176, 184
University of Diponegoro Semarang 179
University of Indonesia 85–90
Urban design 144–5, 190–204
Urban planning 49, 51, 54, 64, 120; Karsten 129–33, 145; nationalism 152; space 135–6
Urban space 97–119, 120–43

Vale, Lawrence 14–15
Van Deventer 16
Van Romondt, Vincent 172–7, 183
Vernacular architecture 92, 173, 176–8
Violence 97–119

Water culture 192–7
Wayang puppets 34–7
Wertheim, W.F. 8, 10, 136
West Guinea see Irian Jaya
Wild, James 37
Wilhelmina, Queen 29
Wilwo Tikto 62
World Bank Development Project 122
Wright, Frank Lloyd 176, 183–5, 188
Wright, Gwendolyn 33

Yamin, Muhammad 63
Yeang, Ken 198, 200–2, 205
Yeoh, Brenda 7
Yogyakarta 33, 62

Zoning systems 81–5, 89, 124, 131–3, 145